YOUTH AND POLITICAL PARTICIPATION

Selected Titles in ABC-CLIO's
CONTEMPORARY
WORLD ISSUES
Series

For a complete list of titles in this series, please visit
www.abc-clio.com

Books in the Contemporary World Issues series address vital issues in today's society, such as genetic engineering, pollution, and biodiversity. Written by professional writers, scholars, and nonacademic experts, these books are authoritative, clearly written, up-to-date, and objective. They provide a good starting point for research by high school and college students, scholars, and general readers as well as by legislators, businesspeople, activists, and others.

Each book, carefully organized and easy to use, contains an overview of the subject, a detailed chronology, biographical sketches, facts and data and/or documents and other primary-source material, a directory of organizations and agencies, annotated lists of print and nonprint resources, and an index.

Readers of books in the Contemporary World Issues series will find the information they need to have a better understanding of the social, political, environmental, and economic issues facing the world today.

$64.00

YOUTH AND POLITICAL PARTICIPATION

A Reference Handbook

Glenn H. Utter

CONTEMPORARY WORLD ISSUES

ABC-CLIO

Santa Barbara, California • Denver, Colorado • Oxford, England

Library of Congress Cataloging-in-Publication Data

Utter, Glenn H.
    Youth and political participation : a reference handbook / Glenn Utter.
        p. cm. — (Contemporary world issues series)
    Includes index.
    ISBN 978-1-59884-661-4 (hardcopy : alk. paper) —
ISBN 978-1-59884-662-1 (ebk.)   1. Youth—Political activity—United States.   2. Political participation—United States.   3. Youth—Political activity.   4. Political participation.   I. Title.
    HQ799.2.P6U77   2011
    323'.04208350973—dc23   2011018927

ISBN: 978-1-59884-661-4
EISBN: 978-1-59884-662-1

15   14   13   12   11   1   2   3   4   5

This book is also available on the World Wide Web as an eBook.
Visit www.abc-clio.com for details.

ABC-CLIO, LLC
130 Cremona Drive, P.O. Box 1911
Santa Barbara, California 93116-1911

This book is printed on acid-free paper ∞

Manufactured in the United States of America

Contents

List of Tables

Preface

Periodically throughout U.S. history, particularly during and immediately following armed conflict, debates have occurred about the appropriate minimum voting age. Many asserted that if people are old enough to be required to risk life and limb during military service, they also should have the right to participate in elections to select those officials who will have the authority to make such life and death decisions. Although free and fair elections often are considered the most crucial ingredient in a democratic system, democracy involves much more than periodically casting a ballot, for there are many ways in which people can participate in politics. They can take part in political discussion, engage in collective efforts to improve the local community, advocate or oppose existing or proposed policies, and take part in election campaigns.

In recent years, especially since ratification in 1971 of the Twenty-Sixth Amendment that established the minimum voting age at 18, political activists and scholars have focused a great deal of attention on investigating the political attitudes and behavior of young people (particularly those aged 18 to 30, the age group with the lowest level of political engagement), often with the goal of increasing political participation levels among those in this age cohort. For the Democratic and Republican parties, attracting young committed adherents can potentially pay large dividends for future political success. And for those concerned about the preservation of democratic values and the institutions of democratic government, the engagement of young people in politics is of critical importance. This book deals with these concerns and with the strategies, many of them the result of social science research, that have been suggested for increasing political participation among the younger population.

Those working to increase youth voter turnout have been encouraged by participation data from the presidential elections of 2004 and 2008 as well as the congressional election of 2006, in which young people turned out in larger numbers than in the past, although still at levels lower than older age cohorts. However, in the 2010 off-year election, the turnout rate of young people fell, due in part to lack of a presidential contest to boost interest as well as a slowing economy and possibly dissatisfaction with the job that government officials had done in the past two years. Also, many of those advocating greater youth activism faulted the two major political parties for failing to focus sufficient energy and resources on motivating young people to cast ballots. Subsequent elections will tell the tale of efforts by partisan organizations and nonpartisan civic groups to attract more young people to political activism. A lesson of the 2010 election is that efforts to politically activate this age group is a perennial task because every two years a new crop of citizens aged 18 to 20 become eligible to vote and many of them do not themselves possess the motivation to engage in politics.

Many have looked to the development of new media technology as a key ingredient in encouraging young people to engage in politics, especially because those in this age group are obviously most likely to use the technology. The Internet and e-mail, Facebook, YouTube, Twitter, as well as classroom technology, including PowerPoint presentations and "clickers" that allow students to participate in class discussion by registering their anonymous views, have become much-used modes of communication not available to previous generations. Levi Baker's recent study, published in the *Journal of Social and Personal Relationships (2010)*, suggests that people who do not interact socially offline find Facebook and other social networking media a much more accommodating way of interacting with others. However, people who use new communication technology for social interaction may not spontaneously use that technology for broader interaction that would lead to political engagement. Only time will tell if political parties, political activists, and organizations wishing to increase participation will be able to achieve continuing success in motivating larger numbers of people to engage in politics.

Chapter 1 examines the background and history of youth and political participation, placing special emphasis on the question of voting age. Chapter 2 focuses on the contemporary situation with regard to young people and political engagement, presenting research on differing methods of increasing interest in and knowledge about the political realm. Chapter 3 presents brief overviews of the governing systems and political participation in six countries in order to provide a comparative context for youth political engagement in the United States. Chapter 4 is a chronology of events related to youth political participation that emphasizes the issue of minimum voting age and the campaign to lower the voting age to 18. Chapter 5 includes biographical sketches of historical and contemporary figures who have engaged in political activity in their youth or who have encouraged youth political engagement. Chapter 6 presents General Social Survey data relevant to the political attitudes and behavior of young people in the United States. In addition, because education is a key variable related to political engagement, the chapter also includes summaries of recent American government textbooks that illustrate the approaches taken to providing knowledge about U.S. politics and encouragement for political participation. Chapter 7 furnishes a list of organizations that either are primarily administered by young people or are focused on engaging young people in political activity. Finally, chapter 8 presents a list of more recent print and nonprint resources relevant to political participation.

I wish to express my appreciation to Thomas Sowers, associate professor of political science at Lamar University, for his assistance with data analysis and to Brenda Nichols, dean of the College of Arts and Sciences, and Stephen Doblin, provost and vice president for academic affairs, at Lamar University, for the generous support they provided in helping me complete this volume. Although recognizing their valuable assistance, I accept full responsibility for any errors of fact or judgment.

1

Background and History

Democracy and Youth Political Participation

Throughout the history of civilizations, youth have represented the hope for the survival of a society, as well as a key threat to its stability and continued existence. The future of a society obviously depends on the next generation assuming the roles of their elders. However, as some thinkers have commented, youth, if not properly prepared for those roles, constitute a major danger to the continuation of various customs and values that distinguish the society from others. In a democratic society, the youth are expected to take on the values and traditions of democracy in order to participate along with older generations in maintaining democratic practices. Plato, in *The Republic*, places great emphasis on the education of the young in order to maintain the "best" regime, which was not necessarily democratic. Aristotle, in *The Politics*, stresses the importance of imitating good examples of human behavior. Both ideas—to gain knowledge and to acquire habits of good behavior—are relevant to the maintenance of a democratic society. For a democracy to endure, youth should acquire knowledge of democratic principles, of the rules governing the political process, and of the actual operation of political institutions; in other words, they should take on the attitudes and habits of democratic behavior.

Democracy involves the claim that all members of a human association, whether a nation or a geographical subdivision (such as a state, province, or municipality; and for some political analysts, educational institutions, private organizations, and even the family) within a country have the right to participate in the making of decisions that require collective, rather than individual or private, choice. As Robert Dahl has emphasized, defining democracy as rule by the people leads to an obvious question: who are to be considered "the people"? The determination of who are considered eligible to participate has varied from society to society and from time period to time period. Age constitutes one of those variables. Individuals are considered competent to make certain decisions or engage in certain activities only after reaching a specified age. There is no "natural" characteristic to determine a person's qualifications for participation in certain endeavors, such as marrying, and different societies create their own standards that contain an element of arbitrariness. For instance, each of the 50 states in the United States has instituted their own rules concerning the minimum age at which a person may marry and whether parental consent must be obtained at certain ages. Although no state permits a person under the age of 15 to marry, other societies do permit such marriages. With regard to voting, a commonly expressed condition for the right to vote is "old enough to fight, old enough to vote." Because the accepted age for military service has been 18, those who supported a lower voting age when the minimum age generally was set at 21 argued that the two activities should have an equivalent minimum age.

Simple age is just one factor in determining a person's qualification to participate in democratic politics. As Robert Dahl (1990) notes, the criterion of competence (usually determined in terms of a minimum age requirement) can be modified by "the principle of affected interests" (49–50). People less than 18, or for that matter 14 and certainly younger, can be affected by political decisions in such areas as education policy, pollution control, and legal protection but generally have not been considered sufficiently competent to take part in making those decisions. There is no obvious criterion to determine when an individual has attained the capacity to participate fully in a society's public affairs. Various institutions determine a minimum age at which an individual can be considered to have attained the right to engage in the activities of a particular institution. For instance, in many Christian churches, youth gain full membership in the church around the age of 14, when they participate in a ceremony to confirm their religious beliefs. Although becoming a full voting member of the church has traditionally been delayed until younger members have reached the age of 18 or 21, more recently some churches have granted the right of full participation following confirmation at the age of 14.

Focusing on voting as a major element in the democratic process, Lester W. Milbrath and M. L. Goel (1977), in their well-known work on political participation, identify age as one of the variables influencing voter turnout. They note that several studies of political participation have concluded that a similar relationship between age and participation can be observed in many nations: "participation increases steadily with age until it reaches a peak in the middle years, and then gradually declines with old age" (114). Focusing on the older age cohorts, Milbrath and Goel report that in the United States of the 1970s, if the criteria of educational and gender differences are controlled, the decline in voter turnout in later years disappears (114). They conclude that the lower political participation rates among older citizens can be attributed to this group's attaining an overall lower level of education than younger groups (115). However, the authors emphasize that younger citizens also have lower levels of participation. Milbrath and Goel consider the best explanation for variations in political participation with age to be the life cycle. Those least likely to participate are the young, who have not yet been integrated fully into the community. Some studies indicate that with marriage, people have higher rates of participation. However, according to the authors, other studies report lower levels of participation for young marrieds, perhaps because many young couples experience the time-consuming pressures of raising children. Nonetheless, although the distraction of raising a family may influence more heavily what the authors term "gladiatorial participation," in other words, involvement in politics beyond simply voting (115), Milbrath and Goel conclude that three intervening variables can be identified in the relationship between age and participation: "integration with the community, the availability of blocks of free time for politics, and good health" (116). As young people marry, find steady employment, and begin a family, their level of political participation, particularly as voters, tends to increase. As their family responsibilities decrease in middle age, the opportunities for more varied political participation increase, and "in the twilight years, physical infirmities probably account for a modest decline in participation" (116).

Undoubtedly due to phenomena of the era in which they were writing, such as the civil rights movement, opposition to the Vietnam War, and the formation of New Left organizations intended to confront existing institutions and authority figures,

Milbrath and Goel observe that "the militant, particularly the rioter, is most likely to be a young male" (1977, 116). They identify possible determinants of such behavior among the young, including large amounts of free time that students and those without regular employment have; weak integration into, or renunciation of, community norms; relative immunity from economic or social retaliation (such as loss of employment or ostracism); and a desire to reform the social and political system that they regard as the cause of their marginal position in society (116).

Participation of Youth in U.S. History

Citizens of the United States historically have taken pride in the youthfulness and inventiveness of the population. Historians and political scientists note that this perception is borne out by the characteristics of delegates to the Constitutional Convention of 1787.

Table 1.1 demonstrates that, with the exception of Benjamin Franklin and the six delegates who were in their sixties, all the other delegates were young men.

The average age of convention delegates was 44 and the median age was 42. Robert Dahl notes that 40 percent of the delegates were 40 years old or younger, and 75 percent were younger than 50. Some of the more influential delegates were especially young: "James Madison was 36, Gouverneur Morris was 35, Alexander Hamilton was 32, and Charles Pinckney was only 29" (Dahl 1981, 8). Nonetheless, these were not men on the margins of American society who just recently rose to political influence. As Dahl comments, "Many had acquired experience and reputation

TABLE 1.1
Delegates to the 1787 Constitutional Convention, by Age

Age (in Years)	Number of Delegates
Less than 30	4
30–39	16
40–49	21
50–55	7
60–69	6
More than 70	1
Total	55

during the Revolutionary War. With few exceptions they were substantial and well-known figures in their states; some were respected throughout all thirteen states" (8). The overwhelming presence of younger persons as delegates was combined with a distinctly high level of ability, accomplishment, and knowledge of politics, qualities that youth generally must have—although not necessarily at the exceptional level exhibited by the writers of the Constitution—during any era in order to engage effectively in the political process and take leadership roles in political ventures.

The Constitution that this largely youthful group of men designed established minimum ages for the various elected offices in the federal government. Members of the House of Representatives must be at least 25 years old, members of the U.S. Senate must have attained the age of 30, and the president must be at least 35 years old. State constitutions also establish minimum ages for members of the state legislature and governors. For instance, Alabama has prescribed the following minimum ages: 30 years for governor, 25 years for state senator, and 21 years for state representative. Young citizens are prohibited from playing an official role in government. At the federal level, an individual who has just turned 18 years old and thus reached the minimum voting age must wait at least seven years before he or she is qualified to run for national office. In contrast to the relative youth of delegates to the Constitutional Convention, the average age of members of the U.S. Senate at the beginning of the 110th Congress in January 2007 was 61.7, and the average age of members of the House of Representatives was 55.9. As of July 2010, only one senator was less than 40 years old. The oldest senator (following the death of Robert Byrd at the age of 92) was 86-year-old Frank R. Lautenberg (D-NJ), and the oldest member of the House of Representatives was Ralph Hall (R-TX), who was 87 years old (Lautenberg and Hall were 5 and 6 years older, respectively, than Benjamin Franklin was at the time he served as a delegate to the Constitutional Convention).

The History of Youth Political Participation

Major studies of voting behavior in the United States conducted prior to ratification of the Twenty-Sixth Amendment in 1971 (which established the right to vote for 18-to-20-year-olds) provide considerable insight into the general historical trends of political participation levels of young voters (those aged 21 to 30). Just one year before the United States entry into World War II, Paul Lazarsfeld, Bernard Berelson, and Hazel Gaudet conducted a survey in Erie County, Ohio, of prospective voters in that year's presidential election ([1944] 1968). The elaborate survey research design involved a systematic sample of every fourth house in Erie County. Assuring that the characteristics of members of each group were closely matched on relevant socioeconomic variables, the researchers created four groups of 600 individuals each (3). The first three groups served as a control and the members of the fourth constituted the research panel, who were interviewed each month from May to the November election in order to track the varied influences on the ultimate vote choice of panel members. Among the questions the researchers asked themselves were: "What is the effect of social status upon vote? How are people influenced by the party conventions and the nominations? What role does formal propaganda [campaign advertisements] play? How about the press and radio? What of the influence of family and friends? Where do issues come in, and how? Why do some people settle their vote early and some late? In short, how do votes develop?" (6).

Lazarsfeld et al. ([1944] 1968) give minimal attention to the age of potential voters but do try to separate the influence of education from that of the age of prospective voters. They observe that by 1940 the general level of education had increased significantly and therefore younger people had attained a higher education level than older age cohorts. Because education is associated with interest in the election, the researchers divided the sample into two education levels: (a) some high school or more and (b) no high school. They discovered that in both categories, those under 45 years of age expressed less interest in the election than those at least 45 years old: "On each educational level the older people are more interested in the election than the younger ones" (44). Associated with this finding, Lazarsfeld et al. report that the largest proportion of those in the sample who failed to vote were among those who reported the least interest in the election. Given the relationship between age and interest, and interest and political participation, the authors ask, "Is it desirable that younger people withdraw from the political scene?" (44–45). Assuming that younger people may be more open to appeals for change, they infer that lower participation levels among young people could promote greater stability in the political process. However, lower participation could "deprive [political life] of a certain amount of energy and vitality and, thus, be regrettable from the standpoint of civic improvement." Lazarsfeld et al. also note that in pre–World War II European countries, in contrast to the United States, "movements on the part of youth were very active" (44–45). With the instability of European democracies prior to World War II, especially the Weimar Republic in Germany, the authors may have intended this observation to be a caution against high levels of youth participation in politics. More recent historians relate the mild protests of some youth against Hitler's regime in Germany, despite the well-organized Hitler Youth. For instance, Richard J. Evans (2005) describes the appetite of youth for swing and jazz music, in defiance of official bans. As Evans comments, the young people did not intend to organize a political protest but "under the Third Reich, everything was political" (206). Commenting on non-voting in general, Lazarsfeld et al. conclude that "non-voting is a serious problem in a democracy" ([1944] 1968, 45).

In a subsequent study, Bernard R. Berelson, Paul F. Lazarsfeld, and William N. McPhee (1954) examined the voting behavior of Elmira, New York, residents during the 1948 presidential election campaign between President Harry Truman and Republican challenger Thomas E. Dewey. Berelson et al. drew a probability sample by randomly selecting housing units in Elmira, a city considered representative in several ways (or at least not exceptional) of the general population of the United States (6–10). The authors did not focus their research and analysis on young voters but did note that young voters (those aged 21 to 30) often conformed to their parents' preferences. The authors attribute this conformity to young people's tendency not to be involved in politics but simply to follow the lead of their elders. They also reject the common belief, even in 1954, that young people tend to be politically radical, concluding instead that young people generally do not take much interest in politics (91). Although youth may possess the seeds of political radicalism because their opinions often are more idealistic and more independent "or at least inconsistent," ultimately they do not "carry through"—in other words, generally they do not participate in politics. The authors state that young people generally do not pay attention to political events and issues, they tend not to turn out in elections, and they have less concern about who wins an election. Consequently, the age cohort that many expect to abandon tradition is "least likely to go through with it in practice" (92). Due to the potential for supporting deviations from tradition among younger people, the authors conclude that the tendency of this age group not to participate in politics provides "an element of stability in the political system" (92).

Berelson et al. (1954) suggest that one factor that may contribute to this lack of active participation may be that potential first-time voters tend to be associated with others who do not necessarily agree with them politically, and hence they fail to receive reinforcement of their political views. As the authors note, many young people who attain voting age are marrying, starting families, and entering employment and new neighborhoods, all of which can lead to exposure to political inconsistencies and disagreements with others (97). On the other hand, those aged 35 and older generally have developed stable social relationships in employment, in a community, and in associations where the chance of interacting with like-minded people is higher (97). With greater political homogeneity comes higher probability of participating in politics. The authors observe that people aged 21 to 24 have friendship groups that to a large degree are heterogeneous in political outlook, and they argue that this situation occurs in part "because [young people] do not care"; but as people continue to age, they adjust conflicting beliefs and choose friends more compatible with their own preferences, a process that continues until about the age of 35 (302–303).

Berelson et al. (1954) note that, important to contemporary interpretations of political participation, there exist "age generations," age groups that matured in distinct time periods. These age generations differ from one another in terms of their voting behavior (301–302). The authors mention that those coming of age during the New Deal had a higher likelihood of voting according to their socioeconomic identification, in contrast to those who reached voting age in the 1920s, who generally did not emphasize political differences along class lines. People who form their political preferences in youth tend to maintain those preferences throughout their life span, a phenomenon that later would be termed the "generation effect." Berelson et al. observe that "people of different ages tend to go to other people of about the same age for discussion of the campaign" (104). Assuming that this observation holds true in contemporary U.S. politics, if there is a decided inclination for a significant proportion of young people not to engage in political discussion or activity, then to the extent that these young people do not converse with people in older age cohorts, who could serve as a source of information or encouragement to participate politically, young people may lack a key factor in initiating political engagement.

Peter Bachrach (1967) offers a critique of voting studies, referring particularly to Berelson, Lazarsfeld, and McPhee's (1954) examination of Elmira, New York, residents during the 1948 presidential campaign. Bachrach places the Elmira study in the context of a theoretical shift in political science following World War II, a shift he terms "democratic elitism." This approach to democracy emphasizes stability of the established system rather than extending political participation in a democracy. According to Bachrach, many political scientists came to the conclusion that democracy is better served if people who have little understanding of democratic principles and express little support for democracy do not participate. Therefore, if many citizens remain politically passive, that situation is beneficial to the maintenance of democracy. At the individual level, many citizens lack the understanding and motivation to participate in politics, but at the societal level, the individual deficiency becomes a virtue because the democratic system is more stable and flexible without the participation of many who do not value the basic principles of democracy (Berelson et al. 1954, 32–33). Berelson et al. (1954) express such a view with regard to young people, who have a predilection for radical change but tend not to be actively involved in politics. In criticizing this approach to nonparticipation, Bachrach (1967) comments, "[Berelson et al.] were in error in implying that because a political system is a viable and stable one, it is therefore also adequately contributing to the growth and well-being of ordinary men and women who live under it" (35). Bachrach asserts that "people generally . . . have a twofold interest in politics—interest in end results and interest in the process of participation" (101), and hence although low voter participation among youth might be considered a support for a more stable political system, on the individual level, those not participating have failed to engage in a key aspect of adulthood in a democracy.

In 1960, Angus Campbell, Philip E. Converse, Warren E. Miller, and Donald E. Stokes, all of whom were associated with the Survey Research Center at the University of Michigan, published *The American Voter*, which at the time was the consummate treatment of voting behavior in the United States. The authors base their analysis primarily on the 1952 and 1956 national elections. The minimum voting age during the 1950s still largely stood at 21, so their analysis of the relationship between voter turnout and vote preference, like Berelson, Lazarsfeld, and McPhee (1954), began at that age. The Michigan team note two interactive characteristics of young people: they vote less than older cohorts, and they tend to be less attached to the prevailing party system. They conclude from their analysis that "strong commitment to a party increases the probability that a person will vote," and therefore one explanation for higher voter turnout among older people involves their greater commitment to a political party (Campbell et al., 1960, 497). In contrast, younger voters, who often regard parties in terms of particular political leaders, are more willing to shift from party to party and to engage only intermittently in electoral politics. The authors speculate further that "in time of crisis [young people] may suddenly flock to the polls in proportions that create great surges in the electoral support of a party promising salvation. And they may in crisis depart from the traditional party structure entirely" (497). The Michigan researchers ask, in passing, whether reducing the voting age would result in "a more fluid electorate," and whether such a circumstance, whether the result of lowering the voting age or instituting a system of compulsory voting, would be "a matter of concern" or would contribute to a more "flexible" political system (498). They cite the voting preferences of young people during the Great Depression of the 1930s as an example of the fluidity of young voters: "the evidence seems to justify our conclusion that the Great Depression swung a heavy proportion of the young electors toward the Democratic Party and gave that party a hold on that generation, which it has never fully relinquished" (155). However, the Michigan researchers note "a substantial tendency for conservatism to increase with age, as we might expect on common sense grounds" (210–211), which can be identified as a life-cycle effect as opposed to a generation effect. Their analysis of voting data from the 1950s led the authors to conclude that "people in their twenties are not particularly concerned about political matters and indeed have a poor record of voting turnout" and that young people in 1930 plausibly were no more likely to become politically active compared to the rest of the population than young people in the 1950s (155–156). However, the New Deal program of Franklin Roosevelt may have attracted a large proportion of young voters, who generally lacked stable party loyalties and therefore were open to "prevailing political tides" (156). With hindsight, we can conclude that lowering the minimum voting age to 18 in 1971 had minimal impact on the

U.S. political party system, given the tendency of young voters to have weak political party loyalties.

Campbell et al. (1960) find in their survey data a striking relationship between age and what they term "class awareness." Those who expressed the greatest awareness of class differences in 1965 were those who were in their 20s and 30s during the Great Depression (357). In contrast, those over 60 years of age in 1956, who likely were "vocationally established" in 1930, appear largely to have withstood the redefinition of politics in class terms that occurred in the 1930s (358). The Michigan team offer support for both the generation effect and the life-cycle effect. Young people who vote for the first time are less likely than older voters to identify with one of the two major parties. If this circumstance results from the life-cycle effect, then older people always should be expected to have stronger ties to a political party and hence are more likely to be regular voters. However, if weaker party ties result from a generation effect, then as younger voters age, their lack of party ties continues, and thus their chance of becoming frequent voters likely would remain lower than previous generations (161).

Norman H. Nie, Sidney Verba, and John R. Petrocik, in *The Changing American Voter* (1979), originally published 16 years after *The American Voter*, provide further insights into the nature of political participation for younger age cohorts. For instance, Nie et al. report the proportion of independents by age from 1952 to 1974, indicating that the proportion of independents in each year consistently decreases with older age groups (60). However, the total proportion of independents increases from 1952 to 1974. In 1952, 25 percent of those 21 to 25 years of age classified themselves as independents, but the average percent of independents among those more than 30 years of age was 22 percent, a difference of 3 percent. However, in 1972 (with 18-to-20-year-olds included in the electorate), the percentage of independents among those 25 years old or younger was 51 percent, and for those more than 30 years old, 19 percent considered themselves independents, for a difference of 32 percent between the two age groups. The data indicate some increase in the percentage of independents in all age cohorts (60), but the major shift occurred among those 25 years old or younger. In 1974, nearly 50 percent of those identifying themselves as independents were less than 35 years old. Correspondingly, Nie et al. note the large gap between young persons and the rest of the population with regard to voter turnout. In the

1972 presidential election, 66 percent of the over-30 population voted, but just 47 percent of those 18 to 20 years old and 50 percent of those 21 to 24 voted (94).

Michael Lewis-Beck, William G. Jacoby, Helmut Norpoth, and Herbert F. Weisberg, in *The American Voter Revisited* (2008), bring the history of voting behavior analysis in the United States to the present, using survey data from the 2000 and 2004 presidential elections to update the findings of *The American Voter*. Lewis-Beck et al. reach the obvious conclusion, as previous researchers have, that the likelihood of voting increases with a person's age. When young voters reach their thirties, voter turnout rates increase substantially (from 57.9 percent for 20-year-olds to 74.5 percent for 30-year-olds) (454). Although young people become "politically legal" at the age of 18, "politics is new to them, with the candidates less familiar, the issues harder to digest, and the parties more vague in image than they are to older citizens" (354). As people age, they gain experience in politics and acquire knowledge and commitments to particular public policies, and thus voting can become a routine and expected activity. The authors note that the relationship between age and voter participation appears to contradict the positive relationship between formal education and political participation: "The younger voters (say under 35) participate less, though they clearly have more education than older voters (say over 35)" (355).

Presenting data from the National Election Studies survey in 2000, Lewis-Beck et al. (2008) observe that the effect of age on voter participation remains strong. For instance, the survey data indicate that the voter turnout of those in the sample with a high school education increases significantly with age. For those less than 35 years old, 59 percent report having voted; those aged 35 to 54, 75 percent; and those at least 55, 85 percent. People with a college education had turnout rates higher than those with a high school education, but the same pattern emerges, with younger people having the lowest voter turnout rate. Lewis-Beck et al. come to the same conclusion that Lazarsfeld et al. ([1944] 1968) did in their much earlier study: a potential for political instability arises when the electoral process experiences the entry of a large number of potential voters who generally have a low level of political bonds with a political party or ideology. However, Lewis-Beck et al. (2008) argue that young persons' lower interest in political engagement limits somewhat the political instability that could result from their participation (356). Should larger numbers of those around 60 years old enter the electorate, the number of people committed to one of the two major political parties is likely to increase. The authors comment that as the baby boomer generation, now reaching their sixties, express their political interests through voting and other forms of political participation, they will have a strong voice in Social Security policy making, in contrast to younger people, whose level of participation remains low relative to other age cohorts.

The instability to which Lewis-Beck et al. (2008) refer involves mainly partisan shifts in favor of one or the other of the two major political parties. They note that young voters usually follow the partisan preferences of their parents. However, when historical circumstances favor one party over the other, younger cohorts conform to the political shift more strongly than older age groups (153). For instance, the authors present data from National Election Surveys that indicate young adults under 30 years of age shifted sharply toward the Republican Party in the 1980s, when Ronald Reagan was president; in 1972, just 30 percent of party identifiers favored the Republican Party, but in 1988, 48 percent chose the Republican Party. However, by 2000 the proportion of Republican identifiers in the youngest age group had fallen to 36 percent. The authors discuss the phenomenon of partisan dealignment, which involves an increasing proportion of the electorate refusing to identify with either major political party, preferring instead to call themselves independents. Although other researchers have attributed dealignment to younger age groups, the authors argue that partisan decline has occurred in all age cohorts of the electorate (157). Conflicting evidence has been offered regarding whether dealignment has continued, or whether the electorate has become more polarized in recent years. In any case, young age cohorts can play a significant role in partisan shifts. Another possible source of such shifts involves the attraction young people potentially have for independent candidacies such as Ross Perot's run for the presidency in 1992. However, Lewis-Beck et al. conclude that such candidates lack the capacity to establish a base for sustained success, perhaps partially because young people in fact often lack strong partisan loyalties, whether to one of the two major parties or to a third party (421).

A major reason offered for the reduction of the voting age to 18 in 1971 by constitutional amendment revolved around the assertion that although young men could be drafted into the armed services beginning at the age of 18, those young people had no formal voice in the making of decisions that could result in their being subject to military duty and having to participate in armed combat. The criteria of competence and affected interests obviously clashed, with the recognition of affected interests leading to the conclusion that those aged 18 to 21 should be considered sufficiently competent to exercise the right to vote. Although 18 is the most frequent age requirement for voting (some countries require voters to be older than 21), more recently there has been a move in the United States and other countries to lower the voting age still further. For instance, 17 states allow 17-year-olds to vote in party nomination events (primary elections and caucuses). In elections other than for the European Parliament, Austria allows those as young as 16 years of age to vote in elections.

The consequences of lowering the voting age further are uncertain, given the history of voting behavior of those 18 to 21 years of age following ratification of the Twenty-Sixth Amendment. The voter turnout rate for this age group has been very low. In the first election following ratification of the Twenty-Sixth Amendment (1972), 18- to 20-year-olds reached a turnout rate of 48 percent, compared to 71 percent among those aged 45 to 64, but 12 years later, in 1984, the turnout rate among the youngest voters had declined to 41 percent, compared to 64 percent among those 45 to 54 and 70 percent among those 55 to 64 years of age. Voter turnout in the youngest age group reached even lower levels in other presidential elections, including 1996 (31 percent) and 2000 (28 percent) (Wattenberg 2008, 99).

The dismal voter turnout rates for young Americans represented an especially disappointing situation, given the belief that those 18 to 20 years old deserve the right to take part in electing their government leaders. Many explanations have been offered for why youth have exhibited such low voter turnout rates, even in presidential election years. Among the suggested explanations are that younger citizens have a lower level of completed education (for instance, many 18-year-olds have not yet completed a high school education), are less well-off economically, and are not as likely as older citizens to own their own home (home ownership provides a person with a large stake in the community and therefore is a strong impetus for civic engagement). Researchers also mention that younger people tend to move more frequently, which can result in their failing to meet residency requirements associated with voter registration (Shea, Green, Smith, and Gibson 2009, 506). Despite these factors that have led to younger

Americans having the lowest voter turnout rate of any age group, recent presidential elections have indicated a turnaround in the proportion of young people who vote. Shea et al. report that although the turnout among those 18 to 24 years old was only a little more than 32 percent in the 2000 election, the voter turnout rate for this age group increased to nearly 42 percent in 2004, and reached 52 percent in 2008. More modest increases occurred in the age group 25 to 44, with turnout increasing from approximately 50 percent in 2000 to a little more than 52 percent in 2004, and to 56 percent in 2008. More modest increases (due to already higher turnout rates and hence less room for improvement) also occurred in other age cohorts, and thus the overall turnout rate increased from approximately 51 percent in 2000 to more than 55 percent in 2004, and reached 63 percent in 2008.

Shea et al. (2009) suggest various reasons for increased voter turnout among young people in recent presidential election years. In 2004, because both Democratic and Republican supporters perceived the campaign to be very close, various organizations such as America Coming Together and MoveOn.org formed to encourage people to vote. In addition, important issues, such as the Iraq war, the controversy over stem cell research, and the question of legalizing gay marriage undoubtedly prompted a greater turnout rate. In 2008, several organizations, including MTV's Rock the Vote and Choose or Lose, Justvotenow.org, the New Voters Project, Smack Down Your Vote!, Youth Vote Coalition, and Generation Engage ran major campaigns to encourage young people to vote. Undoubtedly the candidacy of Barak Obama, the first African American major party presidential candidate, aroused the interest of many citizens, especially younger voters, to cast a ballot. Shea et al. also note the increased participation of young people in the 2008 presidential nomination process. For instance, in the Iowa caucuses, which were the first significant nomination event, three times as many of those less than 30 years of age participated in 2008 as participated in 2000 or 2004. In Tennessee, the turnout was four times greater in 2008 than in 2004. Several other states experienced comparable increases for turnout in primaries and caucuses among those less than 30 years of age (506). Researchers estimate that Barack Obama received approximately 66 percent of the votes of those aged 18 to 24. Analysts express concern about whether this increased voter turnout among young people will continue and increase in the future, especially given that younger people still have the lowest voter turnout rate of any age group (in

2008, 52 percent of those between 18 and 24 voted , compared to 69 percent for the age cohorts 45 to 64 and 65 and older).

Youth Political Participation in the 1960s

Other forms of youth political participation preceded the push to lower the voting age to 18. Although young people engaged in military combat during World War II, and there was some discussion at the time of lowering the voting age, following the war this age group remained essentially politically quiescent. As Eric Foner notes, young people in the 1950s were called "the silent generation" (2005, 998). However, youth activism became more visible during the early 1960s, perhaps due in part to the increased number of young people attending colleges and universities. In 1968 more than 7 million people were attending college (998). One organization, Students for a Democratic Society (SDS), helped to initiate the so-called New Left, which de-emphasized the issues of economic equality that motivated the Old Left of the 1930s—composed of communists, socialists, Trotskyists, and pacifists (Myers 1989, 2)—to emphasize instead efforts to improve the overall quality of life, criticizing many of the basic assumptions of contemporary liberal society. Such an approach to politics did not focus on the more traditional notions of participation in the political realm that include engagement in traditional community structures and electoral politics.

In June 1962 members of SDS met in Port Huron, New York, to develop a statement expressing the organization's principles. The authors of the Port Huron Statement expressed the disillusionment that resulted from being raised into "modest comfort" and being taught to believe in the American values of freedom, equality, and democracy, only to become aware of the contradictions of racism, military expenditures devoted to the Cold War, and what they perceived as the devaluing of genuine controversy for safer public relations in the university. The statement called for the right of each person to participate in the decisions that affect their life (Teodori 1969, 163–172).

One example of youth attempting to participate in the political realm is the Free Speech Movement (FSM) of 1964–1965 at the University of California at Berkeley. In September 1964,

Dean Katherine Towle declared that university policy prohibiting political advocacy for candidates and political causes on campus would be strictly enforced. On October 1, campus police attempted to arrest a former graduate student, Jack Weinberg, who was sitting at a table sponsored by the Congress of Racial Equality (CORE). Students surrounded the police car and did not allow it to move, and for 32 hours the car remained in place and actually was used as a speakers' podium. Subsequently the university dropped the charges against Weinberg, but the movement continued when, on December 3, nearly 2,000 students occupied Sproul Hall in an attempt to force the administration to negotiate with the students regarding the university's policy of limiting political speech. In the early morning of December 4, police surrounded the building and arrested approximately 800 students. When the university brought charges against the students, a protest began that led to closing the university. In January 1965, university officials agreed to allow political discussion for all students at specified hours during the day on the steps of Sproul Hall. Student members of the FSM executive committee, including Mario Savio, a skilled and impassioned speaker, demonstrated a level of political sophistication in representing the various student interests concerned with the issue of free speech. As the United States became increasingly involved in the Vietnam conflict, students at other universities around the country used the FSM at Berkeley as a model for organizing protests against the war.

If the FSM established the framework for protest movements, opposition to the Vietnam War brought disillusioned youth together for protest at the national level. Politically liberal youth perceived the war as the logical result of the failed structure of the U.S. government's Cold War policies. The culmination of the opposition occurred in October 1967 with the march on the Pentagon, when an estimated 100,000 people expressed their opposition to the war, and hundreds were arrested for crossing police lines. Whereas the initial object of the New Left was to advocate equal participation and liberty, many youth shifted the focus to cultural freedom that involved the rejection of any authority or regulation in such areas as clothing, drug use, and sexual behavior (Foner 2005, 1007). In fact, some have argued that the protest movement of the 1960s evolved from a narrowly political cause with explicit goals to a more amorphous counterculture based on the right of individual choice independent of established authority. Youth emphasized community, but a notion of community separate from, and with values distinct from, the overall contemporary culture.

At the center of youth activism in the 1960s and early 1970s was SDS. The Port Huron Statement, composed primarily by Tom Haden, emphasized the importance of personal involvement in politics through direct action to bring about change in the social and political system, and participatory democracy through grassroots-level activity: in other words, ordinary people rather than professional politicians would initiate social and political change (Myers 1989, 3). Founders of SDS quickly split over strategy. One group, following Al Haber, conceived of SDS as an organization situated on college campuses that was dedicated to studying the country's major problems and that would publish recommendations for social transformation. A second group followed Tom Hayden and Rennie Davis along a more activist path, emphasizing the political activation of the less advantaged groups in society. A third group, never very influential, attempted to establish a coalition with liberal groups to pursue common objectives (3–4). The organization quickly gained many new members who showed less interest in the theoretical positions expressed in the Port Huron Statement, instead opting for an activist agenda while at the same time rejecting traditional electoral politics and governmental bureaucracy (5–6).

Directly relevant to youth participation in politics were the efforts of SDS activists to establish branches in high schools and on college campuses. SDS leaders attempted to create organizations on college campuses that would engage student members in political action intended to challenge the authority of the university administration and ultimately of the larger society. Carl Davidson (1969) issued a document in which he offered a strategy for altering the character of universities and ultimately of American society through direct student action. Davidson disapproved of traditional forms of student engagement, such as participating in student government, because, he claimed, such organizations were ineffective in bringing about real change and had been co-opted by an administration he considered authoritarian. According to Davidson, the purpose of student governments was "the containment, or pacification and manipulation of the student body" (326). Davidson suggested that students engaged in activism support those reforms that contribute to "a radical transformation of the university and society" (327). Activists should avoid those reforms that leave the authority of the system unchallenged, that result in divisions among students, and that lead to "co-management" between students and administration, which amounts to co-optation of students to the interests and goals of the administration (328). Davidson recommended support for reforms that advance civil liberties and that lead to the elimination of such "repressive mechanisms" as student courts and other disciplinary groups (328). He urged the formation of various radical student organizations, such as student defense leagues to defend students subject to disciplinary action, teaching assistants' unions, non-academic employees' unions, and SDS chapters (333). Davidson saw the power of such groups lying in their ability to threaten or actually call a student strike that would prevent the university from functioning: "because of this, our constant strategy should be the preparation of a mass base for supporting and participating in this kind of action" (333).

In addition to the prime focus on the university level, SDS engaged in establishing chapters at the high school and even the junior high school level. Mark Kleiman (1969), a student at a Southern California high school in the late 1960s, offered his views about the need for a protest movement in high schools. Kleiman claimed that such acts of vandalism as setting trash cans on fire and pulling fire alarms could be considered forms of political protest against the existing organization of public schools (318). Kleiman identified the major reason for such acts of protest with the condition of public education: "high school is not worth the time we spend there" (319). Students and faculty, Kleiman maintained, are "the tool *and* the product of administrative totalitarianism" (320). He suggested that SDS should become involved in issues he believed were important for students and should play a leading role in student protests against the actions of school administrators. Recognizing that high school student government organizations generally bow to administrative restrictions, Kleiman nonetheless advocated radical student involvement in such organizations in order either to force school administrations to agree to student demands or to "look silly" if the administration denied those demands. Among the goals Kleiman identified for student radicals were the right of students and teachers together to decide on the curriculum, full academic freedom on the high school campus, termination of "student police squads and oppressive Attendance Officers," and the right of students to select the courses they wish to take (323). The ultimate goal, according to Kleiman, should be the creation of a society where all people can experience freedom of expression (323).

The New Left organizers wanted to increase the political engagement of young people, but in directions distinct from those considered appropriate by those in the mainstream of U.S. politics. Rather than participating in party politics, activists challenged the existing party system, as was demonstrated by protests at the 1968 Democratic National Convention. R. David Myers (1989) notes that in 1968, members of the New Left reached the peak of activity. With the Tet Offensive in Vietnam, followed by President Lyndon Johnson's decision not to seek another term as president and the assassinations of Martin Luther King Jr. and Robert Kennedy, many SDS members became further radicalized (9). At the June 1969 SDS national convention in Chicago, the organization divided into the Maoist Progressive Labor party, the Revolutionary Youth Movement, and the Weathermen, which became "the most violent manifestation of the New Left" (10). Myers states that by 1972, the New Left had ceased to be a significant force in U.S. politics. In conjunction with the disintegration of SDS, mainstream U.S. politicians committed to traditional electoral politics began to support the enfranchisement of those aged 18 to 21.

The Campaign for the 18-Year-Old Franchise

Given that the Twenty-Sixth Amendment establishing the right to vote in state and national elections for those at least 18 years old was ratified during the U.S. involvement in Vietnam, it is not surprising that the history of lowering the voting age closely follows various other armed conflicts. Wendell W. Cultice (1992) provides a detailed history of the movement to lower the minimum voting age. Cultice notes that England had established the minimum voting age of 21, and the American colonies followed this precedent. However, in some elections for militia officers in New England, the minimum voting age was less than 21 because militia regiments included males as young as 16 (3). Some colonies established a minimum age for suffrage rights higher than 21 for non-militia-related elections (4). Those states that revised their constitutions to conform to independence from Great Britain established voter qualifications, including a minimum age criterion. Where state constitutions mentioned a specific age, it generally was 21. Although the U.S. Constitution set minimum age qualifications for public office (35 for the presidency, 30 for U.S. senators, and 25 for members of the U.S. House of Representatives), that document did not establish any qualifications for voters, except to state that those qualified to vote in elections for U.S. representatives shall be those who meet the state qualifications to vote for representatives to the largest chamber of the state legislature (U.S. Constitution, Article 1, section 2).

In the first half of the 19th century, debates occasionally occurred with regard to lowering the voting age. Those supporting a reduction argued that because a male 18 years of age was doing the work of an adult, he should be granted the right to vote. However, opponents of such proposals prevailed. Although states eliminated most property qualifications for voting, the age qualification remained unchanged, even though military service and suffrage continued as a popular argument among Americans (Cultice 1992, 9).

Cultice notes that during the Civil War, approximately two-thirds of union soldiers were less than 22 years old, and more than a half million were less than 17 (Cultice 1992, 12). The institution of the draft raised more starkly the premise that if people are old enough to serve in the military, they should be considered old enough to vote in elections to determine those public officials who can make decisions affecting the prospects of life or death for individuals. However, neither state nor national governments took action. For instance, during the New York state constitutional convention in 1867, a proposal to set the minimum voting age at 18 was decisively defeated (13).

In 1917, with U.S. entry into World War I, President Woodrow Wilson's administration instituted a draft, and in anticipation of U.S. involvement in the conflict in Europe and the threat of Japanese aggression, Congress in 1940 passed the Selective Training and Service Act, thus establishing the first peacetime draft (Cultice 1992, 19). The logic of the argument that anyone old enough to serve in the military (especially if compulsory) should have the right to vote became persuasive for many, and in August 1943, voters in Georgia approved an amendment to the state constitution that granted the right of U.S. citizens in the state at least 18 years old to vote in all elections (25). However, no other states followed Georgia's lead. From 1945 to 1952, legislators in 40 states considered approximately 100 proposals to reduce the voting age, while several proposals were submitted to the U.S. Congress to reduce the voting age, but none was successful. Although the statement "old enough to fight, old enough to vote" persuaded many of the wisdom of lowering the voting age, others failed to recognize a clear connection.

In a Senate debate in 1953, Senator Hubert H. Humphrey, who supported lowering the voting age, claimed that doing so would encourage participation "of these people at an age when they are enthusiastic and interested in government and politics" (quoted in Cultice 1992, 38), a claim that, as an overall generalization, lacked empirical support. Data about young people's interest in, and knowledge of, American politics indicates that this age group often lags behind their elders. Contrary to the supporters of lowering the voting age, opponents questioned the level of knowledge that 18- to 20-year-olds possess and concluded that eligibility for the draft represented a poor criterion for determining the qualifications of a voter (48). The hesitancy among legislators about altering the voting age had to do in part with the question of which political party was more likely to gain the greater support among this age group. Uncertainty about partisan support undoubtedly led some members of Congress to hesitate about supporting a constitutional amendment, perhaps rationalizing that the Constitution grants the states authority to establish voting qualifications (at least before the activities of the civil rights movement and passage of the Voting Rights Act of 1965). Lyndon Johnson, in February 1961 shortly after taking office as vice president, commented that the framers of the Constitution intended that the minimum voting age be determined by the states (83).

In 1955, Kentucky became the second state to lower the voting age to 18. In March 1954, the Kentucky General Assembly approved a proposed state constitutional amendment to lower the voting age, and in November 1955, the voters of the state ratified the amendment. When admitted to the union in 1956, Alaska established the voting age at 19, and Hawaii entered the union with a voting age of 20 (Cultice 1992, 58–59). These successes in lowering the voting age represented exceptions to the general rule of defeating such attempts at the state and federal levels. Cultice notes that from 1925 to 1964, approximately 60 proposals for a constitutional amendment to lower the voting age had been introduced in Congress, only to suffer defeat. In December 1963, just short of a month following President John F. Kennedy's assassination, President Lyndon Johnson received the report from the Commission on Voter Participation and Registration, which President Kennedy had established in his first year in office. Concerned generally with encouraging voter registration and participation, the commission also focused on the appropriate minimum age for voters. Noting the low voter turnout among those aged 21 to 30, the commission suggested that the three-year gap between graduating from high school and finally reaching the age at which they are qualified to vote could explain the decline in interest in politics. Therefore, the commission members recommended that each state should consider establishing the minimum voting age at 18 (85). Despite this recommendation, efforts in various states, including Maryland, New York, and Massachusetts, failed to result in adopting the 18-year-old vote.

Centuries-long tradition apparently led lawmakers and voters to conclude that the age of 21 should remain the "age of reason." The argument that because young people are subject to the military draft, they should have the right to vote did not hold sway in most cases, even during the major military conflicts of American history, including the Civil War, World War I, and World War II. However, a limited conflict in Southeast Asia would have a significant effect on the question of voting age. Now youth were not only fighting in that war, but represented a major source of opposition to the military engagement. Youth participation in demonstrations and disruptions, including the march on the Pentagon and the protests at the 1968 Democratic National Convention highlighted the dissatisfaction that many youth felt toward a military engagement in which the government required many to participate through the draft, and with which so many disagreed. The question of voting age to a large extent had been taken out of the hands of public officials and appropriated by those who were both adamantly opposed to government policy and willing to express their opposition by political means other than voting, certainly in part because they were denied the more conventional means of political participation.

In the late 1960s, those committed to lowering the voting age began in earnest to organize to further their cause. In 1968, Dennis Warren, a pre-law student, established LUV (Let Us Vote) at the University of the Pacific in Stockton, California (Cultice 1992, 97). LUV held that young people who have accepted adult responsibilities should be granted the right to participate in the political process. Warren subsequently joined the board of directors of the Youth Franchise Coalition, organized in February 1970 as a clearinghouse for various groups that supported lowering the voting age. Members of the coalition included Americans for Democratic

Action, College Young Democrats, the National Education Association, the National Student Caucus, the Student National Education Association, the U.S. National Student Association, and the U.S. Youth Council. Paul J. Minarchenko Jr. served as chairman, and Ian R. MacGowan, as executive director of the Washington, D.C., office. The coalition members pursued their objective through state as well as federal government action (99). Other organizations working for the lowered voting age objective were Citizens for Vote 18 in New York and the Student Democratic Coalition in Virginia (102).

Although in retrospect the student demonstrations and disruptions related to the Vietnam War are regarded as a major rationale for granting the 18-year-old vote as a means of encouraging more mainstream avenues of political participation for youth and thus providing this age group with a sense of involvement in the political process, at the time supporters feared that such political activity, deemed to be "irresponsible," might jeopardize (or at least delay) action at the state and federal levels to lower the voting age (Cultice 1992, 103). Although both major political parties supported lowering the voting age, the 1968 Democratic Party platform supported an amendment to the U.S. Constitution but the Republican platform called instead for alterations in state policy.

In the national Congress, the issue arose as to whether the voting age could be lowered through legislation, or if a constitutional amendment was necessary. Members of Congress supporting the 18-year-old vote planned to have a provision added to the renewal of the 1965 Voting Rights Act. Cultice notes that the young people who came to Washington to lobby for this legislative provision contrasted with those youth who were protesting the Vietnam War: "Their revolutionary consciousness was zero. . . . They did not issue periodic warnings about what the 'kids' would do if the system failed to respond. Even their issue [voting age] seemed faintly old-fashioned, like something culled from a dusty civics textbook" (Cultice 1992, 134). The congressional leadership had become convinced that taking action through regular legislation rather than by a constitutional amendment would pass judicial muster, so both the Senate and the House of Representatives approved the amendment to the renewed Voting Right Act to lower the voting age to 18, and President Richard Nixon signed the legislation into law. Now supporters would have to wait for challenges to the act's constitutionality in the federal courts.

In the meantime, supporters of lowering the minimum voting age continued to pursue their objective in the states. However, 1970 brought few victories for them, with most efforts being rebuffed in referenda to amend state constitutions. Proposals were rejected in 9 of 14 states considering such a change (Cultice 1992, 158). Voters in Maine and Nebraska approved lowering the voting age to 20, and Massachusetts, Minnesota, and Montana set the voting age at 19. However, the shear number of state efforts to lower the voting age equaled the total number of state referenda from 1943 to 1969, thus indicating a much greater concern for the issue and greatly increased efforts to reduce the voting age (159).

Concerned about the constitutionality of the federal legislation setting the minimum voting age at 18 and the possible consequences for the 1972 presidential election, those on both sides of the issue moved to have the U.S. Supreme Court decide the issue as soon as possible. Four states—Idaho, Arizona, Texas, and Oregon—challenged the constitutionality of the new law (Cultice 1992, 163). In December 1970, the U.S. Supreme Court, in *Oregon v. Mitchell*, reflecting concerns for maintaining the role of the states in the federal system, ruled in a 5–4 decision that Congress possessed the constitutional authority to set the minimum age qualification in elections for president and Congress but that Congress had overstepped its authority by mandating the minimum age for state and local elections. The decision immediately raised significant difficulties for the 47 states that maintained a minimum voting age higher than 18, because in those years in which both national and state offices appeared on the same ballot, they would have to develop a dual voting system that would allow those 18 to 20 years of age to vote for national offices, but prohibit them from voting for state and local offices (178).

Although states could attempt to amend their constitutions in order to coincide with federal law establishing the 18-year-old vote, there was little chance that all states would complete such a cumbersome process prior to the 1972 general election. The more promising option was to propose an amendment to the U.S. Constitution that mandated a minimum voting age of 18. In January 1971, Senator Jennings Randolph (D-WV) introduced a joint resolution proposing such an amendment. On March 10, the U.S. Senate unanimously approved the proposed constitutional amendment, and on March 23, the U.S. House of Representatives followed suit, approving the proposed amendment (Cultice 1992, 188). The amendment calling for lowering the minimum voting age to 18 was then sent to the state legislatures, with the hope that the required three-fourths of the state legislatures would ratify it quickly in order to avoid the administrative complexities and costs of a dual election system in 1972.

Even though the process of state action to lower the voting age proved to be disappointing up to 1970, the ratification of the Twenty-Sixth Amendment proved to be swift, due in part to the constitutional provision that state legislatures approve the amendment without the need for a popular referendum, which was the stage at which most state constitutional amendment efforts failed. Organizations such as Common Cause, the National Education Association and the Student NEA, Project 18, and Youth Franchise Coalition took part in working to have the amendment proposed and ratified, and Youth Franchise Coalition, composed of 23 organizations, lobbied state legislators to support the amendment (Cultice 1992, 190).

During the time the U.S. House and Senate were debating the proposed amendment, state legislatures continued to consider state constitutional amendments to lower the voting age, perhaps as a hedge against the possible failure to ratify the amendment to the national Constitution. At this time, opinion polls indicated that a majority of Americans favored lowering the voting age. Although support for the change declined with increasing age, a majority in all age groups backed the amendment (Cultice 1992, 200). State legislatures began ratifying the proposed amendment almost immediately. Five states ratified the amendment on March 23, and the number of ratifications increased steadily until Ohio became the 38th state to do so on June 30, just 100 days after congressional proposal. With the required three-fourths of state legislatures having approved the amendment, it was now officially ratified as the Twenty-Sixth Amendment to the U.S. Constitution.

Following ratification, President Nixon declared, "I urge them [those 18 to 20 years old] to honor this right by exercising it—by registering and voting in each election" (Cultice 1992, 214). The resulting voter turnout rates for those 18 to 20 years of age tended to confirm the aptness of President Nixon's entreaty to young people to take advantage of the newly granted suffrage right. Subsequently, the focus moved away from portraying young people as anxious to participate in the political process from which they were barred to one of offering reasons for low participation rates and suggesting ways of increasing that participation. Turnout among the newly enfranchised Americans reached

48.3 percent in the 1972 election, but in the 1974 congressional election, the turnout dropped to 20.8 percent among all 18- to 20-year-olds (221, 222). However, at the same time that more than 11 million potential new voters were being added to the electorate, the overall turnout rate among other age groups also had been gradually declining. Therefore, the explanations for low youth participation in elections are related to the overall decline in political participation, but still young citizens are less likely to vote than older Americans. The question to be asked once more is whether the gap in turnout between younger and older citizens is due to a life-cycle effect (in other words, that young people can be distinguished from older age cohorts in their reluctance to participate, but as they grow older, their participation rates will increase) or a generational effect (in other words, that this trend of lower voter turnout will continue into later life).

Voting after the Twenty-Sixth Amendment

In 1993, in order to encourage higher voter turnout, Congress passed the National Voter Registration Act (NVRA), which President Bill Clinton signed into law. Janine A. Parry and Todd G. Shields (2001) analyze the relationship among gender, age, and implementation of the NVRA, also known as the Motor Voter Act because the legislation called for states to provide residents the opportunity to register to vote at motor vehicle and other public offices. Parry and Shields note that the major purpose of the NVRA is to overcome the additional burden that the U.S. electoral system places on potential voters, requiring them to take on the responsibility of validating their qualifications to vote by registering prior to an election. Parry and Shields observe that the act of voting for most citizens "is a marginal (or low-cost/low benefit) action" (507). In their discussion of the effects of age on voter turnout, Parry and Shields present the three major hypotheses used to explain the relationship between age and political participation. First, the life-experience hypothesis notes that as people grow older, they gain additional knowledge and resources that make political participation more likely. Alternatively, the life-cycle hypothesis claims that a lower proportion of younger people vote because they have not yet acquired sufficient involvement that contributes to the belief that political engagement is an important aspect of their lives. Finally, the generational hypothesis argues that each generation has different experiences that lead to differing propensities to engage in politics. The authors suggest, for instance, that contemporary young people vote in fewer numbers because they did not experience the events of World War I, World War II, and the Great Depression, events which energized previous generations to participate in politics (511–512). As a result of their analysis, Parry and Shields conclude that evidence from the 1996 presidential election supports the life-experience hypothesis, which predicts that voter turnout will increase with age. However, they note that this relationship exists only for men; because younger and older women have had differing socialization experiences, younger women can be expected to exhibit higher turnout rates (519) that may overcome other generational factors that militate against higher voter turnout among a younger age cohort.

Richard G. Niemi and Michael J. Hanmer (2010) investigated factors that are associated with the voting behavior of college students. The authors note that although youth turnout in 2004 increased, the gap between the youngest age group and older citizens actually grew (301). In order to determine factors influencing turnout rates among students no older than 24, the authors conducted a national survey following the November 2004 election. They conclude that variations in voter turnout among college students is not associated with traditional demographic measures such as education level, mobility, and home ownership (303). Niemi and Hanmer hypothesize instead that "psychological factors—such as general interest in politics, attachment to political parties, and interest in the presidential election—along with political party mobilization are significant in explaining variation in turnout among college students" (305). They found strong support for this hypothesis, reporting that frequency of political discussions, partisan strength, and mobilization efforts by political parties are strongly associated with voter turnout (310). The authors also found that college-specific variables also were important, especially how far a student's home was from the college or university (319); in other words, the costs of going home to vote are less for those living close to home. Niemi and Hanmer conclude that the results of their survey provide an optimistic picture of youth political participation, given the relatively high turnout rate among students—although they note that turnout was self-reported and hence likely exaggerates actual turnout rates.

The Importance of the Mass Media to Political Participation

In the 20th century, when new technological innovations in communication were introduced, many hailed the new media as offering promising ways to engage more citizens in the political realm. For instance, Matthew Hindman (2009, 130) notes that with the introduction of radio broadcasting in the 1920s and 1930s, political scientists expected the new means of communication to result in greater knowledge about politics and greater involvement in the public realm among the general population. However, although technological advance can result in substantial changes in human behavior, the direction of change may be difficult to anticipate. Hindman reports that when the NBC radio network cancelled of the American Political Science Association's civic education program, political scientists moderated their enthusiasm about the potential beneficial consequences of the new medium. As Hindman summarizes the situation, interested political scientists attributed the less than sterling results of this attempt to reach the general population to such factors as the crucial role of advertising in the new medium, the connection between national networks and their station affiliates, and the costs of producing a radio program (130). Although Hindman could have combined radio with television as an example of a medium with great expected potential for informing the public about politics, he focuses on radio, observing a similarity between the case of radio and that of the Internet with regard to attempts to increase the political knowledge and engagement of the average citizen (including youth) and hence with regard to efforts to enhance the operation of democracy in the United States.

Hindman notes that "political traffic is a tiny portion of Web usage. . . . Noncommercial sources of political information have failed to mount a real challenge to traditional media outlets" (2009, 131). He also refers to characteristics of the Internet that militate against the amount of information to which citizens are exposed. When individuals use search engines, the depth of information received often is limited (132). Contrary to the assumption that the Internet transfers political influence away from political elites, in fact a small group of "A-bloggers" get more exposure than all other bloggers combined (133). Hindman uses the label "missing middle" to refer to the situation in which most online attention goes to two categories: first, the small group of "winners" who receive the greatest amount of exposure, and second, a myriad of small Web sites that receive the remaining attention, with no mid-level group. Hindman claims that the concentration of sources on the Web exceeds that of the more traditional media (134). He observes that the Internet can have an unambiguous effect in reporting scandals, and hence on the nature of political discussion (137). The July 2010 Web posting of Afghan war documents by Wikileaks.com suggests the type of influence the Internet can impose on the political process. However, Hindman argues that although such leaks can have a significant effect on political conversation, such leaks tend to be rare and do not lead to "outsiders" succeeding in gaining attention online (137).

The July 2010 case of Shirley Sherrod, Georgia State Director of Rural Development for the U.S. Department or Agriculture, raises serious questions about the ability of a blogger (in this case, Andrew Breitbart) to influence decisions of government officials. Breitbart posted portions of Sherrod's speech before a meeting of the NAACP, that, taken out of context, gave the impression that Sherrod, an African American, had acted prejudicially against a white farmer in 1986, when she worked for a private firm assisting African American farmers. Only after Sherrod was forced to resign her position in the Obama administration did a full presentation of her speech indicate that Breitbart's excerpt misrepresented her message. The Internet can be used to present undigested information (or misinformation), which in turn can evoke a hasty reply from government officials or political figures. Such incidents possibly can raise the level of cynicism about the political realm, especially among young people, who may be further alienated from political engagement.

Hindman concludes that a person needs to have considerable political skill and an inclination to consult political blogs, and correspondingly few bloggers have the ability to attract readers: "If we consider the ability of ordinary citizens to write things that other people will see, the Internet has fallen far short of the claims that continue to be made about it. It may be easy to speak in cyberspace, but it remains difficult to be heard" (2009, 142). If

Hindman's analysis is correct, then the Internet likely does not offer an obvious way in which a larger proportion of young people can be encouraged to gain greater knowledge of the political process and specific political issues, and to participate more effectively.

Stephen Coleman and Jay G. Blumler present a less critical, but still cautious analysis of the potential for the Internet to "revitalize our flagging political communication arrangements by injecting some new and different elements into the relationship between representatives and represented and governments and governed" (2009, 9–10). Focusing primarily on British politics, Coleman and Blumler describe the condition in which many citizens have become increasingly disengaged from the political processes and institutions of representative democracy and in which citizens express low levels of political efficacy, a situation that can be regarded as a "crisis of disengagement" (1). According to Coleman and Blumler, many people complain that government and the political process fail to acknowledge them and respect their views (2). Meaningful democratic participation, they argue, requires accountable institutions that allow for effective interaction between citizens and elected officials (3). Their definition of "political citizens" has great relevance to an understanding of the involvement of youth in politics: they are citizens who "do not simply spring into life; they are constituted through complex interactions between their own life experiences, traditions of collective action, structures of opportunity and available discourses of thinking and acting politically" (5). The significant question is whether the Internet plays (or can be made to play) a substantial role in the process of creating such citizens. While Matthew Hindman (2009) has raised serious doubts about the overall usefulness of the Internet to democracy, Coleman and Blumler ultimately offer a plan to add greater promise to what they term the vulnerable potential of the Internet to renew declining political communication (2009, 9). I will describe their proposal in chapter 2.

Jim Hightower, editor of the progressive newsletter *The Hightower Lowdown* (2010), has publicized the claimed attempt by the telephone and cable companies AT&T, Comcast, Time Warner, and Verizon, which control approximately 94 percent of the U.S. Internet service providers trade, to offer more efficient and faster service for a fee. Hightower terms the Internet the most democratic of all media but charges that the four companies wish to become "the gatekeepers of content" (2). The companies, Hightower claims, intend to establish corporate control of the Internet, and he argues that they wish to prevent government from regulating the Internet. Hightower quotes Sir Tim Berners-Lee, considered the inventor of the Internet: "When I invented the Web, I didn't have to ask anyone's permission. Now hundreds of millions of people are using it freely. I am worried that that is going to end in the USA. . . . Control of information is hugely powerful. In the US, the threat is that companies control what I can access for [their own] commercial reasons" (2). Those opposing such claimed efforts by large Internet service providers assert that the companies want to determine the nature of service for various users, including the speed of service and whether they have access to the Internet at all, charging fees for different levels of service. These opponents call themselves advocates of "Net Neutrality." Hightower mentions Save the Internet, a group that opposes large communications companies and that advocates net neutrality. The group warns that telephone and cable companies are investing large amounts of money to lobby Congress to gain permission to increase control of the use of the Internet (Save the Internet, 2010). Hightower mentions that Senator John McCain has introduced a bill in the U.S. Senate titled "The Internet Freedom Act," which would ban the Federal Communications Commission from "enacting rules to preserve net neutrality" (4). Supporters of the telecommunications companies such as former congressman and U.S. House of Representatives majority leader Dick Armey has referred to "net brutality" rather than "net neutrality" (3). This case indicates that the Internet still is a fluid entity, and hence the use of this communications technology is dependent on the intentions of several interests with differing stakes—monetary as well as partisan and ideological. Thus, the role that the Internet can play in encouraging the engagement of young citizens in the political realm may depend on decisions made at the highest levels of government.

Scholzman, Verba, and Brady (2010) examine the role of the Internet in facilitating political participation. They present observations about youth, political participation, and the Internet. First, it is well known that young people are less politically active than older age cohorts. Second, young people are those most likely to use the Internet. Third, "among those who use the Internet and e-mail, the young are actually the least likely to be politically active online" (492). However, Scholzman et al. conclude that socioeconomic status plays a much greater role than age in determining whether individuals will be active politically. In attempting to determine the influence of the Internet on political participation, the authors note that the greater likelihood that young people will use the Internet results in this age group being less underrepresented in terms of Internet-based political participation (493). With regard to making campaign contributions, Scholzman et al. note that those in the age group 18 to 24 represent the lowest proportion of those making contributions offline as well as online. However, as could be expected, the difference in the age of online contributions among age groups is much smaller. With regard to political discussion, the authors discovered that "people are much more likely to engage in political discussions offline than on the Internet," and those less than 25 years old participate in such discussions the least; but, once again perhaps due to the larger proportion of youth who use the Internet, online discussions actually decrease with age, a phenomenon of the generational digital divide (496, 498). The authors conclude that "when it comes to online politics—whether political activity, political discussion, or requests for political action on the Internet—younger respondents are less underrepresented than they are offline" (503). Given the relative newness of Internet use, this phenomenon may represent a temporary effect that will lessen as today's youth age; or, as the authors speculate, new generations of young people will continue to use the Internet and social networking sites in larger percentages than older people.

Conclusion

With notable exceptions, young people traditionally have had a minimal voice in politics. Legal limits on the right to vote as well as lack of experiences in the rules of the political game and low levels of engagement in the community generally have militated against high levels of political participation. The Vietnam War era represents a crucial time for focusing on youth political participation. Student demonstrations against the war, although initially giving pause to legislators with regard to lowering the voting age to 18, ultimately contributed to the reasoning that young people who are being asked to fight and possibly die should have the right to participate in making government policy. With ratification of the Twenty-Sixth Amendment, observers quickly discovered that those 18 to 20 years old had the lowest turnout rate among all age cohorts, confirming previous research indicating low participation by young citizens. The development of new communication technologies, especially the Internet, raised hopes that new opportunities for reaching young people and prospective voters generally could increase the level of participation, but so far, as with radio and television, the Internet does not necessarily result in a more informed and interested electorate. Chapter 2 will investigate various procedures suggested to increase youth political participation.

References

Bachrach, Peter. *The Theory of Democratic Elitism: A Critique*. Boston: Little, Brown, 1967.

Berelson, Bernard R., Paul F. Lazarsfeld, and William N. McPhee. *Voting: A Study of Opinion Formation in a Presidential Election*. Chicago: University of Chicago Press, 1954.

Campbell, Angus, Philip E. Converse, Warren E. Miller, and Donald E. Stokes. *The American Voter*. New York: Wiley, 1960.

Coleman, Stephen, and Jay G. Blumler. *The Internet and Democratic Citizenship: Theory, Practice and Policy*. New York: Cambridge University Press, 2009.

Cultice, Wendell W. *Youth's Battle for the Ballot: A History of Voting Age in America*. Santa Barbara, CA: Greenwood Press, 1992.

Dahl, Robert. *After the Revolution? Authority in a Good Society*. Revised edition. New Haven, CT: Yale University Press, 1990. First published in 1970.

Dahl, Robert. *Democracy in the United States: Promise and Performance*. Fourth edition. Dallas, TX: Houghton Mifflin, 1981.

Davidson, Carl. "The New Radicals and the Multiversity." In *The New Left: A Documentary History*, edited by Massimo Teodori, 323–335. New York: Bobbs-Merrill, 1969.

Evans, Richard J. *The Third Reich in Power*. New York: Penguin, 2005.

Foner, Eric. *Give Me Liberty! An American History*. New York: W. W. Norton, 2005.

Hightower, Jim. "Big Biz Wants to Own the Information Superhighway While We the People Bump Along the Backroads." *Hightower Lowdown* 12 (July 2010): 1–4.

Hindman, Matthew. *The Myth of Digital Democracy*. Princeton, NJ: Princeton University Press, 2009.

Kleiman, Mark. "High School Reform: Toward a Student Movement." In *The New Left: A Documentary History*, edited by Massimo Teodori, 246–248. New York: Bobbs-Merrill, 1969.

Lazarsfeld, Paul, Bernard Berelson, and Hazel Gaudet. *The People's Choice: How the Voter Makes Up His Mind in a Presidential Campaign.* Third edition. New York: Columbia University Press, 1968. First published in 1944.

Lewis-Beck, Michael S., William G. Jacoby, Helmut Norpoth, and Herbert F. Weisberg. *The American Voter Revisited.* Ann Arbor: University of Michigan Press, 2008.

Milbrath, Lester W., and M. L. Goel. *Political Participation: How and Why Do People Get Involved in Politics?* Chicago: Rand McNally, 1977. First published in 1965.

Myers, R. David, ed. *Toward a History of the New Left: Essays from Within the Movement.* Brooklyn, NY: Carlson Publishing, 1989.

Nie, Norman H., Sidney Verba, and John R. Petrocik. *The Changing American Voter.* Enlarged edition. Cambridge, MA: Harvard University Press, 1979.

Niemi, Richard G., and Michael J. Hanmer. "Voter Turnout Among College Students: New Data and a Rethinking of Traditional Theories." *Social Science Quarterly* 91 (June 2010): 301–323.

Parry, Janine A., and Todd G. Shields. "Sex, Age, and the Implementation of the Motor Voter Act: The 1996 Presidential Election." *Social Science Quarterly* 82 (September 2001): 506–522.

Save the Internet. Savetheinternet.com. 2010.

Scholzman, Kay Lehman, Sidney Verba, and Henry E. Brady. "Weapons of the Strong? Participatory Inequality and the Internet." *Perspectives on Politics* 8 (June 2010): 487–509.

Shea, Daniel M., Joanne Conner Green, Christopher E. Smith, and L. Tucker Gubson, Jr. *Living Democracy.* New York: Longman, 2009.

Teodori, Massimo, ed. *The New Left: A Documentary History.* New York: Bobbs-Merrill, 1969.

Wattenberg, Martin P. *Is Voting for Young People?* New York: Pearson Longman, 2008.

2

Problems, Controversies, and Solutions

From the 1950s to the 1970s many young Americans took the opportunity to participate extensively in U.S. politics, advocating causes in which they strongly believed. The civil rights movement attracted many idealistic youth to the goal of racial equality, and U.S. involvement in Vietnam energized large numbers of young people who questioned the wisdom, legality, and morality of that military venture, especially because the U.S. government was drafting young males into the Army to take part in the military conflict. However, as these issues receded from the forefront of the public agenda, and political participation declined generally, youth participation in politics diminished. Thus the low level of political participation among youth became an important issue for educators and the civic-minded, given the recognition that the health of a democracy depends on the willingness of its members to engage in the political process, including voting in elections; staying informed about public issues at the national, state, and local levels; and participating in civic organizations.

Low youth political participation accompanies a general decline in political engagement in the United States. Robert Putnam, who brought attention to the general disengagement of many Americans from social and political involvement in recent decades, comments in his article "Bowling Alone: America's Declining Social Capital": "By almost every measure, Americans' direct engagement in politics and government has fallen steadily and sharply over the last generation, despite the fact that the average levels of education—the best individual-level predictor of political participation—have risen sharply throughout this period" (1995a, 67). Putnam notes that participation in parent-teacher associations declined from 12 million individuals in 1964 to 5 million in 1982, with a modest membership increase in the 1990s (68). Also, Putnam notes that the membership in the Federation of Women's Clubs declined by at least half since 1964, and membership in the League of Women Voters decreased by 42 percent since 1969 (69). At all educational levels, Putnam reports that the average number of association memberships dropped by 25 percent in 25 years (1995a, 70). The level of social trust, which Putnam notes is closely associated with civic engagement, also declined.

Those who express concern for low voter participation and a general decline in political engagement suggest various causes for this situation and hence recommend different methods of reversing the trend. Putnam suggests several explanations for the decline in social capital, a term that refers to the level of citizen involvement in social and political affairs. Putnam identifies social capital with "mutual reciprocity, the resolution of dilemmas of collective action, and the broadening of social identities" (1995a, 74). First, Putnam mentions the movement of women into the job market, which may have resulted in women having less time and opportunity to be involved in clubs and organizations (73). Another possible reason involves the mobility of the U.S. population, along with a reduction in the rate of marriage, an increase in the proportion of marriages that end in divorce, a decrease in the number of children in a family, and a decline in real wages (73). Another proposed explanation involves the general availability of television as a means of entertainment that replaced more socially engaged modes of spending leisure time. Putnam asserts that a priority should be given to the discovery of ways to reverse the trend in recent decades of loosening social connections among individuals and thus to the restoration of higher levels of civic engagement and civic trust. Such a task, while true of the general population, appears to be particularly applicable to younger Americans who have been especially influenced by the factors Putnam mentions.

Investigating Youth Political Participation

In attempting to explain the cause of low youth political participation, Martin P. Wattenberg (2008) emphasizes the lack of newspaper reading among younger citizens, noting that the decline in newspaper sales can be attributed largely to "generational replacement," with younger age groups far less likely than older age groups to read newspapers. Wattenberg suggests that because younger generations underwent the socialization process during a time when they were exposed to television, computers, and video games, reading played a secondary role. He observes that this trend in newspaper reading applies to other established democracies and that no alternative to newspapers has yet appeared (10), although electronic readers such as Kindle and the iPad ultimately may provide such an alternative. Wattenberg considers newspapers to be the single most effective way of becoming informed about politics. According to Wattenberg, in 1957, 76 percent of the adult population read a newspaper every day, but by 2004 the proportion had dropped to 41 percent (14). Although many newspapers today have established an online edition, Wattenberg discerns scant evidence that reading newspapers online has become a regular habit for most people (28).

Wattenberg (2008) also notes that, similar to newspaper readers, television news watchers today tend to be from the older age cohorts. Young people either watch other programming or are engaged in activities other than gaining political information from news broadcasts. In the early days of television broadcasting, viewers had a choice among three major networks (CBS, NBC, and ABC), depending on local availability. When significant political events arose, such as the Cuban missile crisis or major political party presidential nominating conventions, all networks delivered reports simultaneously, and thus people had no choice about what to watch. However, with the development of cable television and the vast expansion of station choices, along with videotape and DVD players, individuals could select from numerous news sources or choose to circumvent news coverage entirely (34). According to Wattenberg, survey data indicate that more than 70 percent of those interviewed in 1967 reported that they watched a major network news program every night, but by 2004 that percentage had declined to 29 percent (38).

Although the major networks now face overwhelming competition from the 24-hour news networks (CNN, MSNBC, and Fox News), thus providing younger people much greater flexibility about when to watch a news program, Wattenberg contends that, taking into account the time for commercials, the repetition of stories, and the selectivity of topics, such news broadcasts provide low levels of information. Wattenberg presents data from a Columbia University Project for Excellence in Journalism study of news programming, which reports that just 11 percent of broadcast time is devoted to written and edited stories (2008, 42). Wattenberg notes that in 1972, people in all age groups uniformly reported high levels of watching at least part of the Democratic Party conventions that year (87 percent in the 18–29 age cohort, 90 percent in the 30–44 group, 90 percent in the 45–64 group, and 93 percent in the 65-plus group). By 2000, the percentage had fallen in all age categories, but it had especially declined in the youngest group (35 percent in the 18–29 category, 44 percent in the 30–44 group, 53 percent in the 45–64 group, and 63 percent in the 65-plus category). Similar results were obtained for the Republican conventions (47).

Wattenberg (2008) comments that the only excitement generated in recent presidential campaigns originates in the presidential debates. However, others question the value of such debates in informing the public about the policy positions and qualifications of the candidates. For instance, George Farah (2004) notes that although many citizens initially expect the sort of excitement to which Wattenberg refers, they soon discover that the Democratic and Republican candidates have succeeded in eliminating many of the factors that lead to genuine debate. Farah considers the debates to be no more than "prepared speeches and prepackaged sound bites" (173) and also questions the lack of alternative views that would be expressed by third-party candidates, who could add interest to the debate format and perhaps attract more viewers. The first presidential debates, between John F. Kennedy and Richard M. Nixon in 1960, attracted a large audience (those less than 30 years old were more likely to watch the debates on television than those at least 65 years of age), perhaps in part because they were a new phenomenon and because the three major networks all covered the debates. Today, viewers have a host of other options that allow them to avoid what may be considered an uninformative event.

Wattenberg concludes that "without reading a daily newspaper, watching TV news, or otherwise following current events, even the best-educated people will probably not pick up much knowledge about the political world" (2008, 76). When asked factual questions in surveys, those under the age of 30 invariably score the lowest of among age groups. Wattenberg (90) cites Michael Delli and Scott Keeter (*What Americans Know About Politics and Why It Matters*), who argue persuasively that political knowledge contributes to civic virtues, helps individuals to make informed vote choices, and increases the likelihood of participating in politics. Wattenberg asserts that those who follow the news are more likely to know who is running for which offices, to be familiar with candidates' issue positions, to show interest in the issues, and to understand the importance of an election (96).

As Wattenberg (2008) suggests, the lower participation rates by those less than 30 years old could result from the so-called life-cycle effect, in which younger people have not yet established themselves in a community, including a career and family ties, and therefore do not have as much at stake in public policy making. However, a generation effect also may be at work. Younger people at this time have less exposure to media treatment of political events than older cohorts and therefore are less likely to engage with the community and the political process, a condition that may continue into later years. In 1972, there was a much smaller difference in levels of participation between the youngest voters and older age cohorts than in more recent years, thus suggesting a generation effect as well as a life-cycle effect to explain the difference in voter turnout levels. A third effect that may influence political participation levels is the period effect, which refers to events that may alter the political attitudes and behavior of all age groups in a similar way. For instance, the Vietnam War and the Watergate scandal influenced the attitudes of all age groups, increasing the level of skepticism among citizens of all ages.

Geoffrey Baym (2010), who discusses the change in broadcast news reporting since the 1960s, presents three paradigms, or models, of reporting. These models may help to explain the role that news reporting has played in the decreasing knowledge of and involvement in politics among younger cohorts. Baym calls the first model the high-modern paradigm, which arose following World War II and involved the attempt to provide an objective presentation of the day's events. Listeners and viewers were assumed to be rational individuals who could use the news presentation each day to establish their own conclusions about the political world (169). Because of the limited number of channels available and the absence of videotape and DVD players, television viewing at dinner time—for adults and children—was limited almost entirely to the half-hour news program of one of the three major networks. This model fits well into the traditional understanding of representative democracy, in which the average citizen's responsibility is to stay abreast of political events and issues and to establish informed opinions that can assist in making appropriate choices in elections to fill public offices. According to Baym, the high-modern paradigm, although providing good news reporting, tended to limit the opportunities for political engagement: "it offered no role for the public to play save that of a passive audience, whose requirements for citizenship could be fulfilled simply by watching television" (170).

With the development of cable and satellite television service and the accompanying 24-hour news networks, the high-modern model evolved into what Baym calls the postmodern model. Rather than traditional news programs, stations provided "infotainment" programs, and instead of attempting to provide an accurate depiction of events, the news networks developed the idea of allowing different sides of an issue to present their views, with, Baym claims, an underlying assumption that all sides of an issue simply promote their own self-interest or ideological predisposition (2010, 172). Baym maintains that this type of reporting often results in people withdrawing from the realm of elections and public policy making. We may conclude from this description of the metamorphosis of broadcast news reporting that young people have faced three roadblocks to obtaining adequate knowledge of politics. First, the shift from newspaper reporting to television news limited the amount of information that an individual receives. Newspapers are a space-limited medium, but television is a time-limited medium, which arguably is a more stringent restriction. Second, the shift from a few major networks to cable and satellite television expanded tremendously the viewing options from which to choose. Third, perhaps due in part to increased competition, news programs altered the format of news presentation, placing much greater emphasis on entertainment than objective news reporting that characterized the high-modern paradigm. Therefore, young people growing up after 1970 could reasonably be expected to acquire far less news about day-to-day political developments and minimal detailed background information about political concerns such as U.S. foreign and military policy, health care, and immigration.

Baym (2010) introduces a third, emerging, model for news reporting, which he terms the neo-modern paradigm. He does not consider this model a return to the traditional approach to news broadcasting, but a response to the present dominant model. Baym presents as examples *The Daily Show* with Jon Stewart and *The Colbert Report* with Stephen Colbert, two programs that appear to have gained popularity among young people. Baym claims that these programs succeed in "the harnessing of the power of entertainment in pursuit of high-modern ideals" (173). This news reporting, according to Baym, allows the viewer to question the well-prepared talking-points of the traditional politicians and public officials. However, critics doubt whether the average citizen can depend on such "news" programs to remain informed about the political arena.

Students of political participation and voting behavior suggest several possible solutions to the low level of political participation among young people. Analysts usually turn their attention in two interconnected directions: first, the characteristics of individuals—interest, knowledge, and motivations—that raise or lower the probability of participating in the political realm; and second, aspects of the political process that may encourage or discourage political participation. Possible solutions to systemic factors contributing to low voter turnout include, for instance, greater efforts to simplify the voter registration process. In the United States, voting involves a two-stage process. First, a potential voter must register to vote, and then, a voter must cast a ballot in the election. Many have argued that the registration requirement dampens voter turnout (Brians and Grofman 2001, 170), and have recommended dispensing with voter registration entirely by placing the responsibility of registration on public officials rather than the individual person or by allowing for election day registration. If an individual has registered to vote, or may register at the same time as voting, then the probability of casting a ballot in a particular election obviously increases significantly. The single most accurate predictor of whether a person will vote in an election is whether they are registered: if so, there is a positive probability that they will vote; if not, the probability (excluding fraud or error) is zero. Government has taken various steps to encourage the participation of people of all ages. For instance, in 1993 Congress passed the National Voter Registration Act, often called the Motor Voter bill because it required states to offer citizens the opportunity to register to vote at public agency offices, including motor vehicle bureaus. By 2000, an additional 10 million people had been registered, but voter turnout did not increase accordingly (Hudson 2010, 145). However, from 2000 to 2008, the rate of registration rose from 68 percent to 74 percent, and the turnout rate in the 2008 presidential election also rose, perhaps in part due to the appeal of the Democratic presidential candidate, Barack Obama, and the efforts of supporters to get voters to the polls. Turnout in future elections will show if trends toward increased participation will continue.

Other possible explanations for low voter turnout include the frequency of elections. In contrast to other nations, U.S. citizens are asked to turn out to vote on numerous occasions for federal, state, and local elections. With well over 80,000 governments in the United States, many elections are required to fill the large number of public offices. Often these elections are held at different times, thus requiring voters to participate in several elections in a four-year period. With numerous candidates running for various public offices, young people's more limited knowledge of the political process may discourage participation in elections in which candidates are unfamiliar to the potential voter. Also, elections in the United States, unlike other established democracies, are regularly held on weekdays when people have to find time during the work day to vote.

The operation of the electoral college, in which the popular vote outcome in each state must be translated into a number of electoral votes equivalent to the number of senators and representatives to which a state is entitled in the U.S. Congress, has been a major target of those scholars who argue that this system represents a major restriction on democracy in the United States. The electoral college can result in complex outcomes, largely because most states employ the winner-take-all system: the plurality winner of the popular vote in a state is awarded all of the state's electoral votes. Arguably on four occasions (most recently the 2000 election), the candidate who received the most popular votes failed to win the election. In the 1876 presidential election, Republican Rutherford B. Hayes won the presidency by one electoral vote even though Democrat Samuel Tilden undoubtedly had received more popular votes. The bitter fight over the allocation of electoral votes resulted in disillusionment with the political process for a generation.

Contemporary campaign techniques, including negative campaigning and structured media advertising, may also leave potential voters dissatisfied with the electoral process. As candidates came to rely on the mass media for campaigning, political parties became less effective as voter mobilization organizations, which contributed to low voter turnout generally. Some political scientists have suggested that political parties and candidates have tended not to make specific appeals to younger voters because this age cohort already has a record of low voter turnout. Candidates consider spending time and resources appealing to this age group a waste as such efforts often fail to bear adequate results in higher voter turnout. Therefore, the expectation that a large proportion of young people will not turn out to vote results in a self-fulfilling prophecy.

Solutions to Low Participation

In order to encourage higher voter turnout in all age cohorts, some states have introduced election day registration (EDR). Citing Raymond E. Wolfinger and Steven J. Rosenstone's *Who Votes?* (1980), Craig Leonard Brians and Bernard Grofman (2001, 171) note the claim that the last day to register prior to an election is the single most important legal restriction preventing people from voting. The states of Maine, Minnesota, and Wisconsin adopted EDR in the 1970s. Brians and Grofman argue that allowing voter registration closer to election day can be expected to lower the cost of voting for those less likely to become voters, which includes younger citizens, and EDR reduces the costs significantly by combining the registration and ballot casting acts into one step (172). Brians and Grofman hypothesize that "statistically visible turnout increases should develop only when the registration procedure changes yield substantial enough cost reductions to move a significant number of people over all of the threshold barriers to voting" (178). Brians and Grofman conclude from available data that in those states that have adopted EDR, average voter turnout has increased by approximately 4 percent and has remained higher than states without EDR. Their analysis also leads them to conclude that middle-class individuals tend to benefit the most from EDR. It seems reasonable to surmise that especially young people, who often are preoccupied with daily activities of work and family, may find EDR a convenient way of participating in electoral politics because the costs of voting (primarily inconvenience) have been reduced.

Community Engagement

As with any social activity, individuals likely will not possess the inclination to participate in politics if they have not gained basic knowledge about political participation, either through personal experience or by the efforts of family members and teachers. Political scientists have experimented with different instructional methods to encourage political engagement among students. William J. Ball (2005), in his study of the relationship between community engagement and political engagement, notes that previous researchers discovered that volunteering for various community activities is not necessarily related to more explicit political activities such as voting (287). Furthering this research, Ball conducted a study in which students were given the opportunity to combine community service and political engagement. The Leadership in Public Affairs (LPA) program used a modified version of the community-based research (CBR) model to develop a program for political participation that moves students from involvement in community service to active participation in politics by offering an acceptable paradigm of political behavior (288). The experiment involved two courses offered in the 2002–2003 academic year. In one course, work involved a small-group CBR project in which students collaborated with a local citizens group, serving in effect as political consultants for the organizations. The second course was meant to develop student research skills and collaboration with local organizations.

Ball reports that students who completed the two CBR courses expressed greater interest both in helping others as well as in influencing the political system and becoming community leaders (2005, 289) and concludes that the initial analysis of the courses indicates that they succeeded in increasing favorable student attitudes toward service and volunteer programs as well as toward interest in political engagement. The students in the experimental groups, as opposed to those in the control group, expressed increased interest in "influencing the political structure . . . influencing social values . . . and becoming a community leader" (289). Ball especially notes, contrary to previous research, the increased interest in influencing the political structure. Ball concludes that implementing the CBR model shows promise of increasing the ability to translate "positive experience with community-based collaboration into greater political engagement" (289). Ball asserts that the purpose of emphasizing a community-based deliberative democracy project in the LPA program is "not to politicize community engagement, but to do just the opposite, to 'communitize' political behavior" (290).

Joseph Kahne and Joel Westheimer (2006), dealing with a similar question regarding community engagement and political engagement, are concerned with the level of political efficacy that may result from such engagement. They note that the level of volunteerism among young people has risen significantly in recent years. Can this increased volunteerism then have a positive effect on the level of political engagement, primarily through bolstering young people's sense of political efficacy (in other words, their belief that they can have a positive effect on the political process) (2006, 289)? The authors conclude that although negative experiences students have in community engagement can discourage political involvement, emphasizing only positive outcomes can result in a limited understanding of political engagement. With that caveat in mind, a positive relationship can occur between the development of a sense of political efficacy and civic and political engagement.

Youth and Voting

Daniel M. Shea and Rebecca Harris, in their report on mobilizing young voters (2006), note the importance of voting turnout to a democracy. They cite a report from the Center for Information and Research on Civic Learning and Engagement (CIRCLE) that indicates young people participate in volunteer work more often than older citizens (Shea and Harris 2006, 341). However, that participation is not necessarily associated with political activity, for as the authors note, "the decline in election turnout among young Americans has been stunning" (341). They report that in 1972, the first year in which 18-to 20-year olds throughout the United States were granted the right to vote, just under 50 percent exercised that right. However, 28 years later, in the 2000 presidential election, only 35 percent of that age group voted, and in the 2002 congressional elections, the turnout rate dropped to 20 percent. In the 2004 presidential election, the turnout rate among young people increased to 51 percent, but many expressed reservations with the notion that the increase represented a more long-term trend (341). Shea and Harris further note that according to the University of Michigan's American National Election Study, from the 1950s to the 1980s, approximately 30 percent of those citizens less than 25 years old stated in interviews that they cared "very much" or "pretty much" about the outcome of congressional elections in their district. In the 2002 survey, although 67 percent of all respondents stated that they cared "very much" or "pretty much" about the results of congressional elections, only 47 percent of those respondents younger than 25 responded in the same manner. Shea and Harris conclude that "the withdrawal of young citizens from politics has been rapid, deep, and broad" (341). Given the asserted importance of citizen participation to the continuance of representative democracy, the authors focus on projects that might have a positive effect on youth political participation.

First, Shea and Harris (2006) identify the more likely explanations for low political participation on the part of young people. They cite Thomas E. Patterson's research (2002) that low levels of political participation is associated with the especially high level of mistrust that young people have for political activity. Other researchers have focused on changes in civic education curricula in high school instructional programs. Karl T. Kurtz, Alan Rosenthal, and Cliff Zukin's study (2003) shows that just 64 percent of those between the ages of 15 and 26 report having completed a high school civics course. The Campaign for the Civic Mission of Schools (2003) noted that "one-third of high school seniors lacked a basic understanding of how government works" (Shea and Harris 2006, 341). Results of the 2011 National Assessment of Educational Progress, a national civics examination administered by the Department of Education to 27,000 4th-, 8th-, and 12th-grade students, indicated that only about 25 percent of 4th- and 12th-grade students, and just 20 percent of 8th graders, scored at the proficient or advanced levels (Dillon 2011, A23). Although Richard G. Niemi and Jane Junn (1998) reported the fairly obvious conclusion that completing a civics course can increase political knowledge, Shea and Harris (2006) doubt whether traditional course work can achieve the objective of increasing interest and participation in politics, and they suggest changes in the content of such courses in order to avoid the abstract presentations that fail to emphasize the citizen's active role in a democracy.

The authors suggest that a peer-to-peer learning experience, without the immediate involvement of a teacher, encourages civic engagement. Shea and Harris refer to the Center for Political Participation's (CPP) summer 2004 program, which was intended to spark high school seniors' greater interest and participation in politics (342). Two students at Allegheny College, where Shea serves as director of the CPP, developed a 45-minute PowerPoint presentation titled "Why Bother? The Importance of Voting in America," which included information presented in images and animations about the relevance of issues for young people, the differences between candidates for public office, the effect a small number of votes can have on an election outcome, and the rights as well as the obligations of citizens in democracies (342). In September and October 2004, four college students made the presentation to students at eight high schools in western Pennsylvania. In each school, the researchers established an experimental group, which viewed the presentation, and a control group. Following the 2004 election, the researchers returned to six of the high schools to administer a survey to 370 students in the experimental and control groups, asking students about various areas of political behavior (343), including questions about the level of attention paid to politics and attitudes toward politics and government. They discovered that the experimental group students were more likely than control group students to have registered to vote (51 percent versus 38 percent) and, among those registered, more likely to vote (74 percent compared to 58 percent).

Shea and Harris also reported that experimental group students were more likely than control group students to report "quite a bit" of discussion about the election (44 percent versus 34 percent) and to express the view that government "listens to young people 'a good deal of the time'" (2006, 343). The authors discovered some similarities between the two groups. For instance, more than 90 percent in each group expressed the view that "young people can make a difference in elections," and more than 70 percent said they believed government could be trusted "to do the right thing at least some of the time" (344). The study results suggest that "peer programs and 'super treatments' can encourage civic engagement in younger populations" (344). The authors state that the program, in addition to changing behavior, "instilled new attitudes about the ability of young people to make their voice heard in government" (344), and conclude that attitudinal changes in youth can result in long-term modifications in political behavior as a result of newly acquired views.

Youth and Citizenship

Lonnie R. Sherrod, in his study of the development of a conception of citizenship in youth (2003), notes that although youth in the United States, particularly poor and minority individuals, often are described as disaffected from the political process, in focus group discussions these youth do express opinions about political issues relevant to such areas as family, race, and religious belief (287). Sherrod's research involves examining youth's political views and socialization in order to discover a possible link ("'hook' or 'handle'") that "could be used to redirect youth attention and interest to citizenship" (287). Sherrod operates under the assumption that the development of a sense of citizenship requires identification of some kind with the nation. This identification with the country then becomes the basis for developing political attitudes, which in turn encourage political participation as a citizen of the country. Because groups other than the nation can influence the development of attitudes, an important research question is how particular groups affect the acquisition of values and attitudes (287). Sherrod asks, "what then is the socialization process that leads to participation as a citizen in the social group that defines loyalty to country, and how does this process vary by specific group with the country, such as by race or class membership?" (287). Sherrod mentions as possible avenues for developing citizenship membership in organizations such as 4-H and Boys and Girls Clubs, civics or government courses in the public schools, and political discussions with teachers and friends about what they have observed in the mass media. These avenues can provide initial practice for citizenship in venues outside the standard political arena.

Noting that poor and minority youth do not participate in extracurricular activities, service to the community, and other activities as frequently as other youth, Sherrod focuses on the way in which poor and minority youth may come to develop a sense of social group identification that ultimately is applicable to developing an association with the nation's political system (2003, 287). Sherrod states that his objective is to provide an overview of the two-year long Fordham University Applied Developmental Psychology Program (ADPP). Rather than focusing on knowledge or behavior, this program emphasizes attitudes and political views, operating under the assumption that even youth with "insufficient knowledge" can acquire political attitudes that may influence behavior as well as develop "a political self-concept" (288). In fact, Sherrod asserts that "the formation of political attitudes constitutes one form of civic engagement" (288).

The citizenship portion of the ADPP survey attempts to determine respondents' understanding of citizenship, including rights as well as responsibilities, their own relationship to citizenship, and their level of political knowledge. Other questions attempt to determine the socialization experience of youth within the family regarding race and class identification; the level of participation in extracurricular activities at school and in the community; and the level of knowledge that students have attained. Factor analyses resulted in three factors of expected future political behavior: (1) traditional political behavior, including voting; (2) volunteerism; and (3) activist behavior. The ADPP then conducted bivariate correlations and regressions to determine "correlations between attitudes, knowledge, and behavior, and to determine which attitude and knowledge variables predict which behaviors" (Sherrod 2003, 289).

Sherrod (2003) presents initial results from surveys conducted at high schools and colleges in the New York City area. For instance, the study discovered that youth who express concern about political issues involving concern for others tend to become involved in service "for altruistic reasons," but youth who express interest in political issues for self-interested reasons also become involved in service activities but out of concern for personal advancement (for instance, to develop a record for future education or employment) (290). Even youth with "inadequate knowledge" acquire political attitudes, but those with more political knowledge are more likely to vote: "knowledge predicts whether or not youth vote, but it does not predict how they vote" (290). Sherrod notes that preliminary findings indicate that, when asked to express their own understanding of citizenship, youth have rather limited conceptions, mentioning such things as obeying the law or helping others (290).

Interestingly, Sherrod (2003) states that "marginalized youth" (in other words, those in a racial minority or who are poor) do not express attitudes about citizenship that differ significantly from others. Sherrod also notes that although minority youth in focus groups mention obeying the law and other forms of "good behavior" as a part of good citizenship, many minority youth are prone to delinquency. He interprets this response among minority youth to the citizenship question as a meaningful notion of their development of a view of citizenship (291). Subsequent research will involve further examination of the role that race plays in the formation of attitudes toward citizenship: "how does racial identity and experienced discrimination relate to ideas of citizenship?" (291). In addition, the Fordham program will engage in developing a program included in civics classes that "uses what youth 'are into'" (Sherrod mentions the example of political music) as a basis for "redirecting attention to and involvement in citizenship" (291).

Classroom Methodology

Although many research projects dealing with methods of increasing the political engagement of youth focus on service learning and increasing the amount of volunteer activity in which young people participate, Stacy Ulbig (2009) has concentrated on improved student learning through modifying classroom methodology. The results of Ulbig's study suggest that rather simple alterations in the lecture method can result in greater engagement with the subject of the course as well as possibly greater political engagement. Noting reports of significant trends toward disengagement and the efforts of organizations to reverse this trend, Ulbig has attempted to alter the traditional lecture format in the college classroom to spark greater interest in politics. He refers to studies that have introduced such classroom activities as having current events discussions, holding pseudo elections, and introducing democratic practices. To overcome a limitation of the lecture method, which has been criticized for failing to allow for active student participation, Ulbig reports that he attempted "to make introductory political courses as engaging as possible" (386) by introducing "concrete visual cues" that possibly could assist students in recalling the material covered in class. Studies suggest that the use of visual images during lecture presentations can increase the amount of information that students are subsequently able to recall. Such enhanced visual presentations allow students to use more of the five senses than traditional lecture methods. Ulbig investigated the effects "simple, colorful still (e.g., photographic, illustrative, clip art) images have on students enrolled in a college-level introductory political science course" (386).

Ulbig used two separate 65-student sections—a treatment (experimental) group and a control group—of an introduction to political science course. Each section received the same lecture materials but different PowerPoint slides. The treatment group viewed slides containing the lecture outline, plus "colorful, iconic, and sometimes comical still images" (2009, 387), while the control group viewed slides containing the same lecture outline, but without the additional images. Ulbig expected that the added visual images would ameliorate the more abstract nature of lecture material by providing students with concrete images. Ulbig designated as the dependent variable subsequent student engagement, measured by a pretest and a posttest. Students in both groups were asked whether they were considering a major or minor in political science; how often they discussed politics with family members or friends; how interested they were in the recent political campaigns; to what extent they had trust in the federal government; and their level of knowledge about politics (387).

Ulbig monitored the two groups as the semester proceeded, in order to track the amount of change in attitudes within each group. With regard to majoring in political science, at the beginning of the semester, more than 95 percent of students in both groups stated that this did not describe their intent. At the end of the semester, nearly 5 percent more students of the experimental group, compared to the pretest responses, replied that they were considering to some extent majoring in political science. Among the control group students, more than 3 percent fewer students responded positively about choosing political science as a major in the posttest than did so at the beginning of the semester. The percentage of students in the control group that reported discussing politics actually dropped from the pre- to the posttest, while the percentage of experimental group students increased. Ulbig concludes that experiencing the visually enhanced lectures has the potential for increasing political interest and action beyond the classroom (2009, 389). To measure political knowledge, students were asked to identify the positions held by Nancy Pelosi and Harry Reid; to state who is in line to succeed to the presidency after the president and vice president; and to state how many justices there are on the Supreme Court. Although the average knowledge score of the control group exceeded that of the experimental group on both the pretest and posttest, Ulbig notes that the experimental group students had the largest average gain. Ulbig concludes that the introduction of visual enhancements to a political science class constitutes a "low-investment opportunity to improve the general-education experience of college students." Students who are given visual enhancements in a political science class tend to be more engaged in the class and "appear to be more civically engaged" (389).

The Possibility of Political Indoctrination

Attempts to increase youth political involvement, especially in more formal educational settings, raises the issue of whether the instructor's political preferences could be considered a form of indoctrination accompanying instruction in political engagement. Mack D. Mariani and Gordon J. Hewitt (2008) explore this concern regarding higher education. They site David Horowitz's argument that politically more radical members of college faculties introduce their own political agenda into the classroom, thus "engaging in propaganda rather than scholarship and indoctrinating students rather than teaching them" (773). In order to test this claim of indoctrination, Mariani and Hewitt employ data from the Cooperative Institutional Research Program (CIRP) Freshman Survey, the College Student Survey, and the Higher Education Research Institute (HERI) Faculty Survey to evaluate the influence of faculty political preferences on the attitudes of undergraduate students during the four years of undergraduate education (773).

Mariani and Hewitt note that several conservative authors in recent years have criticized institutions of higher education as purveyors of liberal doctrine (2008, 773). According to the authors, evidence does indicate that there exists a decided liberal bent among college and university faculty. Mariani and Hewitt's own investigation of 38 private colleges, including nearly 7,000 student respondents, demonstrated that faculty members overall tend to hold liberal political positions and identify with the Democratic Party. In addition, the authors cite a 2001 Brookings Institution survey of 550 professors of economics, history, political science, and sociology in which only 8 percent of respondents described themselves as conservative or very conservative, 31 percent described themselves as liberal or very liberal, 77 percent identified to some extent with the Democratic Party, and just 13 percent with the Republican Party (774).

Assuming that such information about faculty political preferences is accurate, the concern then has shifted to whether this political imbalance has resulted in unfair treatment of conservative faculty and students. Mariani and Hewitt interpret indoctrination to involve the question of change: "whether there is a significant relationship between the liberalism of faculty at an institution and changes in the political orientation of students over the course of their college careers" (2008, 775). Among the results of their analysis, Mariani and Hewitt report that by the time students in the study graduated, their political orientation shifted to the left, and there were 8 percent more liberal students than conservative students, even though when they began their educational career, there were somewhat more conservative than liberal students. However, the authors conclude that the shift is not sufficient to conclude that faculty political orientation significantly affects the political orientation of students and that student orientation does not differ significantly from the general population. They note that female students tend to move to the left more than male students (779). Movement to the left can occur for several reasons other than faculty influence, such as the stage of personal development, the result of peer pressure, and exposure to current events.

Mariani and Hewitt conclude from their own research that "there is no definitive empirical evidence of widespread or systematic ideology-based bias on the part of faculty" (2008, 775) and that the political orientations of a majority of college students do not change during their college career (780). To the extent that student political orientations do alter, change at an institutional level apparently does not occur due to the influence of faculty ideology. It appears from this study that college and university students often already have acquired political attitudes before entering the classroom. If individual professors in a course do not have significant influence by themselves on the political attitudes of students, the question remains to what extent such courses influence students to greater involvement in the public realm.

April Kelly-Woessner and Matthew C. Woessner (2006), also concerned about professors' political ideology and partisan preference entering the classroom as a potential source of bias, examine the effect of "students' perceptions of professors' ideologies on their experiences in the classroom and, correspondingly, their assessments of the professors' performance" (495). The authors suggest that among the possible consequences of professors making their political views known in the classroom is that students, who wish to maintain their own political orientation, can attempt to argue for their own position in class, at least appear to accept the professor's position, or simply dismiss what the professor says in class. The latter strategy may be the most unfortunate because students can reject the credibility of all the professor is trying to convey.

The authors developed a survey that 30 instructors administered in their undergraduate classes at several colleges and universities across the nation. The authors were not interested in whether students could accurately categorize their professors' ideology but were concerned instead with student perception of instructors' political views and what effect such perceptions may have on student experiences in the classroom (Kelly-Woessner and Woessner 2006, 497). They concluded from the data that students evaluated professors they considered to be liberal more favorably on various characteristics, including "encourage students to express their own viewpoints," "work to provide a comfortable learning environment," and "cares about students and their success" (2006, 497). Because students' evaluations of professors may result in part from their own political positions, the authors note that the highest proportion of students reported that they identify themselves as liberal (43 percent), and a lesser proportion (29 percent) reported having moderate or conservative views.

Kelly-Woessner and Woessner report that "greater ideological and partisan differences between professors and students result in lower evaluations of the courses, lower evaluations of the instructors, and less student interest in the subject" (2006, 499). The authors conclude that instructors face a dilemma when trying to convey information: if they convey their own views, they risk having students reject the subject matter being taught; but if they try to reinforce the already existing views of students, the instructors may not provide as much useful information. The authors suggest that although "some level of sensitivity to students' values may be in order," exposing students to new and possibly controversial views can expand their perception of the world, even if a certain level of discomfort occurs (499). When the objective is to raise the level of interest in the political realm in order to counteract the low levels of political engagement among young people, the professor can search for some political balance between maintaining students' level of comfort and challenging students to confront political orientations with which they disagree. The authors conclude that this objective may be pursued without professors making their personal ideological and party preferences explicit (500).

Political Engagement and the Rational Choice Approach

In addition to the question of indoctrination to a professor's political views, some have raised concern about the effects of specific methods of teaching political science and American politics and government. For instance, Sue E. S. Crawford (2007) investigates the consequences of using a rational choice approach in introduction to political science and American government courses. Past studies have focused on the possibility that the rational choice orientation, or the "simple instrumental utility model of voting," discourages students from participating in elections. According to this model, the utility of voting for the individual hinges on two factors: the probability that the individual's vote will alter the election outcome and the strength of the preference the individual has for one candidate over the others (387). The result of this calculation often will lead to the conclusion that the costs of voting (for instance, the time needed on election day to travel to the polling place) outweigh the benefits. Crawford investigates the possibility that using the rational choice model as a basis for political science courses may lead students to the individually rational decision not to take the time to vote. Crawford (2007, 388) focused her research on three questions: Does a teaching method emphasizing the rational choice model lower the level of generalized trust that students have in others? Does the method increase the level of student internal efficacy ("a citizen's sense of his or her competence to engage in politics")? Does the method affect the expectation students have for future civic engagement?

Crawford constructed a quasi-experimental design, in which some students were introduced to the rational choice approach in four class sections, and other students were presented with non-rational choice methods in three sections of introduction to political science courses at Creighton University. A questionnaire was administered to students in these sections at the beginning of the course and then again at the end. The questionnaire contained questions dealing with level of political trust, efficacy, and anticipated civic engagement. At the end of the study, Crawford concluded that "the results demonstrate little evidence that teaching rational choice wreaks havoc on students' civic attitudes." In addition, "the results offer no evidence that a rational choice curriculum performs better than other curricula in increasing students' internal efficacy" (389). However, Crawford notes that the rational choice students showed a decrease in the expected civic activity measure from the pretest to the posttest; however, the decrease was small. As one possible explanation for failing to find significant differences between the control groups and experimental groups, she suggests that the students in the experimental groups may not have grasped rational choice theory sufficiently in one semester to alter their conception of human behavior (390). However, Crawford indicates that on examinations students generally were able to apply the rational choice material to practical problems. Crawford concludes that exposure to rational choice theory does not lower general levels of trust and that students in traditional and rational choice sections experienced similar increases in internal efficacy. She raises the possibility that more forceful presentations of the rational choice perspective might generate different results and suggests that comparisons be conducted over longer periods and more course work, such as in students' major program of study (390).

Voter Mobilization Efforts

Researchers have investigated techniques not directly associated with the educational process that could increase political participation, particularly voting in elections. For instance, David Niven (2004) investigated the success of a face-to-face mobilization conducted by two groups—a coalition of municipal union members and a coalition of church and civic organizations—prior to the March 13, 2001, municipal election in Boynton Beach, Florida. Niven's interest in the mobilization effort originated in the finding that low voter turnout can be attributed in part to a lack of mobilization efforts by political parties and other groups. One reason already mentioned for low voter turnout among young people is that political parties tend not to solicit votes from this age group because of already low voter turnout rates. Niven refers to other studies that concluded that "contacting prospective voters and asking them to vote appears to increase turnout" (869). Those who express an active interest in politics likely will vote regardless of mobilization efforts, and those essentially uninterested in politics tend to disregard any attempt to mobilize them to vote. Niven is interested in discovering whether mobilization efforts can activate those less likely to go to the polls and hypothesizes that "it is those in the middle [intermittent voters] who are neither fully disengaged from politics nor fully committed to it, where the potential lies for mobilizing contact to be accessible and influential" (871).

In order to determine the effects of mobilization efforts on voter turnout, Niven (2004) analyzed data derived from four voting precincts where members of the two groups canvassed prospective voters. Niven concluded that even when other possible independent variables (age, race, number of voters in the household, and voter turnout in the precinct) are taken into account, direct contact with prospective voters remains a significant factor in influencing turnout, increasing turnout by as much as 10 percent (877–878). The data analysis supported three of Niven's hypotheses: that mobilization efforts will have greater effect on intermittent voters, that contact by someone known to the person being contacted has a greater chance of success, and that two contacts (in other words contact by representatives of both political parties) will be more influential.

However, face-to-face contact can have fairly high costs: "clearly, even as face-to-face mobilization has an effect, it is a grueling process to activate any large quantity of voters" (Niven 2004, 880). Niven estimates that to motivate an additional voter among those considered most active requires three hours of work, while an additional voter among those least likely to vote mandates eight hours of effort (880). Therefore, whether face-to-face mobilization efforts are considered effective depends on whether emphasis is placed on the observed success of such efforts, or the focus instead is on the large amount of time and effort required (881). How successful such efforts would be with younger potential voters may depend on whether such people would be best categorized as consistent, intermittent, or seldom participants. Given Niven's conclusion that "many, indeed most people, appear beyond the reach of mobilization efforts," this strategy to increase youth political participation may have limited appeal, unless canvassing efforts can be well organized and reach large numbers of people.

Allan S. Gerber, Donald P. Green, and Christopher W. Larimer (2008) conducted a study to determine whether adding social pressure to mobilization efforts could affect the level of voter turnout, thus increasing the positive results for the time expended. Although the study did not confront directly the issue of youth political participation, the results could apply to individuals in all age cohorts. Focusing on the question of whether social norms can be used to increase voter turnout, the authors conducted a mailing to 80,000 households prior to the August 2006 Michigan primary election. The households were divided into four groups, with each subsequent group receiving a mailing involving an increased level of social pressure: the first received a mailing that simply reminded the recipients that it was their civic duty to vote; the second informed recipients that researchers would study their turnout as recorded in public records; the third contained the turnout record of those in the household; and the fourth disclosed the turnout of household members as well as of their neighbors (33–34). The authors identify three categories of social norm: the perception of the existence of social norms; the internalization, or acceptance, of specific norms; and the enforcement of norms, including such actions as ostracism and violence (34). Gerber et al. observed that publicizing behavior relevant to norms tends to increase compliance with those norms. Referring to compulsory voting laws, they observe that Italy formerly had such a provision, but the penalty for failing to vote involved nonvoters having their names posted at the town hall and a "certificate of conduct" marked "Did not vote" (35). Therefore, the pressure to vote involved avoiding the embarrassment of being labeled a non-participant.

As the level of social pressure increased across the experimental groups, the level of voter turnout increased. Gerber et al. conclude that "in terms of cost efficiency, mailings that exert social pressure far outstrip door-to-door canvassing" (2008, 38). They then asked whether there may be an interaction between the effects of social pressure and a sense of civic duty, measured by past voting behavior. The authors wished to test two alternative hypotheses: first, that social pressure can increase turnout because it augments an already present inclination to vote; and second, that "extrinsic incentives extinguish intrinsic motivation, resulting in greater treatment effects among those with low voting propensities." Their analysis of the data lead them to conclude that there is no significant association between social pressure and a feeling of civic duty (39). Gerber et al. assert that, unlike other attempts to increase voter turnout, which rely on an internalized sense of civic duty, their intervention into the tendency of individuals to vote involves the employment of "one of the most formidable forces in social psychology, pressure to conform to social norms" (40). Although more intense use of social pressure can result in a contrary reaction on the part of those targeted, the authors conclude that overall, people accede to social norms "in order to avoid shame and social ostracism" if they perceive that others are watching their behavior (40).

Applying the results of this study to youth, one could hypothesize that increasing the proportion of young people who engage in politics (voting and other activities) may depend in part on external pressures as an incentive separate from internalized social norms. The specific nature of such external motivations are unclear but could involve judgments by others that the individual who does not to participate is failing to live up to what is expected of a citizen in a democracy to some form of ostracism for failing to engage in politics. Assuming that social norms play a significant role in human behavior, their operation in the case of election participation could increase youth political participation.

David W. Nickerson's (2008) discussion of two field experiments provides insight into what factors might increase youth voter turnout and political participation generally. Nickerson notes that voting can be seen as an action involving "interactions among friends, neighbors, and members of the family." Individuals stimulate each others' interest in politics and elections, and attempt to persuade each other to vote for particular candidates (49). Nickerson faces the task of moving away from an alternative assumption—the basic atomist postulate that individuals make the decision to vote and for whom to vote without any "contagion" from those around the individual. In order to test the claim that voter contagion does occur, Nickerson analyzed results from two "placebo-controlled" experiments conducted in Denver, Colorado, and Minneapolis, Minnesota, in which randomly selected households containing two registered voters received a personal visit from a researcher, who encouraged the person answering the door to vote. The study then attempted to determine if the frequency of turnout for the second member of each household increased. Recognizing that the similar political behavior among the members of a two-voter household results from "innumerable shared experiences rather than interpersonal influence," Nickerson suggests that factors such as "high level of interaction, familiarity, respect, and trust" among two persons living together encourages political discussion and similar political views and political behavior (50).

Nickerson sites previous research suggesting that one person's decision to vote on average influences four other individuals' decisions to vote (2008, 50). Nickerson attempted to measure both the increase in turnout among the persons directly contacted in each household, as well as the indirect increase of the other individuals in the two-voter households (51). In order to control for other possible factors that could explain similar behavior, households were assigned to three separate circumstances: one group received the "Get Out The Vote" message, the second received a message about recycling, and a third was not contacted at all. The first two groups received the message the first weekend before the primary election, which was held the following Tuesday. In order to assure that contagion, and not some other influence was involved, the experimenters selected only two-voter households and administered "the treatment" (in other words, they received the encouragement to vote message, the recycling message, or "placebo" message). Following data analysis, Nickerson estimates that the indirect mobilization effect resulting from the "Get Out The Vote" message was 5.5 percent in Denver and 6.4 percent in Minneapolis, and the "contagion effect" amounted to 64 percent in Denver and 59 percent in Minneapolis. According to Nickerson, "the unavoidable conclusion is that voting is a highly contagious behavior and an important determinant of turnout" (54). Nickerson's findings contradict the initial atomistic assumptions regarding the decision to vote.

Although Nickerson (2008) recognizes possible threats to the external validity of the findings, he concludes that the experimental results support the assertion that voting behavior is susceptible to the kind of contagion he hypothesizes. As an implication of the study, Nickerson states that declining turnout can be a self-reinforcing phenomenon: "as turnout declines, a person encounters fewer people who vote and the social pressure to vote declines," but with increasing turnout, an individual likely interacts with more voters, and hence the likelihood of voting increases (55). Applying these results to youth political participation, one can surmise that the more frequently youth are exposed to political discussion and political behavior among family members, friends, and classmates who are active politically, the greater is the probability that they also will become engaged politically.

College Elections

Kimberly M. Lewis and Tom W. Rice (2005) conducted an examination of voter turnout in undergraduate elections for student government president. The authors mention several reasons for studying student elections. For instance, the different rules governing these elections provide the opportunity to investigate the ways in which these variations may affect turnout, and investigating this topic may lead to recommendations for increasing student interest and participation in these elections and possibly in local, state, and national elections as well (723). Lewis and Rice sent questionnaires to 400 randomly selected schools of varying student population size and received responses from approximately 24 percent of them. The questionnaire asked for such information as the number of students who voted in the last student government presidential election, the number of candidates for president, the vote totals for the top three candidates, whether online voting was permitted, and the number of days the polls were open.

Lewis and Rice (2005) divided the variables that potentially influence voter turnout into two categories: contextual variables (including institutional characteristics, student demographics, and election rules) and election-specific variables (including the level of electoral competition [number of candidates and winner's percentage of the vote] and campaign activity [amount of advertising and the use of debates]). Lewis and Rice conclude from their analysis that, similar to the findings of previous voter turnout studies of elections, "contextual variables influence turnout in student government elections far more than election specific variables" (727). Several of these contextual variables, the authors argue, represent the influence of the socioeconomic status of students' parents. They estimate that average voter turnout would increase more than 4 percent if schools elected student government presidents separately from other offices, and a similar increase would occur if schools introduced online voting.

Lewis and Rice (2005) conclude from the data analysis that varying the time during which the election polls are open did not affect the turnout rate. Contrary to previous research on voter turnout, the authors discovered that close campaigns (in other words, situations in which the vote totals of the winning and losing candidates were close) did not result in higher voter turnout. They speculate that unlike many elections for government officials, there generally are no polls taken in student government campaigns that would indicate that the competition between candidates was intense (728). However, similar to the findings of other studies, Lewis and Rice conclude that campaign advertising can positively influence turnout.

Lewis and Rice (2005) note that the average turnout in the student elections is no better than 20 percent, which is considerably lower than the turnout rates in national general elections (approximately 50 percent in presidential elections and 40 percent in congressional elections), but roughly equivalent to turnout rates in some state and many local government elections. Because comparable turnout rates in student government elections and many municipal and state primary elections are achieved, the authors conclude that student turnout rates should not be viewed pessimistically. However, although such a comparison in relative terms leaves a favorable impression, taken absolutely, turnout rates of 20 percent and often even lower can be regarded as deplorable. Perhaps recognizing the extremely low level of turnout, the authors conclude that developing strategies to increase turnout in student government elections could result in increasing voter turnout among young cohorts in public elections.

Cynthia J. Bogard, Ian Sheinheit, and Reneé P. Clarke (2008) present the results of a project at Hofstra University prior to the 2004 and 2006 general elections. The project involved a voter registration drive among undergraduate students. Members of the League of Women Voters and the Association of American University Women volunteered to work voter registration tables during summer orientation and during lunch time in the student center in the weeks leading up to the general election (542). Bogard et al. report that nearly 80 percent of students in a sample they drew registered for the 2004 election, 14.5 percent of whom did so with the assistance of the voter registration effort. This registration level compared favorably with U.S. Census data that indicate 64.8 percent of those 18 to 24 years of age with education including "some college" are registered to vote.

Bogard et al. (2008) identify two possible explanations for voting (or nonvoting). The first is the amount of social capital that individuals possess. Many potential young voters lack the civic engagement that would lead to their considering voting as something they ought to do. They have not yet developed the requisite norms and level of political trust that many claim are required to lead to the act of voting. Other researchers argue that sufficient knowledge about the political process leads to the act of voting. According to this view, young people lack specific knowledge about such things as how to register and where to vote, and information about particular candidates and issues. The authors choose to combine these two explanations in their attempt to discover what will motivate youth to vote. Bogard et al. refer to evidence indicating that when youth become involved in school government activities and community service projects, they likely will continue that political participation and civic engagement after graduating (541).

In addition to the voter registration drive, a group of faculty organized several political events prior to the 2004 general election, including separate activities (with a progressive [in other words, liberal] viewpoint) and a "Day of Dialogue" in which various points of view—including the ROTC, College Republicans, and campus religious groups—were aired. The authors estimate that approximately 40 percent of students attended one or more of the civic engagement events. Reasons for attending included individual interest in the events, the expectation of receiving extra credit in a course, and a professor taking students to the event during class time. The authors note that of those who were registered to vote, 89.3 percent of those who attended the Day of Dialogue voted, whereas 82.4 percent of those who did not attend voted: "those who attended the Day of Dialogue voted in statistically significantly higher numbers than other registered student voters regardless of why they had gone to the events" (Bogard et al. 2008, 543). In 2006 the faculty did not organize the Day of Dialogue (perhaps because there was no presidential election that year); instead, a series of separate events were held and students attended as they wished. The authors' investigation indicates that just 22 percent of students attended the 2006 events, and the voter turnout rate dropped to just 23.5 percent (544).

Bogard et al. (2008) conclude, first, that reducing the costs of registration by simply making it easier to register can raise the voter turnout rate considerably. They further surmise that the participation of large numbers of students in the Day of Dialogue contributed to the belief that becoming familiar with the issues and participating was expected of everyone: "thus, the Day of Dialogue may have proved an effective vehicle for civic literacy development as well as civic-involvement-focused social capital development" (544–545). The analysis suggests that voting levels of young people can be increased by promoting knowledge of the political process ("civic literacy")—including, as the authors see it, information that young people can trust due to the open nature of presentation—along with the view that becoming involved in politics has a normative aspect to it: the individual is expected to participate in democratic politics.

Faculty Civic Engagement and Civic Education

According to Susan Hunter and Richard A. Brisbin Jr. (2003), the predilection of college professors to emphasize civic education in their courses may depend on their scholarly interest. The authors received survey responses from approximately 600 faculty who completed an online survey, and an additional 200 political scientists returned a mailed questionnaire to determine the extent to which they consider citizenship education a major goal of their teaching (759). Hunter and Brisbin state that those who responded to the survey generally agreed that teaching civic engagement is an important objective; and a smaller number, but still a majority, said that it was appropriate in courses to require students to engage in civic activities. However, those faculty who are not themselves engaged in civic activities are not likely to encourage such activity in their students. Therefore, Hunter and Brisbin conclude that a way to move students toward greater civic engagement is to have faculty who themselves engage in civic activities (762). In order to assure the teaching of civic engagement, the authors recommend that the political science profession "add pedagogical and civic components to the graduate education of political scientists" (762). Finally, Hunter and Brisbin recommend that colleges and universities assist faculty in including greater reflection and assessment in service-learning courses (762).

Susan Dicklitch (2003) presents an example of teaching service learning for a college course in an area that she personally finds especially meaningful. Dicklitch perceives the purpose of service learning to combine academic theories to the actual life experiences of civic engagement (773). She developed a senior political science seminar titled "Human Rights/Human Wrongs" at Franklin and Marshall College that actively involved students in immigration cases. Dicklitch required students to read literature relevant to immigration, including human rights documents and associated topics in political philosophy. The Coalition for Immigrants Rights at the Community Level assisted Dicklitch and her students with the project. Asylum seekers awaiting judicial decision in their cases were being held at a local prison, where the students could interview individual persons to gain insight into the background of each case and to determine if the asylum seekers met one of the conditions for being granted asylum (774). Dicklitch states that in participating in the course, the students learned that they could make a difference in another person's life, which she considers an important aspect of civic engagement. At the end of the service-learning course, the students had assisted three asylum applicants who won their cases (five cases were still pending, and one asylum seeker was in the final stages of deportation). Dicklitch notes that for a service-learning activity to be successful, the faculty member must establish a solid connection with a community partner (775). Also, for the course to be effective, the students, in addition to having a genuine learning experience, must have the opportunity to provide substantive service to the community (776). Referring to the low level of civic engagement in the United States, Dicklitch concludes that her course potentially provides a means of involving students in more long-term civic engagement.

Deliberative Skills and Collective Action

J. Cheri Strachan (2006), concerned with young people's involvement in forms of political participation that go beyond voting, discusses the development of a course at the University of Albany that emphasizes civic engagement and deliberative collective action. Strachan proceeds under the assumption that enhancing communication skills contributes to citizenship (911). Recognizing that younger citizens tend to distrust government and group interaction in general, Strachan, following Robert Putman's findings, suggests that youth have been socialized during a period when the country has experienced declining participation in associations of all kinds. Consequently, young people express low levels of political efficacy because they have not been taught the skills of group participation (912). Strachan suggests that including the formation of deliberative skills in civic education can possibly provide young people with a paradigm for engaging effectively in politics. She mentions three possible caveats to offering opportunities for building deliberative skills: first, deliberation with others can be difficult and involve uncomfortable situations for the individual; second, any consensus that a group may establish can be the result of the influence of "those with greater oratory skills"; and third, when a group comes to a genuine consensus, the result may simply be presented to public officials who show little interest in the recommendations. Strachan contends that teaching deliberative skills to support collective action can play a role in overcoming these three caveats (912).

When the University of Albany adopted an oral discourse requirement, the opportunity arose to establish a one-hour communication course that emphasizes deliberative communication skills in support of collective action to achieve political influence (Strachan 2006, 913). The course emphasized the skills of negotiation and compromise, which are considered crucial to successful collective action. Students in the class completed a questionnaire before starting the course and again after its completion. The questionnaire attempted to determine students' trust in others, attitudes toward several political activities, and possible future involvement in political and nonpolitical endeavors. The first portion of the course included readings, lectures, and discussions intended to inform students about the value of deliberative communication skills, which, when combined with collective action techniques, could contribute to exercising political influence (913). Subsequently, students were divided into small groups in which they chose a public affairs issue to study and then develop a position on the issue to present to the class. This exercise was intended to emphasize the ability to compromise and negotiate, which are skills necessary for collective action (913).

Strachan reports that the posttest did not indicate any increase in students' sense of internal efficacy (an individual's confidence in his or her ability to act effectively), nor did it show improvement in students' belief that they could make a difference in the political realm. Students maintained their cynical attitude toward government institutions, continued to have limited expectations about the effectiveness of voting, and expressed the belief that political outcomes were difficult to influence. Although Strachan notes that students' trust in others improved, perhaps due to the collective action project, the students in the pretest generally reported that collective activity at the local level could be effective, so there remained little room for improvement to be measured on the posttest. On both tests, students considered the activities of attending a local meeting and speaking out at a meeting the most effective local (as opposed to national) tactics (914). In both the pre- and posttest, students tended to favor participating in nonpolitical as opposed to political activities. However, students' reported potential for engaging in a political campaign increased.

Although the overall results of the study did not prove unequivo-
cally positive, Strachan concludes that the extension of such com-
munitarian projects to other courses could strengthen the lessons
of deliberative civic education.

The Public Schools and Learning Civic Engagement

Michelle L. Frisco, Chandra Muller, and Kyle Dodson (2004) conducted a study to determine whether adolescents in junior high
school who join youth-serving non-school organizations ultimately have higher rates of voter turnout in young adulthood
(661). Frisco et al. note that the organizations they studied "provide connections to extra-familial adults and mentors who offer
supervision, guidance, and pro-social norms for behavior" and
therefore may help to develop "early adult civic participation"
(662). They wished to determine if some nonschool voluntary
association may have greater influence than others on later civic
engagement (663). The authors use data from the National Education Longitudinal Study (1988–1994) to determine which adolescents participated as a member or officer in scouting or religious
youth groups, nonschool team sports, 4-H clubs, the YWCA and
YMCA, and Boys and Girls Clubs in order to assess whether organization membership was associated with voter registration in
1992 and whether respondents voted in the 1992 election.

Data indicate that "participation in scouts, religious youth
groups, nonschool team sports, and 4-H positively predicts young
adults' voter-registration status, and scouting, religious youth
group membership, and leadership positions in voluntary organizations are positively related to voting in a presidential election" (Frisco et al. 2004, 673). Organizations that have a traditional
objective of "building moral and civic responsibility" appear to
have the greatest success in encouraging civic engagement. Although recognizing that their findings are relevant only to middle
school student membership in voluntary associations and that
membership in such organizations may be self-selective in that
students who already are well-integrated into the community are
more likely to join, the authors conclude that their findings contribute to the literature of group membership and civic engagement. Of particular concern is Robert Putnam's finding (1995) that

membership decline in volunteer organizations has a negative effect on civic engagement and the development of social capital.

The Internet and Civic Engagement

Stephen Coleman and Jay G. Blumler, professors of political communication in Great Britain, in their analysis of the Internet and democratic citizenship (2009), propose a policy to improve the use of the Internet for political action that, given the attraction of Internet use to young people, could have a positive effect on this age group's participation in politics. However, given that U.S. citizens and elites tend to support free enterprise over any government entity, Coleman and Blumler's recommendation may have limited applicability to the United States. They propose the development of "more effective and sensitive ways of hearing and acknowledging the millions of voices and actions, not to mention silences and inactions, that constitute meaningful human interaction" (168). They envisage in the United Kingdom an online civic commons involving a nongovernmental agency funded by public resources that would promote public deliberation and consultation on civic issues. The authors assert that "democracy requires a trusted civic space to which all know that they can come when they have something to discuss with their fellow citizens and elected representatives" (173). Coleman and Blumler state that the new agency's democratic role should be to encourage and moderate social interaction, and create summaries of public conversations, allowing various voices in a highly diverse society to be heard: "the agency running the civic commons would be entrusted with the political responsibilities of helping diverse social networks to be fully open and accountable to one another; connecting local experience, habits, knowledge and common sense to official structures of political representation; and promoting deliberative mechanisms that are sensitively responsive to asymmetries of social power between and within networks" (180). The authors perceive important roles for journalists, including encouraging and moderating conversations among citizens, providing accounts of "social reality," interpreting differing views, and adding to the general appeal of public discussion (181).

Coleman and Blumler perceive a crucial need for a civic commons, along with an agency funded by the government that would be "charged with the promoting, publicizing and facilitating public deliberation between government at its various levels and the dispersed networks which constitute the contemporary communicative landscape" (2009, 183). Confronting the possibility of implementing their proposal, the authors first speculate about whether citizens would use a civic commons as they have described it. Referring to a 2005 survey of Internet users conducted in the United Kingdom, Coleman and Blumler note the lower voter turnout rate among those aged 18 to 25. Sixty-one percent of those in this age group reported not having voted in the 2005 election, and 25 percent of them disagreed with the survey statement that they had a civic duty to vote. In addition, just 25 percent of those in the youngest age group expressed confidence in politics as a means of solving problems (185). Coleman and Blumler report that whereas 84 percent of respondents more than 60 years of age stated they were interested in being consulted online, 69 percent of those aged 18 to 24 expressed an interest, and 19 percent stated that they were undecided—hardly an expression of major support for electronic-based political engagement. The authors conclude that much needs to be done to persuade young people (as well as women and the less affluent) of the personal relevance of online consultations.

A second difficulty involves the willingness of government officials to take online consultations seriously in order to avoid "consultation fatigue" and frustration among citizens. The authors recommend that consultations be conducted during the early stages of the policy making process so that public officials may give adequate consideration to citizen views (Coleman and Blumler 2009, 190). Therefore, the civic commons agency must have authority independent of government to gain entry into the decision making process of government agencies (192). Coleman and Blumler caution that "the short history of e-democracy is littered with failed projects, dead web sites, earnest intentions that were never taken up and thoughtful dialogues that led nowhere" (195).

A major conceptual shift that they believe should occur is from viewing citizens as policy consumers to regarding them as "politically responsible citizens" (Coleman and Blumler 2009, 196). In order to be successful, the civic commons must bring citizens together into a community capable of political deliberation. This proposal includes an expectation that citizens (perhaps especially the youngest of them) can be encouraged to engage in politics more effectively than was possible in the past. However, even if such a proposal could gain sufficient support in the United

States, there remains the critical question about whether citizens in general, but particularly those aged 18 to 30, are willing to participate in this enhanced conception of democracy.

An Overview of Political Participation

Anne Colby, Elizabeth Beaumont, Thomas Ehrlich, and Josh Corngold (2007) offer a comprehensive presentation of methods for educators to prepare undergraduates for political engagement. Colby et al. initiated the Political Engagement Project (PEP), which involved analyzing the objectives and teaching strategies for courses at 21 colleges and universities, students' perceptions of the programs, and the effects of these strategies on student development (8). In an earlier work, Anne Colby, Thomas Ehrlich, Elizabeth Beaumont, and Jason Stephens (2003) discuss various strategies to include moral and civic education for undergraduates and describe the approaches that 12 colleges and universities have used to further moral and civic education. In the later work, the authors focus on those teaching approaches that will lead students toward good citizenship in a democracy, a governing system in which it is important that "as many people as possible possess a set of capacities that are intrinsically valuable and also support responsible citizenship by helping them thoughtfully evaluate political choices and effectively contribute to political outcomes" (2007, 6). The authors conclude that five strategies are important to developing political engagement: "political discussion and deliberation, political research and action projects, invited speakers and program-affiliated mentors, external placements, and structured reflection" (18).

Although Colby et al. note that education "is a powerful predictor of political knowledge, civic values, and active engagement in the political realm," they observe an apparent inconsistency: although the proportion of the population who attend college has sharply increased, the level of political knowledge and engagement has not grown accordingly (2007, 49, 51). Therefore, colleges and universities should focus greater attention on preparing undergraduates for engagement in the political realm. In addition to increasing students' interest in politics, most of the faculty involved in the PEP project endeavored to have their students acquire basic knowledge about the political process as well as understanding of the contemporary political world (109), and to encourage the development of the skills of democratic citizenship that are necessary for political engagement, including the ability to collaborate with others and to compromise. The authors also emphasize the importance of acquiring the motivation for demo-cratic citizenship, which includes "hopefulness about the future and indignation about injustice," "emotions like anger or passion for a particular issue or problem," and the minimization of such attitudes as "anti-institutional beliefs and emotions like cynicism, distrust, alienation" (147).

A sense of political efficacy plays a key role in engaging students in politics. As previously noted, political scientists divide political efficacy into two categories: external and internal. External political efficacy involves "faith in government responsive-ness," while internal efficacy refers to the belief that one has the ability to achieve objectives by participating in politics (Colby et al. 2007, 142). A practical way to develop political efficacy is involving students in "action projects," where hopefully they will have a politically efficacious experiences (152); but faculty should attempt to protect students against demoralization that may result from failed projects that possibly result from unrealistic expectations (195). Internships and placements in community organizations also can provide better understanding of public policy and the political process.

Discussion plays an important role in education to political engagement because through discussion, students can learn what qualifies as a reasoned argument and what types of behavior are (and are not) considered acceptable in public discourse (Colby et al. 2007, 157). Because people often believe deeply in a political position, they may tend to reject compromise. Colby et al. indicate that situations arise, as during the Vietnam War, when "intoler-ance toward and vilification of the opposition is taken as signs of political commitment, integrity, and purity, indicating a strong resolve to resist the ongoing press to compromise one's principles for the sake of expedience" (285). The authors consider face-to-face interaction especially important because students gain practice in speaking coherently in a discussion situation (164). In addition, involving students in research can provide a more detailed un-derstanding of the operation of governmental and community organizations (178). Colby et al. recommend the use of outside speakers, who can provide a more practical perspective on a sub-ject, offer more detailed knowledge, and discuss the potential eth-ical issues that may arise in a policy area (202–203). The final step is for faculty to afford students the opportunity for structured reflection, both in discussion and writing assignments.

Summarizing their discussion of the PEP, Colby et al. (2007) state that development of informed citizenship includes acquiring understanding of public institutions, processes, and political issues; developing basic modes of behavior that support knowledgeable engagement in politics; learning how to acquire and evaluate information and to express views on current issues; and developing the capacity to discuss political questions and to collaborate with others in the political realm (2007, 277). We can conclude from the authors' discussion that political engagement requires some definite skills that can be nurtured by undergraduate faculty.

A program closely related to the PEP that encourages youth political participation is the American Democracy Project (ADP), a creation of institutions associated with the American Association of State Colleges and Universities (AASCU). The ADP published a monograph, *Democracy and Engagement: A Guide for Higher Education*, the result of a conference attended by several university leaders in June 2004 (American Association of State Colleges and Universities n.d., 7), which contained several reports from campus leaders about how specific institutions are establishing civic engagement programs. Noting the potential negative consequences of the decline in civic activities reported by scholars such as Robert Putnam, the AASCU reports that approximately 200 member institutions have become involved in various projects geared to encourage student civic engagement. The report invites universities to take three essential steps to increase student civic engagement. First, the institution should perform a "campus audit" to determine to what extent the existing curriculum and extracurricular program are facilitating student engagement. Second, "campus conversations" should be held to assess the present situation and to propose campus-wide strategies for civic engagement. Finally, appropriate organizations are to be established to achieve the goal of greater civic engagement (14). The AASCU suggests that various "experiential opportunities," such as service-learning projects, senior capstone courses, professional internships, and "action-research projects," which most campuses already offer, be associated with the student's role as a citizen in a democracy (24). General education requirements can contribute to the basic skills for civic engagement, including critical thinking, proficiency in writing and speaking, and acquiring a basic understanding of the origins and principles of democracy (26). To this end, the AASCU recommends a basic cultural change on college campuses to shift away from the individual professor's research efforts to a focus on achieving a collective goal of civic engagement. The AASCU suggests such methods as : "creating effective professional development programs for faculty, transforming the evaluation and reward system, [and] redefining scholarship to include engagement with the curriculum" (29).

Conclusion

Political participation levels, particularly voting, are low in the United States compared to other established democracies. Researchers such as Robert Putnam (1995a, 1995b) have observed a decline in civic engagement for the past 30 years and have attempted to explain this phenomenon by referring to such trends as the rising proportion of the female population in the workforce, the development of television and other forms of home-based entertainment, and the decline in newspaper reading. Young citizens (those aged 18 to 30) have the lowest rate of political participation. Because youth are the established citizens of the future, many have investigated the participation patterns of young people, and those involved in education have developed strategies to increase the political engagement of younger Americans, especially those attending institutions of higher education. One possible way to view college courses and other activities aimed to increase political participation is that they are similar to the remedial courses some institutions offer to bring the mathematics, reading, and writing skills of some students up to college-level performance. The process of political socialization, which involves young people acquiring from the family and the public school system knowledge and attitudes about the political process, may be considered to have fallen short in many cases in the major objective of preparing adult citizens who care about and want to participate in the operation of the political system. The various experiments and proposals described here largely are meant to remedy this lapse in the political socialization process.

For many analysts, another aspect of low levels of political participation lies in characteristics of the U.S. political system that fall short of an ideal representative democracy. For instance, legal scholar Sanford Levinson (2006), in his analysis of the U.S.

Constitution, finds several crucial undemocratic aspects, such as granting to each state, regardless of population, equal representation in the U.S. Senate, and establishing the electoral college as the method of electing the president, which has led in some cases (for instance, 2000) to the election of the candidate who received fewer popular votes than the losing candidate. Such constitutional provisions may contribute to increased cynicism and withdrawal from political engagement. Other factors, such as the single-member district plurality system of electing representatives to legislative bodies, including state legislatures and the U.S. House of Representatives, may lead many to shy away from participating in politics. Every 10 years, when state legislatures reapportion legislative districts, the political party controlling the legislature undoubtedly will draw district lines to their own advantage—a process called "gerrymandering." Anyone residing in a gerrymandered district may conclude that participating in the election is a futile exercise because the candidate of one of the two major parties almost surely will be elected. Although Alan I. Abramowitz, Brad Alexander, and Matthew Gunning (2006), in their examination of redistricting and competition in U.S. House elections, express doubt about the effects of redistricting, they nonetheless note that competition in House elections has markedly declined in recent years. They observe that in the 2004 election, "only 22 House races in the entire country were decided by a margin of less than 10 percentage points—a record for the postwar era" (75). In the 2002 and 2004 elections, 99 percent of incumbents won reelection. Such a situation is certainly not one that will offer strong motivation for anyone—whether they support or oppose the incumbent representative—to become politically active. The role of money in political campaigns, although not always the determining factor in who will win the election, also may add to the cynicism of prospective participants.

In order to encourage civic engagement among those young people who are not otherwise likely to participate, educators and others must employ strategies to spark interest in politics and a sense of allegiance to the political realm, and also impart knowledge about political structures (including government institutions and the rules of political engagement) that includes a realistic understanding of why the system operates as it does and how to participate in it most effectively, including ways in which the political process might practically be altered to facilitate closer adherence to democratic principles and greater citizen involvement.

References

Abramowitz, Alan I., Brad Alexander, and Matthew Gunning. "Incumbency, Redistricting, and the Decline of Competition in U.S. House Elections." *Journal of Politics* 68 (February 2006): 75–88.

American Association of State Colleges and Universities. *Democracy and Engagement: A Guide for Higher Education*. n.d.

Ball, William J. "From Community Engagement to Political Engagement." *PS Political Science and Politics* 38 (April 2005): 287–291.

Baym, Geoffrey. *From Cronkite to Colbert: The Evolution of Broadcast News*. Boulder, CO: Paradigm Publishers, 2010.

Bogard, Cynthia J., Ian Sheinheit, and Reneé P. Clarke. "Information They Can Trust: Increasing Youth Voter Turnout at the University." *PS Political Science and Politics* 41 (July 2008): 541–546.

Brians, Craig Leonard, and Bernard Grofman. "Election Day Registration's Effect on U.S. Voter Turnout." *Social Science Quarterly* 82 (March 2001): 170–183.

Campaign for the Civic Mission of Schools. "Civic Mission of Schools." http://civicmissionofschools.org/campaign/cms_report.html, 2003.

Colby, Anne, Elizabeth Beaumont, Thomas Ehrlich, and Jason Stephens. *Educating Citizens: Preparing America's Undergraduates for Lives of Moral and Civic Responsibility*. San Francisco, CA: Jossey-Bass, 2003.

Colby, Anne, Elizabeth Beaumont, Thomas Ehrlich, and Josh Corngold. *Educating for Democracy: Preparing Undergraduates for Responsible Political Engagement*. San Francisco, CA: Jossey-Bass, 2007.

Coleman, Stephen, and Jay G. Blumler. *The Internet and Democratic Citizenship: Theory, Practice and Policy*. New York: Cambridge University Press, 2009.

Crawford, Sue E. S. "Will We Ruin Them for (Civic) Life? Analyzing the Impact of Teaching Rational Choice in Introductory Courses." *PS Political Science and Politics* 40 (April 2007): 387–391.

Dicklitch, Susan. "Real Service = Real Learning: Making Political Science Relevant Through Service Learning." *PS Political Science and Politics* 36 (October 2003): 773–776.

Dillon, Sam. "Failing Grades on Civics Exam Called a 'Crisis'." *New York Times* (May 4, 2011): A23.

Farah, George. *No Debate: How the Republican and Democratic Parties Secretly Control the Presidential Debates*. New York: Seven Stories Press, 2004.

Frisco, Michelle L., Chandra Muller, and Kyle Dodson. "Participation in Voluntary Youth-Serving Association and Early Adult Voting Behavior." *Social Science Quarterly* 85 (September 2004): 660–676.

Gerber, Alan S., Donald P. Green, and Christopher W. Larimer. "Social Pressure and Voter Turnout: Evidence from a Large-Scale Field Experiment." *American Political Science Review* 102 (February 2008): 33–48.

Hudson, William E. *American Democracy in Peril: Eight Challenges to America's Future*. Washington, DC: CQ Press, 2010.

Hunter, Susan, and Richard A. Brisbin, Jr. "Civic Education and Political Science: A Survey of Practices." *PS Political Science and Politics* 36 (October 2003): 759–763.

Kahne, Joseph, and Joel Westheimer. "The Limits of Political Efficacy: Educating Citizens for a Democratic Society." *PS Political Science and Politics* 39 (April 2006): 289–296.

Kelly-Woessner, April, and Matthew C. Woessner. "My Professor Is a Hack: How Perceptions of a Professor's Political Views Affect Student Course Evaluations." *PS Political Science and Politics* 39 (July 2006): 495–501.

Kurtz, Karl T., Alan Rosenthal, and Cliff Zukin. "Citizenship: A Challenge for All Generations." *National Conference of State Legislatures* (2003): 1–14.

Levison, Sanford. *Our Undemocratic Constitution: Where the Constitution Goes Wrong (and How We the People Can Correct It)*. New York: Oxford University Press, 2006.

Lewis, Kimberly M., and Tom W. Rice. "Voter Turnout in Undergraduate Student Government Elections." *PS Political Science and Politics* 38 (October 2005): 723–729.

Mariani, Mack D., and Gordon J. Hewitt. "Indoctrination U? Faculty Ideology and Changes in Student Political Orientation." *PS Political Science and Politics* 41 (October 2008): 773–783.

Nickerson, David W. "Is Voting Contagious? Evidence from Two Field Experiments." *American Political Science Review* 102 (February 2008): 49–57.

Niemi, Richard G., and Jane Juun. *Civic Education: What Makes Students Learn*. New Haven, CT: Yale University Press, 1998.

Niven, David. "The Mobilization Solution? Face-to-Face Contact and Voter Turnout in a Municipal Election." *Journal of Politics* 66 (August 2004): 868–884.

Patterson, Thomas E. *The Vanishing Voter*. New York: Random House, 2002.

Putnam, Robert D. "Bowling Alone: America's Declining Social Capital." *Journal of Democracy* 6 (January 1995a): 65–78.

Putnam, Robert D. "Tuning In, Tuning Out: The Strange Disappearance of Social Capital in America." *PS: Political Science and Politics* 28 (December 1995b): 1–20.

Shea, Daniel M., and Rebecca Harris. "Why Bother? Because Peer-to-Peer Programs Can Mobilize Young Voters." *PS: Political Science and Politics* 39 (April 2006): 341–345.

Sherrod, Lonnie R. "Promoting the Development of Citizenship in Diverse Youth." *PS Political Science and Politics* 36 (April 2003): 287–292.

Strachan, J. Cherie. "An Argument for Teaching Deliberative Collective Action Skills in the Political Science Classroom." *PS Political Science and Politics* 39 (October 2006): 911–916.

Ulbig, Stacy. "Engaging the Unengaged: Using Visual Images to Enhance Students' 'Poli Sci 101' Experience." *PS Political Science and Politics* 42 (April 2009): 385–391.

Wattenberg, Martin P. *Is Voting for Young People?* New York: Pearson Longman, 2008.

3

Worldwide Perspective

Researchers have focused attention on youth political participation in various countries. In order to provide comparisons
to the United States, this chapter will summarize findings regarding political participation among young people in countries
that have enjoyed stable democratic politics since World War II.
Most of these countries are in Europe (England, France, Germany,
and Italy), but one (Costa Rica) is located in Central America,
and another (Japan) is situated in Asia. Background information
about each country is presented, including the type of governing system (parliamentary versus presidential), voting system
(single-member district plurality, a form of proportional representation, or a combination of the two), and a brief look at the
history of electoral politics and political participation generally.
Also included for each country is a discussion of recent events
and political conflicts that may influence the political attitudes of
youth as well as citizens in all age groups. Some of these countries
have experienced in the recent past instances of corruption and
inefficiency in government that could lead to political cynicism,
especially among young people.

Because much research has been conducted on youth participation in community service, and because of the potential link
between this form of engagement and various kinds of political
participation, such community service activities are also discussed
where information is available. Researchers disagree about the relationship between activities that are generally considered nonpolitical and more obvious political engagement such as voting in
regional and national elections and participating in efforts to have
the government take action, for instance, to control air and water

pollution. However, if a broader understanding of the boundaries of politics is accepted, such volunteer endeavors may quickly cross over to the political realm.

Youth Populations and Birth Rates

The percentage of a country's population that is under 30 years old, as well as a country's birth rate, may influence the overall attention that young people receive in the political process and the actual influence they may exercise. Table 3.1 presents estimates of this information for the six countries treated in this chapter, plus the United States, as well as comparable data for eight countries that generally are not considered democratic.

In countries with democratic regimes, the two measures correspond very closely, with those countries with a higher percentage of the population under 30 years old having the highest birth

TABLE 3.1
Percent of Population under 30 Years Old (estimated 2011) and Birth Rate per 1,000 Population (estimated 2010)

	1,000 Population	
Democratic regimes		
Costa Rica	52.1	16.65
United States	41.0	13.83
United Kingdom	37.2	12.34
France	37.0	12.43
Germany	30.3	8.21
Italy	29.7	8.01
Japan	28.8	7.41
Nondemocratic countries		
Somalia	70.6	43.33
Sudan	70.6	36.58
Mauritania	68.4	33.67
Syria	65.9	24.44
Egypt	60.7	25.02
Libya	60.0	24.58
Saudi Arabia	60.0	19.43
Tunisia	50.1	15.31

Source: U.S. Census Bureau (percent of population under 30 estimates), www.census.gov/ipc/www/idb/region.php; Index Mundi (birth rate estimates), www.indexmundi.com.

rate. Therefore, young people should be expected to constitute a comparable proportion of the population in the future. A possible conclusion might be that those countries with the highest proportion of young people in the population would grant the greatest attention to this age group in making public policy. However, countries with undemocratic regimes have young populations that constitute much greater proportions of the total population. The uprisings in several of these countries in late 2010 and early 2011 indicate that young people can play a crucial role in regime change if other factors (such as government inefficiency and high unemployment) lead to general dissatisfaction among the population. Many have pointed to the importance of communication technology such as social networking sites on the Internet and mobile phone texting regarding the success of protests (Ghosh 2011, 32). These communication devices tend to be the province of younger people.

A reasonable hypothesis is that democracies with higher proportions of young people (those under 30 years old) face a much greater task in educating this age cohort to the principles and procedures of democracy in order to assure a continuing commitment to the democratic system. And for nondemocratic regimes, which tend to have much larger proportions of the population under 30 years old, the transition to democracy depends on the ability of the nascent democratic regime to gain the loyalty of the younger population.

Costa Rica

Costa Rica has come to be recognized as the most stable and long-lasting democracy in Central and South America. Although the country flirted with democracy much earlier, a long-lasting democratic system emerged following World War II. In 1948 a brief (44-day) civil war erupted when a coalition of Social Conservatives and Communists led by Rafael Angel Calderón and Teodoro Picado refused to recognize that Otilio Ulate, candidate of the National Unity Party, had won the presidential election. When government troops laid down their arms, José María Figueres headed a junta that established a new constitution (which is still in effect) and in 1949 the ruling group handed political authority to Ulate. The new constitution provided for universal suffrage and free elections and abolished the military. In 1951, Figueres established the National Liberation Party (PLN) and subsequently won the 1953 presidential election. The party remained influential in the parliament until the 1970s. Under the PLN, the Costa Rican government introduced public spending measures in the areas of health, education, and infrastructure expansion.

Two political parties—the PLN and the Social Christian Unity Party (PUSC)—tend to dominate the political process, typically receiving more than 95 percent of the vote (Daling 2002). Family loyalties strongly influence voting behavior, with family members transferring party preferences from one generation to the next. Election campaigns exhibit a carnival atmosphere, with party supporters publicly displaying banners and appropriately colored clothing. The minimum voting age is 18 and voting is compulsory, although the requirement is not enforced and there are no legal sanctions for nonvoting.

Political analysts attribute Costa Rica's stable democratic system to several factors, including relative economic prosperity, an educational system that has contributed to establishing a stable middle class, and a leadership committed to democratic values. Costa Rica can boast relatively high salaries and the region's highest standard of living, a life expectancy longer than any other Latin American country, a literacy rate greater than 95 percent, and a growing eco-tourism industry (Cruz 2005). Costa Rica traditionally has been known for its production of bananas and coffee, but pineapples have exceeded coffee as an agricultural export.

In addition to a president and two vice presidents, the Costa Rican government is composed of a unicameral Legislative Assembly of 57 deputies who are elected for four-year terms. The constitution provides for term limits for both the president and members of the Legislative Assembly. Former presidents may run for reelection only after two subsequent presidential terms (eight years), and deputies may seek reelection only after sitting out for one term (four years). The ultimate judicial authority resides in the Supreme Court of Justice, consisting of 22 judges chosen by the Legislative Assembly for eight-year renewable terms. The Supreme Court of Justice selects the members of the Supreme Elections Tribunal, whose duty is to guarantee free and fair elections. The country is divided into seven provinces, which are further divided into 81 cantons. Although there are no elected provincial officials, in 2002 municipalities began to elect mayors to four-year terms.

For many years, the U.S. Peace Corps has provided assistance to Costa Rica in many areas, including environmental protection, education, small business development, and youth development. The Peace Corps's youth project assists in various ways young people and youth organizations, especially in poorer communities, and provides various training opportunities and assistance in the control of violence and the dissemination of information about reproductive health (Peace Corps n.d.). The constitution mandates universal public education and a primary school education is required of all youth. There are public as well as private universities and students from poor families are eligible for subsidies (U.S. Department of State n.d.).

Young people became disaffected with the conservative government policies of the 1950s and 1960s, and resulting protests are credited with greater democratization of the Costa Rican system of higher education. Beginning in the 1970s, Costa Rica experienced severe economic problems, resulting from high government spending, the need to import oil, and a sharp fall in coffee prices later in the decade. In April 1970 high school and university students engaged in protests against government concessions to Alcoa, a multinational mining corporation. When the government approved a contract with the corporation, young people stoned the legislature and violent encounters between students and police followed. In 1981, President Rodrigo Carazo suspended interest payments to foreign creditors. In 1982, the country received a new loan from the International Monetary Fund but was required to reduce the number of government employees, increase taxes, raise excise duties, and cut social spending. Economic difficulties continued into the 1990s, with the two major political parties attempting to collaborate in instituting policies to deal with the situation. One consequence was that the public infrastructure has not been sufficiently maintained due to lack of new investment. In 2000, many young people participated in large public demonstrations against an attempt to privatize the Costa Rican Institute for Electricity (ICE), the government-owned hydroelectric and telephone company. High school and university students joined with workers and state employees in nationwide protests until the privatization plan was suspended indefinitely (Cerdas 2004).

In 2010, in the 15th presidential election since 1953, Costa Rican voters elected Laura Chinchilla to the presidency, the first woman to serve in that position. Chinchilla served as one of the country's two vice presidents during Oscar Arias's presidency and is considered his protégé. Political analysts concluded that Chinchilla's victory resulted from voters' wish to continue the status quo that included sufficient salaries and near-universal literacy. Arias had won the Nobel Peace Prize in 1987 for initiating a successful Central American peace plan that the presidents of El Salvador, Nicaragua, Guatemala, Honduras, and Costa Rica signed in August 1987. Arias continued to engage in peace initiatives, which included working to abolish the Haitian military in 1995 and, along with former U.S. President Jimmy Carter, assisting Peru and Ecuador in resolving a border dispute. In line with Arias's peace initiatives, Costa Rica has continued to have no military and has proposed treaties to prevent a future arms race in the region. During the election campaign, Chinchilla promised to continue Arias's economic policies and to extend free trade agreements. A social conservative, Chinchilla has opposed gay marriage, abortion, and any alteration in the position of the Roman Catholic Church as the state religion. She also proclaimed that she would increase education spending and has focused on reducing crime, a growing concern among Costa Ricans. As the country's youth continue to receive educational opportunities and the economy remains strong, barring unforeseen circumstances, the future of democracy in Costa Rica appears secure (Steven Palmer and Iván Jiménez's edited work [2004] contains several articles that present background information about Costa Rica, which can be helpful in evaluating the prospects for continued democratic governance in that country).

England

Historians have maintained that the minimum voting age of 21 in many Western democracies originated in English tradition, which required a candidate for knighthood to be at least 21 years old. English common law continued this tradition, regarding 21 as the age at which both men and women reached full adulthood and possessed the ability to reason for themselves. The right to vote originated with the signing of the Magna Carta in 1215, when the English feudal barons and the church forced King John to concede to them certain rights. The document, which originally protected baronial privileges from the king's interference, ultimately came to be regarded as a guarantee of various freedoms, including protection against taxation without representation and excessive royal power. The notion that suffrage rights (with gender and property limitations) began at the age of 21 spread throughout the British Commonwealth (Cultice 1992, 2).

The Reform Act of 1832 mentioned ownership of property and residence as voting qualifications but imposed no minimum age requirement, stating simply that a male "of full age" had attained suffrage rights. By tradition, the age of 21 was assumed to establish the right to vote. In 1912, Parliament rejected a proposal establishing universal suffrage, largely because the legislation would have enfranchised women as well as men. The Reform Act of 1918 granted to all men at least 21 years of age the right to vote who satisfied a six-month residency requirement (Cultice 1992, 72). However, men who had served in the military during World War I acquired the right to vote at the age of 19, which indicated that the government recognized a connection between military service and the right to vote. Men as young as 19 with military service during World War II were also granted the right to vote. Women did not achieve full suffrage rights until 1928, nearly a decade after women in the United States had achieved the right to vote. Following World War II, Parliament approved the Representation of the People Act of 1949, which enfranchised all British subjects who had reached the minimum age of 21, were a resident of the voting district, and had been added to the voter rolls. Voter registration became the responsibility of the government, not the individual voter.

The effort to lower the minimum voting age to 18 began in 1958. In that year, a Conservative member of Parliament suggested that a committee on electoral reform be established to consider various changes in the election system, including lowering the voting age to 18. However, Douglas Home, the Conservative Party leader at the time, rejected the suggestion. In subsequent years, further steps were taken to consider a lower minimum voting age. In July 1967, a committee of inquiry released the results of its investigation of the appropriate legal age of marriage and engaging in contracts. The committee recommended reducing the general "age of majority" from 21 to 18, although a Speaker's Conference called by the prime minister concluded that a minimum voting age of 20 should be established. Nonetheless, the government, in formulating a proposal, opted for the minimum age of 18, and the Representation of the People Act went into effect on January 1, 1970. In addition to granting the right to vote to those aged 18 to 20, the act also made young people legally qualified to take part in various adult activities such as entering into contracts, marrying without parental consent, buying property, and borrowing money. In 2006, the Electoral Administration Act reduced the age at which an individual may run for elective office from 21 to 18.

Since 1999, there has been consideration of proposals to reduce the minimum voting age still further to 16. Although a measure proposed in Parliament to effect that reduction was unsuccessful, a general debate began regarding the advantages and drawbacks to further reducing the voting age. Although 18 is considered an arbitrary age, some minimum age must be established, and the argument can be made that a sufficient number of those aged 16 and 17 have not yet reached maturity to be trusted with the vote. In response, others argue that at the age of 16, an individual may leave school, marry, join the military, and pay taxes (White 2009, 3). Opponents respond that, as with present younger voters, 16- and 17-year-olds will tend not to participate in elections. The Liberal Democrats introduced a proposal in the party's 2001 manifesto to reduce the voting age to 16 and renewed this position in 2005. However, in 2002, Prime Minister Tony Blair of the Labour Party expressed his opposition to lowering the voting age. In 2003, more than 40 youth and democracy organizations established the Votes at 16 Coalition to support lowering the voting age.

England's political system is similar to that of the United States in that both employ the single-member district plurality system of electing representatives, with the territory divided into districts with just one representative elected from each district and with the candidate who receives the most votes (not necessarily a majority) elected to the seat in the legislature. However, the two systems differ in that the United States has a presidential system, with the chief executive selected independently of Congress, while England has a parliamentary system in which a majority of the members of Parliament selects the prime minister. The single-member district system has often been associated with a two-party system, and the United States generally follows that expectation. However, in England, three political parties vie for seats in parliament: the Labour Party, the Conservative Party, and the Liberal Democrats. Although the latter party attracts the lowest level of voter support overall, as a result of the May 2010 parliamentary elections, this party gained significant influence in the government through negotiations with the other two parties, neither of which won a majority of seats in Parliament.

A characteristic of the single-member district system that likely adds to the reported cynicism of young voters as well as voters of all ages is that the system does not equitably translate popular votes into parliamentary seats. In the 2010 election, the Conservatives received 36.48 percent of the popular vote but gained 47.2 percent of parliamentary representation (307 seats); Labour received 28.99 percent of the popular vote but 39.7 percent of the representation (258 seats, which represented a loss of 91 seats); and Liberal Democrats received 23.03 percent of the popular vote but just 8.8 percent of the representation (57 seats). The Liberal Democrats also lost electoral support since the last election, which went instead to the right-wing British National Party (Burns 2010). Neither Labour nor the Conservatives could muster a majority to form a government on their own and so one of the major parties had to form a coalition with the Liberal Democrats. To many, a Labour–Liberal Democrat coalition appeared to be the more likely alliance, especially because the Labour Party had won the highest number of seats, and because of speculation that Labour leaders would more likely combine with the Liberal Democrats to introduce a system of proportional representation, an electoral system more advantageous to third parties. Although England faced serious economic difficulties and whatever party gained power would have to face onerous policy choices, the Labour and Conservative parties undoubtedly represented very different public policy approaches. Although England had not faced this situation since World War II, its occurrence at this time raised serious questions about the legitimacy of the governing coalition and the potentially controversial policies it would pursue.

Nick Clegg, leader of the Liberal Democrats, guided his party into a governing coalition with Conservatives, thus raising Conservative leader David Cameron to the position of prime minister. In the agreement with the Conservative Party, Clegg would become deputy prime minister and the Liberal Democrats would claim as many as five cabinet seats (Guttenplan and Margaronis 2010, 11). However, the Liberal Democrats' hope for electoral reform that would allow it to gain a greater share of representation in Parliament apparently would not be fulfilled. Nonetheless, with the necessity for a coalition government, a political party that received less than 25 percent of the popular vote had the power (along with its chosen coalition partner) to greatly influence which policies would be implemented.

This electoral outcome appears to add credence to the view that young people and citizens in general are skeptical about the way in which the political process operates and that many have become increasingly disaffected with the functioning of democracy in England. Some researchers contend that people in general view politics as a system managed by those who remain remote and unresponsive. Studies have reported that younger people tend to vote less in elections, participate less in political organizations, are less likely to identify with a political party, and show less interest in politics. Some have concluded that the gap in political engagement between young people and older age cohorts has widened to the point that a major separation of young people from the political system has occurred.

Political analysts point to a key phenomenon in recent decades: the increasing professionalism of politics. The influence within political parties has become more centralized, and electoral politics has been characterized by greater professionalism that has replaced grassroots voluntary organizations. Party-related organizations, such as Young Labour and Conservative Futures, have become training venues for a smaller group of potential candidates and political advisers rather than recruiters of volunteers in the general population. People generally, it is argued, become consumers of politics rather than active participants.

However, in a 1999 panel survey and a series of focus groups, Henn, Weinstein, and Wring (2002) discovered greater participation in politics among youth than would be expected from the findings of past research. They concluded that a majority of young people do show interest in politics. A majority of young people discuss politics with friends and family members, a finding that, the authors note, differs from the traditional view that youth have little interest in public matters. Young people blame political parties for much of the lack of interest in politics because the party organizations do not make the effort to involve them in political affairs. Instead, many young people believe that they are being encouraged to be quiescent. The authors conclude that youth show heightened interest in those issues that concern them, such as militarism, civil liberties, animal rights, educational opportunities, and conditions in underdeveloped countries.

Roker, Player, and Coleman (1999), in their examination of youth involvement in volunteer work and campaigning, also challenge the view that young people in England are "uninterested, apathetic, uninvolved, and self-centered," claiming that this perception is "inaccurate and simplistic." They assert that young people are no less altruistic nor more hesitant than other age groups to become involved in community affairs. The authors define "campaigning activities" broadly to include actions to bring about some change, including involvement in environmental concerns, support for animal rights, engagement in political party activities, and defense of particular groups or issues (71). Correspondingly, the authors hold to an expansive understanding of altruism that includes various forms of political activity. Thus altruism includes young people's involvement in voluntary community activities as well as political campaigning. Roker, Player, and Coleman note that, unlike the United States, "most community service and volunteering opportunities [in England] are still organized informally," and schools seldom require such service in their curriculum (59). However, beginning in the early 1990s, more concerted efforts were initiated to introduce students to the knowledge and skills that support active participation. The Citizenship Foundation and the Centre for Citizenship Studies in Education offer materials to be used in the educational system (59–60). As evidence that many young people are availing themselves of the opportunity for community service, the authors note that membership in the youth sections of Amnesty International and Greenpeace has grown considerably; 6 of 10 applicants for volunteer work with Community Service Volunteers are under the age of 18; and more than 50 percent of those aged 18 to 24 have engaged in some form of voluntary service. Based on their case studies of young people and staff at three schools, Roker, Player, and Coleman report that just under 10 percent of the students were members of a group involved in campaigning, and a majority in the past year had engaged in activities such as giving money to charity, taking part in a boycott, or campaigning in favor of changing a school rule. A majority of the students questioned supported more opportunities for community involvement but generally opposed any formal requirement for participation: they supported the notion of choice regarding voluntary community engagement.

Roker, Player, and Coleman (1999) conclude from their research that there is no evidence that young people are less interested in social problems or that their motives for community engagement are less altruistic than older age groups. Certainly youth can have self-interested motives for involvement, such as the hope of being better regarded by others, but altruistic concerns also play a role in engagement. They also focus attention on the special situation of youth in rural areas who may have difficulty becoming involved due to prohibitive distances, and those with disabilities, who often may be regarded as recipients of assistance from organizations rather than active participants.

In July 2007, Prime Minister Gordon Brown, reporting to the House of Commons on constitutional reform, spoke of the need to engage young people in politics and to improve citizenship education. He expressed support for a commission to examine these issues and to consult with young people regarding the possible effect of lowering the voting age on voter participation. The commission was to determine what support English schools required to assure that young people are prepared for adult citizenship and the exercise of voting rights. A Youth Citizenship Commission was established to examine possible strategies intended to expand young people's understanding of the nation's history, to consider the meaning of British citizenship, and ultimately to engage greater numbers of youth in the political process. In June 2009, the commission published a report that did not include a recommendation to reduce the voting age, but a majority of those who responded to the commission's invitation to provide input favored lowering the voting age to 16. Those aged 16 and 17 generally supported such a reduction, but all older age categories tended to oppose any reduction in the minimum voting age. The commission concluded that although the voting age issue is worthy of further consideration, it is not the most important ingredient in the formulation of a strategy to increase youth political engagement.

Young people in Britain face the economic downturn that has plagued the country. Economic growth remained modest prior to the 2010 election, which contributed to a general lack of enthusiasm for either of the two leading political parties. With the economic downturn, there appeared to be no consensus over where the country was heading and who was best qualified to handle the troubling situation. A part of the difficulty, as Catherine Mayer (2010) noted, was the increasing inequality between the wealthy and the poor.

The Cameron government's decision to increase tuition charges for attending British universities as a key part of its austerity measures led to student protests in London and other cities. Young people were upset especially because the Liberal Democrats, who now were within the governing coalition, had pledged during the election campaign to do away with college tuition fees. Members of the National Union of Students declared that they would initiate efforts to recall legislators who voted in favor of tuition increases that resulted in tripling student fees. In November 2010, thousands of students in London protested against the fee increase and some of the protesters attempted to enter Conservative Party headquarters. Police arrested 32 of the protesters on various charges, including violent disorder and criminal damage. College students around the country, including the cities of Bristol, Liverpool, and Leeds, took part in marches and sit-ins. In Cambridge, several hundred students reportedly climbed the Senate House fence and moved into King's College grounds waving signs and shouting. In December, students again held protest gatherings in the streets when Parliament approved the tuition hikes. Police placed barricades around the Houses of Parliament. The demonstrators attacked a car in which Prince Charles and his wife Camilla were riding; although the couple was unhurt, 6 police officers and some 20 students reportedly were injured in the demonstrations.

The demonstrations against increased tuition fees perhaps reflect the long-standing disengagement of many young people from the traditional political process. The combination of the single-member district electoral system with the moderate success of third parties that necessitated bargaining between two of the parties to achieve a parliamentary majority may have contributed to the mass protests. Given no clear majority preference, the students were frustrated with a policy they considered unreasonable, and they entered the political fray in a climate already characterized by deep political divisions. As Henn, Weinstein, and Wring (2002) have concluded, young people in England are politically engaged, but they are "engaged sceptics" in that they are interested in the political realm but often do not trust those who have been elected to office. Whether young people can be brought back to the more traditional political path depends on several factors, including an improved British economy and perhaps reforms in the electoral system that ensure fairer representation to political parties that currently fail to receive a level of representation closely related to electoral strength. This and other reforms also apply to the United States, where the political engagement of young people, although on the increase in recent elections, still lags behind the electorate as a whole.

France

Since the 1960s, youth in France have periodically engaged in the politics of protest, at times bringing crucial parts of French society to near-standstill. In 2005, riots involving primarily disaffected youth in immigrant communities centered in poor housing projects shook the country. In 2006, students protested the government's attempt to increase employers' ability to hire and fire young workers. Although largely peaceful, the protests sometimes became violent as demonstrators smashed store windows and set automobiles on fire. The government ultimately abandoned proposals to alter hiring policies. In fall 2010, students joined unionized workers in protests against President Nicolas Sarkozy's plan to institute an increase in the retirement age from 60 to 62. Youths throughout France took part in demonstrations and confronted police. High school (lycee) students aged 15 to 18 and younger students from middle schools ("colleges") united with university students in the protests. Across France, young people disrupted hundreds of high schools by walking out of classes or blocking entrances. President Sarkozy and his Union for a Popular Movement (UMP) party had suffered a setback in the March 2010 regional elections when the Socialist Party and left-wing allies won nearly 54 percent of the popular vote and control of 23 of France's 26 regions, in contrast to 35 percent voter support for the UMP.

In addition to the electoral defeats, in August 2010, French president Nicolas Sarkozy came under suspicion for claimed misuse of campaign funds when allegations arose that his minister of labor, Eric Woerth, had engaged in dealings with L'Oréal cosmetics heiress Liliane Bettencourt. Sarkozy, in his successful 2007 election campaign, flouted French tradition by celebrating the quest for affluence and criticizing the tax system. That year, voter turnout reached nearly 74 percent (as opposed to a turnout rate of just over 50 percent in the 2010 regional elections). Sarkozy's position on wealth received a measure of acceptance until the global economic downturn in 2008. Although the president quickly backed government intervention to help the economy and pointed to the role of the banks in the economic recession, one of his government ministers reportedly spent large sums on personal items and another housed relatives in elaborate government housing at the same time that cabinet members were advising citizens to work more and retire later. In mid-2010, Sarkozy's approval rating in opinion polls had dropped to 35 percent. A columnist in the journal *La Tribune* commented that the administration was a "new ancien regime," referring to the corrupt government of King Louis XVI, who was guillotined during the French Revolution of 1789 (Dickey and McNicoll 2010, 9). Yet another event that brought into question the integrity of the political process was the March 2011 corruption trial of Jacques Chirac, president from 1995 to 2007, who was charged with securing jobs for political supporters when he served as mayor of Paris.

The French electoral process resembles that of the United States in that both countries employ the single-member district system to elect representatives. However, the two countries differ in other ways, including the method of electing the president (the U.S. Constitution established the electoral college while France elects its president by direct popular vote). The present French governing system, known as the Fifth Republic, was established when Charles De Gaulle came to power in 1958 in reaction against right-wing military personnel in French-controlled Algeria who threatened a coup d'état.

The multi-party system of the Fourth Republic tended to converge into two major voting blocs with the introduction of the single-member district system and the election of the president by a two-tiered electoral process in which the two top candidates in the first round compete in a run-off election. The country is composed of 555 single-member districts, each of which elects one member to the National Assembly (overseas territories and departments elect a few other deputies). The second chamber of the French parliament, the Senate, includes 321 members who are chosen indirectly by an electoral college composed of various public officials. All French citizens at least 18 years old have the right to vote. The voter turnout rate in France since the 1950s has remained high relative to the United States but lower than other European democracies. Turnout tends to be considerably lower in elections for France's representatives to the European Parliament.

In addition to elections for the National Assembly, French voters participate in local elections, selecting members of municipal councils. Also, voters take part in cantonal elections to select members of the General Council. France uses a two-round system of elections. If no candidate receives a majority of the popular vote, a second election is held between the top vote getters in the first election. In the 2007 presidential election, Nicolas Sarkozy of the UMP party received 31 percent of the vote, and Ségolèn Royal, the Socialist Party candidate, received 26 percent, with 10 additional candidates sharing the remaining votes. In the second round, Sarkozy received 53 percent of the vote to Royal's 47 percent. Some election researchers have argued that a system of preferential voting, in which voters rank each candidate in order of preference, would more accurately reflect the wishes of the electorate than does a runoff election. Rather than a separate runoff election, the votes of losing candidates in the first election would be transferred to voters' second choices.

A combination of factors appear to have led to lower voter turnout in French elections as well as a resort to more unconventional methods of political participation on the part of young people: an electoral system that may not accurately reflect voter preferences; perceived corruption; and crucial issues that the government in power appears not able to resolve to the satisfaction of the majority, or substantial segments, of the population.

Germany

Following Germany's defeat in World War II, the allied nations divided the country into East Germany (the German Democratic Republic), under the influence of the Soviet Union; and West Germany (the Federal Republic of Germany), administered by England, France, and the United States. West Germany established a democratic constitution, the Basic Law, and first held elections in 1949. The West German government was composed of a two-house legislature: the lower house (the Bundestag, members of which were elected directly by the people) and the upper house (the Bundesrat), composed of representatives from the 16 federal states. The chief executive is the chancellor, who is elected by the Bundestag. West Germany and East Germany reunified in 1990, following the dissolution of the Soviet Union and the fall of the communist regimes of Eastern Europe.

Prior to the Nazi takeover in 1933, the Weimar Republic used a strict form of proportional representation that allowed numerous political parties to gain representation in the Reichstag. The newly established Federal Republic of Germany established a mixed system in order to prevent the fragmented representation associated with a large number of parties gaining representation. Citizens vote for individual candidates in single-member districts but also vote for political parties, which gain representation in the legislature in proportion to electoral support. The election of individual candidates establishes a certain level of accountability that the representative owes to his or her constituency. In order to gain representation in the national legislature, political parties must receive a minimum of 5 percent of the total vote. Elections are held for municipal, district, regional, and federal positions. The individual regions, or Lander, govern how municipal and district elections are to be conducted. The minimum voting age varies from 16 to 18, depending on the region, but the national standard is 18. The regional state parliament in each of the 16 Lander is directly elected, and those parties that receive at least 5 percent of the popular vote may receive additional seats. German parties do not hold primary elections to determine candidates, as is the case in the United States, but rather party officials select the candidates. Candidates for the Bundestag may decide to run for a seat as an individual constituent candidate as well as on the party list. In the national elections, citizens at least 18 years of age who have resided in Germany for at least three months have the right to vote (Roberts 2009, 52). Unlike the tradition in the United States, where general elections are held during the week, in Germany, they take place on Sunday. Also in contrast to the United States, the government automatically registers citizens to vote and the relevant municipality notifies each person of their voting status. Voter turnout in Germany has averaged around 90 percent. However, in the first election following reunification, turnout declined to less than 80 percent. In recent years, political campaigns have become longer, thus necessitating larger campaign budgets and more campaign staff.

An electoral college composed of members of the Bundestag plus an equal number of individuals selected by the parliaments of the Lander elect the president. The president lacks political influence and plays a role equivalent to a constitutional monarch. In 2010, President Horst Koehler resigned, and Chancellor Angela Merkel nominated Christian Wulff as the candidate of the conservative Christian Democrats to replace Koehler. In a special parliamentary assembly in July, Wulff won 625 votes and opposition candidate Joachim Gauck received 494 votes, with 121 abstentions, mostly from the Left Party. With Wulff's victory, Merkel avoided a political embarrassment. However, in December 2010, Merkel suffered a defeat in parliament when the Bundesrat failed to approve a welfare reform proposal. The Christian Democrats had lost their majority in the Bundesrat in the May election, and thus political analysts expected that Merkel's party would experience further defeats during her remaining three years as chancellor.

An examination of post–World War II Germany allows for the comparison of youth political views and political involvement between a democratic regime and an authoritarian one. In 1990, when East Germany (the German Democratic Republic [GDR]) rejoined West Germany (the Federal Republic of Germany [FRG]) following the collapse of the communist regime, questions arose about the integration of younger people into the Federal Republic. Hans Oswald (1999) has contrasted the political attitudes of adolescents in the former GDR to those of young people in the former FRG. Oswald notes that indoctrination played a key role in the GDR's educational system and calls the GDR a "paternalistic-authoritarian system inside and outside schools" that attempted to educate all citizens to socialist conformity and loyalty to the communist party and government. The communist regime established a day-care system in which most children participated, so that the indoctrination process began at the very earliest years. The intense efforts of the regime to socialize young people to communist ideology, including civic education in the schools as well as the party youth organization, Freie Deutsche Jugend (FDJ), proved less than successful, and during the 1980s the legitimacy of the regime declined (98). The availability of Western television and radio broadcasts from the FRG undoubtedly had an influence on political attitudes. Students generally considered the Marxist-Leninist doctrine conveyed in school and university civics courses just a formal requirement, and young people tended to withdraw from the political realm. Oswald categorizes youth in the GDR into four categories: the "loyal socialists" who benefitted from the regime; the "politically interested, well educated critics of the system" who wished to improve socialist society; the "politically interested opponents of the system" who desired a change of regime; and the "politically disinterested," a large group of mainly working youth who simply withdrew from the political realm (99). Following reunification, youth as well as older citizens in the former GDR showed greater interest in politics than residents in the FRG, but surveys indicated decreased interest in subsequent years.

In Germany, the notion of community service traditionally has referred to "voluntary and continuous unpaid work within an organization that is performed in the interest of others during one's spare time" (Hofer 1999, 114). However, Manfred Hofer asserts that the traditional understanding of community engagement is being replaced by activities "that allow creativity, adventure, and personal initiative, and that may enhance social reputation as well as individual gratification" (115). Hofer also notes that the structure of the German welfare system plays a key role in the nature of community service. As the extent of government-administered welfare programs in the FRG increased beginning in the 1960s, the need for voluntary assistance decreased significantly. Currently, community service does not play an integral role in the social system. Young people who want to volunteer find only limited opportunities in the applicable organizations. According to Hofer, given the professionalization of social work, many young people may participate in community service in order to gain experience in anticipation of gaining a paid position. However, since the economic difficulties experienced in the 1980s, which were accompanied by a decrease in public assistance programs, the need for voluntarism has expanded (116). Although community service participation is low in Germany compared to other Western nations, it is estimated that 10 percent to 18 percent of the population engage in voluntary service activities. The types of community engagement considered community service include participation in sport clubs, helping people with special needs, and service within the political realm. Hofer states that the latter category includes youth becoming involved in school organizations and auxiliary groups for young people. In his investigation, Hofer discovered that adolescents mentioned various examples of engagement, including church activities, sports, social welfare, politics (for instance, being a member of a peace advocacy group), and school (such as becoming a school or class representative). Studies indicate that individuals who become involved in service activities generally come from higher socioeconomic backgrounds, leading to the conclusion that parents may play a key role in youth involvement (119). A related finding is that the more that adolescents discussed the issues of pollution and the environment with family members and friends, the more likely they were to support taking action to remedy the problem (120). Hofer also notes a study that identified a feeling of responsibility as a significant motive for community involvement. Other factors include "seeking leisure contacts," "seeking approval," and "needing knowledge about oneself" (121).

Prior to unification in 1989, the East German population was expected to engage in Communist Party–related and workplace-related activities. Since unification, Hofer (1999) notes that many former East German young people have participated in political and school activities. The overall low level of youth community participation, Hofer suggests, may be associated with what has been termed "individualization," which involves an increase in individual freedom as well as "loss of traditional bounds, controls, and values as society has lost its orienting function for the individual" (123). Because youth generally are concerned with their own status, they tend not to contribute time to activities that have low expected value for themselves. Symbolic values, such as a sense of satisfaction, self-awareness, and increased prestige that result from community service may motivate youth to voluntary engagement. Relevant to the potential relationship between community service and political engagement is the notion of transcendence, which Hofer borrows from Yates and Youniss (1996). "Transcendence" is defined as the process by which abstract concepts are derived from concrete experiences (Hofer 1999, 124). At the most advanced level, individuals look for the cause of social problems they encounter in their community work, and consider possible solutions and what they can do personally to remedy the immediate situation. Hofer has applied the transcendence idea to a group of German adolescents, and in a subsequent study, he and colleagues investigated whether adolescents engaged in community service differ from nonparticipants. They discovered that transcendence scores for service volunteers were significantly higher than for nonparticipants.

Hofer concludes that unpaid community service contributes to the public interest shown by young people and also is crucial to the operation of a democratic political system (1999, 130). He notes that economic downturn—including the costs of unification that Germany experienced in the 1990s—have led to a greater spirit of communitarianism. Volunteering activities can operate as intermediate institutions that offer people a basis for understanding social circumstances. Community service can help young people to transcend immediate encounters and thus have beneficial effects on the individual's bond with society (131). Young people, reflecting on present experiences, discover the importance of affiliation to family and social institutions. Hofer suggests that youth could be encouraged to engage in volunteer work in such areas as libraries, hospitals, and the elderly. Also, schools could offer educational programs that encourage young students to volunteer and provide training. In a broader, politically relevant context, schools could serve as the realm for discussions relevant to such issues as morality and justice (133).

Italy

Following World War II and the fall of Benito Mussolini's fascist regime, Italy became a republic with a president, a prime minister, and a democratically elected parliament. Italian governments were extremely unstable in the years following the war, due in part to the system of proportional representation used to elect members of parliament that led to many political parties gaining legislative seats. From 1945 to 1993, 52 governments ruled, with the average length of each regime less than one year. In 1993, electoral reform brought about a mixed electoral system in which three-fourths of parliamentary seats were decided by single-member district elections, and the remainder resulted from a proportional representation arrangement. However, in 2005, the country returned to a form of proportional representation. The bicameral parliament, composed of the Chamber of Deputies and the Senate, elects the president, who is the head of state. The president officially appoints the prime minister, who is the leader of the majority party or ruling coalition in parliament. The voting age has been set at 18; however, the minimum age for voting in senatorial elections is 25. In addition to parliamentary elections, voters may participate in regional, provincial, and municipal elections, as well as national referenda. Residents in 8,101 municipalities elect members of a municipal council, who serve a term of five years.

Silvio Berlusconi, who served as prime minister from 1994 to 1995 and from 2001 to 2006, and resumed the position once more in 2008, faced charges of corruption and sexual indiscretions, a circumstance not conducive to encouraging young people to become more actively engaged in politics. In March 2010, Berlusconi's political coalition did well in regional elections, winning four districts from the opposition and ultimately registering electoral victories in 6 of the 13 regions. Viewing the election results as a mandate, the prime minister began to push for several reforms, including restructuring the judicial system and changing the method of electing the president from parliamentary election to direct election. In January 2011, the Constitutional Court rejected a law that granted to the prime minister automatic immunity from prosecution, thus opening the door for prosecutors to conduct criminal investigations of Berlusconi's questionable activities and alleged abuse of power during the previous 16 years. Prosecutors in Milan charged that Berlusconi had engaged in sex with several prostitutes and were investigating allegations that the prime minister had paid to have sex with a 17-year-old Moroccan girl. Despite the various allegations against him, Berlusconi managed to maintain political power. Before entering politics, Berlusconi developed a mass media conglomerate, and he has successfully transferred that prominence to his political career. Some claim that the prime minister's ownership of several Italian media outlets provides him with significant influence on public opinion.

Prior to Berlusconi's rise to power, political parties representing class interests and social groups dominated the political scene, including the Communist Party and the Christian Democrats. Following the fall of the Soviet Union and the Communist regimes of Eastern Europe, the Christian Democratic coalition in Italy quickly dissolved under charges of corruption and incompetence, thus opening the door for an alternative to the traditional political divisions. With great influence in the mass media, Berlusconi had the advantage of general popularity and name recognition. Stille (2010) asserts that television program preferences, rather than social and economic status, have become the most reliable predictor of voter choices. Berlusconi brought into the government business associates and various television personalities and executives from his media companies that include major television channels. He initiated changes in election rules so that voters no longer had a choice among the candidates that the political parties offered. That function was assumed by party officials who determined which candidates would run for which positions. This situation appears to leave little room for youth to exercise genuine influence over the electoral process. Nonetheless, Berlusconi's popularity among Italian voters continued, as his center-right coalition made gains in the March 2010 elections.

Elena Marta, Giovanna Rossi, and Lucia Boccacin (1999) discuss the involvement of Italian youth in voluntary organizations, which have a long tradition of ministering to various human needs. The authors examine volunteers' social characteristics and motivations. Their investigation was conducted in a context in which young people often were regarded as disillusioned, pragmatic, and lacking in strong ethical convictions. However, the authors suggest that many youth have developed a greater sense of the importance of human relationships in the determination of the quality of life (74). This development, the authors contend, is associated with the evolution of the Italian political and social system, including the decline of traditional political parties, difficulties with maintaining the welfare system, and the decreasing importance of political ideologies and large political movements. Youth, wishing to engage in "prosocial action," engage in voluntary activities in order to deal more effectively with the bureaucratic structure of Italian society that reportedly neglects the increasing emphasis on "the personal dignity of its citizens" (75).

The areas in which young people (aged 18 to 29) tend to participate include assisting the sick and the elderly, youth and troubled children, and those suffering from drug addiction. Environmental concerns also attract the attention of youth (Marta et al. 1999, 76). The authors report on a sample study of 225 young volunteers and the organizations in which they participate in the region of Lombardy in northern Italy. They administered a questionnaire to the young volunteers that asked them about their social and cultural characteristics, motivation for volunteering, how they joined the organization, and how much time they allot for service activities (79). The authors discovered that most volunteers became involved through their own initiative, and many were invited by a friend or relative. Political engagement generally was not a major concern of the volunteers, and they tended to disapprove of a greater political role for their organization. However, some of the expressed concerns appeared to have a political component, such as "protecting the rights of vulnerable members of society" and "protection of the environment and the artistic heritage" (82). The most often mentioned motivation for involvement was a sense of solidarity and civic responsibility to help others. A small proportion (15 percent) of those expressing this motivation agreed that the organization could become politically involved. A second motivation involved the wish to belong to a group. Finally, a small proportion of the sample expressed a religious motive for engaging in volunteer activities. This group expressed little interest in political engagement (84).

The authors emphasize that recent voluntary participation, unlike the past, generally does not assume a political character and has little to do with political parties. They conclude that volunteers appear to reject and avoid traditional political engagement, and they suspect that this retreat from the political is associated with the contemporary difficulties that the Italian political system has faced. According to the authors, "political commitment and volunteer commitment have never been, even in the past, closely related phenomena; rather they are distinct areas of action" (92). The authors note that the only significant difference between youth-oriented volunteer organizations and predominantly adult groups is that youth organizations tend to focus greater attention on activities intended to protect the environment.

Japan

Following World War II, after losing 3 million lives and suffering the atomic bombing of the cities of Hiroshima and Nagasaki, Japan became a parliamentary democracy with a largely symbolic hereditary monarch, the emperor. When Emperor Hirohito died in 1989, the monarchy continued with his son, Akihito, who succeeded to the throne. Immediately following the war, the Allied powers governed Japan through the U.S. military commander General Douglas MacArthur. A new constitution went into effect in May 1947, which established the structure of Japan's government, guaranteed certain rights, such as universal adult suffrage, and prohibited the development of a large military. The nation has a parliamentary form of government, with a two-house legislature, the Diet—consisting of a House of Representatives (designated the lower house) with 480 seats and the House of Councillors (called the upper house) with 242 seats. Candidates for the House of Representatives must be at least 25 years old, and candidates for the House of Councillors must have reached the age of 30. Every four years, an election is held to fill all seats in the House of Representatives. The electorate chooses half the members of the House of Councillors every three years. In addition to parliamentary elections, there are also elections every four years for the 47 regional prefectures and for municipal governments. The minimum voting age is set at 20.

At least five political parties—the Democratic Party of Japan (DPJ), the Liberal Democratic Party (LDP), the Social Democratic Party (SDP), the New Clean Government Party (Komeito), and the Japan Communist Party (JCP)—compete in elections, although the DPJ and the LDP currently are the two dominant parties. The prime minister is the leader of the majority party in the Diet. From the 1940s, Japan experienced relative political stability and economic growth. Following electoral reforms in 1994, the election system became mixed-member majoritarian, combining a single-member district system that elects 300 seats in the House of Representatives, and a proportional representation system that elects an additional 180 members. A voter casts two ballots, the first for a candidate in a single-member district and the second for a political party or group. Each party receives seats equal to the number of candidates that win in single-member districts plus the number of seats apportioned to the party based on the proportion of votes it received.

Rosenbluth and Thies (2010, 101) conclude that the 1994 electoral reform has led to a more consolidated, bipartisan political system, greater emphasis on party platforms and party leaders, nationwide campaigns, and more (but not completely) homogeneous parties and weakened factions. Factions, especially in the

LDP, which represent special interests, previously played a dominant role in Japanese politics. In addition, campaigns are more issue oriented, with parties seeking to attract the "mythical median voter" rather than depending on the support of particular segments of the population, such as farmers. Although the LDP and DPJ have become the two dominant political parties, the proportional representation aspect of elections allows third parties to gain representation in the Diet. The emergence of the DPJ as a rival to the LDP, which dominated the electoral scene for more than three decades, may provide young citizens greater incentive to participate in the electoral process. However, as Hayes (1995, 132) notes, campaign activities that are taken for granted in the United States are extensively restricted in Japan, which may tend to discourage citizens from engaging in electoral politics.

Continued economic prosperity in the 1970s and 1980s made Japan the second largest economy after the United States. However, during the 1990s, the country experienced economic reversals as well as scandals involving government officials, bankers, and industrialists. The economic and political difficulties were reflected in the speed at which prime ministers were replaced. In 2001, Liberal Democrat Junichiro Koizumi became the nation's 11th prime minister in 13 years. In August 2005, Koizumi retained the prime minister's position in an election in which his Liberal Democrat Party won a large majority in the Diet. Soon thereafter, Shinzo Abe succeeded Koizumi as prime minister. In the 2007 parliamentary elections, the LDP suffered defeat, losing control of the House of Councillors to the Democratic Party. In August 2009, the DPJ won a strong victory in the election for the House of Representatives, giving the party a majority in the House and the position of majority coalition in the House of Councillors. However, due to continuing public concern over a finance scandal, Prime Minister Yukio Hatoyama, along with the party's secretary general, resigned in June 2010, and Minister of Finance Naoto Kan became the new prime minister. Another issue that had plagued Hatoyama involved his promise to have the U.S. Marine base removed from the southern island of Okinawa. Hatoyama, who stepped down after just 8 months in office, became the 4th prime minister to resign in 4 years. In September 2010, Kan won a party election to maintain his position as party president and hence became prime minister. Kan proved to be a flexible politician and government official. For instance, although he had criticized the Liberal Democratic Party for bowing to U.S. interests, once he became prime minister, Kan indicated that he would not disturb the United States–Japan relationship, and that he would honor the agreement with the United States regarding the U.S. Marine base on Okinawa.

Japanese society possesses characteristics that would appear to contribute to political engagement on the part of youth and the population in general. The literacy rate stands at 99 percent, and the country has a very low crime rate (Japan recorded only 1,281 homicides in 1996; the homicide rate in 2008 was 0.5 per 100,000 population compared to 5.4 per 100,000 in the United States). The right to vote developed relatively slowly in Japan, with just 1 percent of males possessing the franchise in 1890. In 1925 all males at least 25 years old had gained the vote, but females were still excluded from the electorate (Takahashi and Hatano 1999, 225). Leading up to and during World War II, the military limited popular political participation.

Following the war, universal suffrage was instituted and U.S. occupation authorities attempted to introduce into the educational system principles conducive to democracy, including equal opportunity, learning that is focused on personal growth, and appreciation for academic freedom (Hayes 1995, 201). However, the pre-university schools came to emphasize the ability of students to pass university admissions examinations, which meant intense preparation in testing skills and information recall. The pressures of test preparation, which can begin at the pre-school level, has tended to limit participation in extracurricular activities such as clubs and sports. However, once they gain admission to one of the nation's more than 500 public and private universities, students tend not to be confronted with challenging academic work.

Hayes (1995, 212) considers the lack of demanding course work at the college level to be one of the reasons why students became especially politically active in the 1950s and 1960s: they could afford to take time away from studies to engage in protest movements. Takahashi and Hatano (1999) note that students "protested against U.S. military aggression in Vietnam, American military bases in Japan, the Japanese government's policies in South Asia, the revised Japan-U.S. Security Treaty, and the introduction of atomic weapons to Japan" (226). In 1960, both high school and college students expressed their opposition to the renewed security treaty with the United States. Students also sought more democratic college administration, including improved teaching methods and public reporting of school budgets.

With the attainment of educational reforms and the end of the Vietnam War, student activism subsided. In the early 1980s, the government proposed educational reforms, including altering the testing system and making education more responsive to social needs. At the pre-university level, the government called for greater emphasis on socializing students to citizenship (Hayes 1995, 216). Takahashi and Hatano (1999) maintain that young people "indulged themselves in conservative ways of living" (240) and that currently adolescents and young adults tend to be conservative and shy away from political engagement. Reports indicated that two-thirds of those aged 20 to 29 failed to vote in the 1996 elections for the House of Representatives. However, the authors discuss three areas in which Japanese youth and the population in general have engaged in community activity: feminist movements, community service, and environmental protection (226). The feminist movement gained strength in Japan in 1945 when occupation officials assured that women received the franchise, and in the 1946 elections, 39 women gained seats in the Japanese House of Representatives. In the 1970s, a women's liberation group was established, and although feminist organizations subsequently have not been very active, Takahashi and Hatano claim that many young women support the movement's moderate aims.

As for community service, Takahashi and Hatano (1999) note that such involvement traditionally originated in Buddhist or Christian beliefs. They cite a 1993 survey in which 81 percent of more than 2,000 respondents between the ages of 13 and 25 expressed interest in participating in community activities, but only a third had actual experience, and only 5 percent were currently involved in such activities as "protecting the earth's resources," "taking care of the elderly and handicapped," and "teaching children" (229). Rather than relying on self-initiated involvement, the authors note that the educational system may be an alternative way of engaging young people in community activities, a step that the Ministry of Education took in 1989. High schools began to offer opportunities in such areas as social welfare and community service, and by 1994, 11,000 elementary and high schools had instituted community service programs (229). Takahashi and Hatano note that Japanese youth engage in three types of environmental protection efforts. The first, begun in the 1890s, involves protests against pollution from various sources, including mining. The second, antinuclear protests, began in 1954 and became one of the more active political movements in which youth participated. Citizens have campaigned against plans to construct additional nuclear power plants. However, the authors note that those involved in environmental protection generally are not directly political because they focus primarily on consumer concerns such as food additives, natural food, and organic farming methods. Other activities include attempts to reduce energy use, recycling campaigns, and protests against the abuse of the natural environment. Nonetheless, the authors note that at least some young people regard environmental protection to be an economic and political issue.

Takahashi and Hatano conclude that "a great majority of youth are indifferent to politics" and do not regard political parties as representative of their concerns (1999, 232). Hayes (1995, 144) concurs, stating that "the great majority of students are politically apathetic and do not participate actively in politics." From their studies of youth's knowledge of economics, Takahashi and Hatano (1999) conclude that "a majority of Japanese adolescents and young adults, including college students, do not fully understand the banking business" (237). Given that economics and the operation of the banking system constitute a significant part of the public policy arena, such lack of knowledge among students, if generalizable to the overall population, does not speak well of the ability of young people to engage in politics. The authors assert that more nongovernmental organizations could assist in promoting civic engagement.

Takahashi and Hatano (199) conclude that, given complaints from people who say they cannot find opportunities for community engagement, there may be a large number of people who are interested in participating: "the goodwill of the Japanese people has generally been untapped" (242). They observe optimistic signs of increasing support for civic engagement with the development of nonprofit organizations and citizens' networks (243).

On March 11, 2011, Japan experienced a major earthquake and a resulting tsunami, which caused significant loss of life and extensive damage, including the shutdown of the Fukushima Daiichi nuclear power plant and the possible spread of harmful radiation among the general population. Thousands of people were killed in the earthquake and tsunami and nearly 100,00 were required to leave their homes near the nuclear facility. Japan's economy suffered from the devastation. The political consequences of the disaster were uncertain. It was much too early to evaluate the reaction of the Japanese population to the performance of TEPCO (the nuclear power company) and the government during the crisis, but Prime Minister Naoto Kan announced in May that the government would reevaluate its nuclear energy policy. As a more long-term result of the disaster, the Japanese population, especially young people, could become more engaged in matters involving the relationship between the economy and the political realm.

References

Burns, John F. "Brown's Exit Pushes Conservatives to Power." *Houston Chronicle* (May 12, 2010): A1.

Cerdas, Rodolpho. "On the Recent Protests against the Privatization of the Costa Rican Hydroelectric Company (ICE)." *The Costa Rica Reader*, edited by Steven Palmer and Iván Molina, 345–348. Durham, NC: Duke University Press, 2004.

Cruz, Consuelo. *Political Culture and Institutional Development in Costa Rica and Nicaragua*. New York: Cambridge University Press, 2005.

Cultice, Wendell W. *Youth's Battle for the Ballot*. Santa Barbara, CA: Greenwood Press, 1992.

Daling, Tjabel. *Costa Rica: A Guide to the People, Politics and Culture*. New York: Interlink Books, 2002.

Dickey, Christopher, and Tracy McNicoll. "Original Sin in France." *Newsweek* (August 2, 2010): 9.

Ghosh, Bobby. "Rage, Rap and Revolution." *Time* (February 28, 2011): 32–37.

Guttenplan, D. D., and Maria Margaronis. "Shakeup in the UK." *Nation* (May 31, 2010): 11–12.

Hayes, Louis D. *Introduction to Japanese Politics*. Second edition. New York: Marlowe, 1995.

Henn, Matt, Mark Weinstein, and Dominic Wring. "Youth and Political Participation in Britain." *British Journal of Politics and International Relations* 4 (2002): 167–192.

Hofer, Manfred. "Community Service and Social Cognitive Development in German Adolescents." In *Roots of Civic Identity: International Perspectives on Community Service and Activism in Youth*, edited by Miranda Yates and James Youniss, 114–134. New York: Cambridge University Press, 1999.

Marta, Elena, Giovanna Rossi, and Lucia Boccacin. "Youth, Solidarity, and Civic Commitment in Italy: An Analysis of the Personal and Social

Characteristics of Volunteers and Their Organizations." In *Roots of Civic Identity: International Perspectives on Community Service and Activism in Youth*, edited by Miranda Yates and James Youniss, 73–96. New York: Cambridge University Press, 1999.

Mayer, Catherine. "U.K. Election Ends in a Hung Parliament." *Time* (May 7, 2010). http://www.time.com/time/world/article/0,8599,1987773,00.html.

Oswald, Hans. "Political Socialization in the New States of Germany." In *Roots of Civic Identity: International Perspectives on Community Service and Activism in Youth*, edited by Miranda Yates and James Youniss, 97–113. New York: Cambridge University Press, 1999.

Palmer, Steven, and Iván Jiménez, editors. *The Costa Rica Reader: History, Culture, Politics*. Durham, NC: Duke University Press, 2004.

Peace Corps. "Costa Rica." www.peacecorps.gov/inde.cfm?shell=learn.wherepc.centralamerica.costarica.

Roberts, Geoffrey K. *German Politics Today*. Second edition. New York: Manchester University Press, 2009.

Roker, Debi, Katie Player, and John Coleman. "Exploring Adolescent Altruism: British Young People's Involvement in Voluntary Work and Campaigning." In *Roots of Civic Identity: International Perspectives on Community Service and Activism in Youth*, edited by Miranda Yates and James Youniss, 56–72. New York: Cambridge University Press, 1999.

Rosenbluth, Frances McCall, and Michael F. Thies. *Japan Transformed: Political Change and Economic Restructuring*. Princeton, NJ: Princeton University Press, 2010.

Stille, Alexander. "The Corrupt Reign of Emperor Silvio." *New York Review of Books* (April 8, 2010): 18, 20, 22.

Takahashi, Keiko, and Giyoo Hatano. "Recent Trends in Civic Engagement among Japanese Youth." In *Roots of Civic Identity: International Perspectives on Community Service and Activism in Youth*, edited by Miranda Yates and James Youniss, 225–244. New York: Oxford University Press, 1999.

Underhill, William. "Britain Under Siege." *Newsweek* (December 20, 2010): 4.

U.S. Department of State. "Background Note: Costa Rica." www.state.gov/r/pa/ei/bgn/2019.htm.

White, Isobel. "Reduction in Voting Age." London: Library of the House of Commons, July 2009.

Yates, Miranda, and James Youniss. "Community Service and Identity Development in Adolescents." *Journal of Research on Adolescence* 6 (1996): 271–284.

4

Chronology

The following chronology includes significant events in the participation of youth in political and civic affairs, and landmark policies that have sanctioned and encouraged such participation. Not surprisingly, the most important events tend to concentrate in the post—World War II era, when young people, particularly the baby boomer generation (those born in the decade or so following the war), greatly increased their involvement in public policy issues such as civil rights and foreign policy. In fact, the popular culture of the nation revolved around its youth. Ratification of a constitutional amendment in 1971 lowering the minimum voting age to 18 played a key role in opening opportunities for youth political participation, and this chronology describes in detail the events leading up to that important event. (Those events related to the enfranchisement of 18- to 20-year olds have been derived primarily from Cultice's *Youth's Battle for the Ballot*.) Although many instances of franchise extension occurred earlier in U.S. history, policy makers did not consider fully the qualifications for the franchise that citizens less than 21 years old should possess and possibly simply assumed, according to long tradition, that the age of reason came only with the 21st birthday. However, an examination of the history of political participation brings to light a more complex account of the role that youth might play in politics and society.

1619   The Virginia House of Burgesses declares that every man and manservant at least 16 years old must serve in the militia and be subject to taxation to pay for public safety and for public officials' salaries.

1220   Miles Standish, selected to serve as a military officer in the colonies, includes those as young as 16 in the group of men designated to defend the colony of New Plymouth.

1639   In the colony of Rhode Island, militia members can select their own officers, and because the militia is composed of men aged 16 to 60, those as young as 16 are allowed to participate in the voting.

1647   Plymouth colony establishes 20 as the new minimum age requirement for militia members.

        Massachusetts sets the minimum age requirement at 24 for non-freemen (those under legal constraint) who wish to vote or hold public office.

1664   Massachusetts establishes the minimum age requirement at 24 for non-church members who wish to become free men in the colony.

1776   Service of people younger than 21 in the fight for independence raises the issue of the relationship between military service and the right to vote: "old enough to fight, old enough to vote" is recognized by many as a factor in determining rights of franchise.

1787   Delegates to the Constitutional Convention establish minimum age requirements for holding federal office: 25 years of age for the House or Representatives, 30 for the Senate, and 35 for the presidency. However, the convention leaves to each state the determination of voting qualifications.

1819   The Connecticut legislature allows residents to serve one year in the military as a substitute to paying a state tax, further establishing the link between military service and citizenship.

1820   Some delegates to the Missouri constitutional convention propose lowering the minimum voting age for males from 21 to 18, arguing that men that young already have families and are independent. The convention fails to adopt the proposal.

1821   The New York constitutional convention debates the issue of suffrage for those who have served in the militia.

The convention decides to accept military service for men at least 20 years old as an alternative qualification to property ownership.

1861 During the Civil War, nearly two-thirds of union soldiers are estimated to be less than 22 years old, and as many as 500,000 are less than 17.

1862 The Confederacy institutes a draft law that requires all white males aged 18 to 35 to undergo three years of military service. Subsequently, the minimum age is reduced to 17 and the maximum age is raised to 50.

1863 On March 3, the Union Conscription Act goes into effect, which mandates that all able-bodied men between the ages of 20 and 45 are subject to military service in the Civil War. Initially, anyone who pays the government $300 or supplies a substitute is absolved of his military obligation. The act's unpopularity leads to protests around the nation, especially in New York City, where extensive rioting occurs.

1864 Colonel Arthur McArthur, 19 years old, leads his regiment to the polling place to cast a ballot in the presidential election, but his own right to vote is challenged because he is not yet 21 years old.

1867 A majority of delegates to the New York constitutional convention reject proposals from Marcus Bickford and Anthony L. Robertson to lower the minimum voting age to 18.

1868 The states ratify the Fourteenth Amendment, Section 2 of which states that if a state denies the right to vote in federal elections to any male citizen at least 21 years old, that state's representation in Congress will be reduced.

1892 James Francis Burke, a 25-year-old law student at the University of Michigan, establishes the American Republican College League, predecessor to the College Republican National Committee.

1917 Congress passes the Selective Service Act, which mandates that males aged 21 to 30 register for the draft.

1920 Following the Allied victory in World War I, the draft is discontinued and Congress passes the National Defense

Act instituting a policy of voluntary recruitment. Many suggest that, given the large number of young people who have served in the war, the minimum voting age should correspond with the age of military service. However, no formal action is taken at this time either at the national or state levels.

1931   President Herbert Hoover asks West Point graduate George H. Olmstead to head the Young Republican affiliate of the Republican Party.

1932   College Democrats of America is established. The organization provides youth support for Franklin Roosevelt's presidential election campaign.

Young Democrats of America is established to attract young people to the Democratic Party.

1935   The American Youth Congress, a coalition of youth organizations, is established. The organization quickly receives encouragement from Eleanor Roosevelt, the wife of President Franklin Roosevelt.

The Young Republican division of the Republican Party becomes the Young Republican National Federation (YRNF). George H. Olmstead is chosen as the organization's first president.

1936   The American Youth Congress disseminates a Declaration of the Rights of American Youth, which includes what the organization considers the fundamental rights of young people, including educational opportunities without discrimination; freedom of speech, the press, and religion; stable employment; and adequate wages.

1939   A Gallup poll estimates that just 17 percent of the population supports lowering the minimum voting age.

1940   Congress passes the Selective Training and Service Act, which requires all males from 21 to 35 years of age to register for the draft. A national lottery is held to determine which men will be selected for military service.

1941   The Young Voters League adopts the objective of reducing the minimum voting age to 18.

1942   Congress amends the Selective Service and Training Act, lowering the minimum draft age to 18.

During the debate in the Senate over the Selective Service Act, Senator Arthur Vandenberg (R-MI) states that if young people can be drafted at the age of 18, they also should have the right to vote to choose the government for which they are willing to fight. Vandenberg proposes a constitutional amendment that would lower the voting age to 18, but the proposal fails to receive the necessary two-thirds vote in either the Senate or the House of Representatives.

The National Education Association announces its support for the youth suffrage movement.

1943   Senator Arthur Vandenberg (R-MI) and Representative Jennings Randolph (D-WV) reintroduce the proposed amendment to lower the voting age. Randolph notes that 37 percent of Navy personnel and 50 percent of Marine Corps personnel are below the age of 21.

Joy E. Morgan of the National Education Association supports the proposed amendment, stating that, given the expansion of high school enrollment in the past 30 years, those aged 18 to 20 are well qualified to make vote decisions.

Senator Harley M. Kilgore (D-WV) backs the proposed amendment, arguing that military personnel should enjoy the suffrage right for which they are fighting. This and similar proposals are referred to committee, where no further action is taken.

On August 3, Georgia voters approve an amendment to the state's 1877 constitution that lowers the minimum voting age to 18.

On August 13, an editorial in the Washington *Times-Herald* criticizes the lowering of the voting age in Georgia. The editorial calls fallacious the argument that if someone is old enough to fight, they are old enough to vote, noting that although women are not combat soldiers, no one argues that they should be denied the right to vote.

Kenneth W. Colsgrove, professor of political science at Northwestern University, claims in a radio round-table discussion that voting is a responsibility and government can determine who should be granted that responsibility. He argues that 18-year-olds are too closely tied to their parents' political opinions and need time to develop their own views.

Alonzo F. Myers, chairman of the department of higher education at New York University, criticizes Georgia's lowering the voting age to 18, claiming that, were it not for the war, voting age would not be an issue. Myers doubts whether students are receiving sufficient citizenship training and whether young people under the age of 21 genuinely want the right to vote.

1944   A national poll indicates that 52 percent of citizens support granting the right to vote to 18-year-olds.

Following ratification of an amendment to the Georgia state constitution establishing a minimum voting age of 18, approximately 50 percent of Georgia residents aged 18 to 20 have registered to vote, and 67 percent of those registered ultimately vote in the November election.

1947   President Harry S. Truman recommends that Congress allow the Selective Training and Service Act to expire, to be replaced by a system of voluntary recruitment.

The National Student Association, the forerunner of the United States Student Association, is established following the formation of the International Union of Students the preceding year.

1948   Adlai Stevenson, Democratic candidate for the Illinois governorship (and future presidential candidate), includes in his platform a call for the 18-year-old franchise.

President Truman proposes the reintroduction of the draft, and Congress passes a new Selective Service Act to draft men between 19 and 26 years old.

1950   With the start of the Korean Conflict, those men between the ages of 18.5 and 35 are made subject to conscription.

1951   Representative Edwin Hall (D-NY) introduces a measure to grant voting rights, regardless of age, to members of the armed forces, but it fails to be approved.

Congress passes the Universal Military Training and Service Act, which mandates that all men between 18 and 26 years of age register for the draft.

1952   Senator Blair Moody (D-MI) introduces a joint resolution to establish a minimum voting age of 18. The measure does not reach the floor of the Senate.

The American Legion, AMVETS (American Veterans), and the Veterans of Foreign Wars announce their support for lowering the minimum voting age.

In June, Republican Party presidential nominee Dwight D. Eisenhower expresses his support for the 18-year-old vote.

Attitude surveys indicate that 60 percent of respondents support lowering the voting age.

1953   Representative Clyde Doyle (D-CA) introduces a joint resolution proposing the 18-year-old vote. Doyle declares that his proposal is nonpartisan, and states that members of the Republican and Democratic parties should not take a position on the issue based on speculation about which party will benefit most from the measure, but rather according to the basic principle that citizens should have the right to vote at the age of 18.

Senator Hubert Humphrey (D-MN), who will serve as vice president in the Lyndon Johnson administration, states that lowering the minimum voting age to 18 will strengthen democracy by including in the electorate young people, who he claims are especially interested in government and politics.

George W. Williams, former U.S. district judge for the Virgin Islands, submits testimony to the Senate Subcommittee on Constitutional Amendments in which he claims that the large majority of young people are unqualified to participate in politics. Most young people, he asserts, are ignorant of U.S. and world history.

Focusing on the "old enough to fight, old enough to vote" argument, an editorial in the July 11 issue of *Collier's Weekly* questions whether being old enough for military service qualifies a person for the responsibility of voting and recommends careful study before Congress proposes a constitutional amendment to lower the minimum voting age.

The Gallup organization releases a poll in July indicating that 60 percent of college students support, and 38 percent oppose, lowering the minimum voting age to 18.

Frank Chodorov establishes the Intercollegiate Studies Institute to promulgate on college campuses basic principles of conservative philosophy, including limited government, personal responsibility, and the superiority of the market economy.

1954   In his State of the Union address to Congress, President Eisenhower declares his support for lowering the minimum voting age to 18. The president emphasizes that young people are called on to fight for the country and therefore should have the right to participate in the political process. He asks Congress to propose a constitutional amendment to lower the voting age to 18.

Former President Harry S. Truman disagrees with President Eisenhower on the voting age issue and even expresses the view that a minimum voting age of 24 would be better than 21.

Senator Kenneth B. Keating (R-NY), who in 1953 introduced a joint resolution to lower the minimum voting age to 18, says in a radio debate that simply because young people at the age of 18 have the right to vote in the Soviet Union is not an argument against the 18-year-old vote in the United States. Besides, Keating comments, voting doesn't amount to anything in the Soviet Union anyway.

Representative Emanuel Celler (D-NY), in a forum broadcast, states that he considers the identification of draft age with voting age to be invalid and asserts that democracy will suffer if the franchise is granted to those under 21 years old. Celler mentions that Communists in other countries have concentrated their activities on university campuses to reach youth aged 18 to 21.

On May 21, the U.S. Senate fails to reach the required two-thirds vote to propose a constitutional amendment to lower the voting age to 18.

The American Institute of Public Opinion administers a quiz of historical and political knowledge to a nationwide sample. Those 18, 19, and 20 years old outscore older citizens on six of the seven questions included in the quiz.

1955 In August, Congress passes the Federal Voting Assistance Act, which establishes uniform voting regulations for members of the armed forces stationed overseas.

In the November election, Kentucky voters approve an amendment to the state constitution lowering the minimum voting age to 18.

1956 In his state of the union address, President Eisenhower again urges Congress to submit a constitutional amendment to the states that would lower the voting age to 18 in federal elections.

Delegates preparing a constitution for Alaska's entrance into the union write a governing document that sets the minimum voting age at 19. Voters in an April election approve the constitution.

1957 In the November election, South Dakota voters reject a proposal to lower the voting age to 18.

Two years after Kentucky voters approved a state constitutional amendment lowering the minimum voting age to 18, a study reveals that the voter turnout rate of those aged 18 to 20 is disappointingly low.

1958 South Dakota voters, for the second time, reject a proposal to lower the minimum voting age to 18.

1959 In January, Alaska enters the union with a minimum voting age of 19.

In August, Hawaii enters the union as the 50th state with a minimum voting age of 20.

Delegates to the National Education Association meeting in June and July approve a resolution supporting a minimum voting age of 18.

Idaho voters defeat a resolution proposed by the state legislature to lower the voting age to 19.

In a November survey, 31 of 46 governors in states with a voting age of 21 report that they have no objection to lowering the minimum voting age. Eight governors oppose lowering the voting age, 2 are undecided, and 3 fail to complete the survey.

1960   Following the presidential election, polling agencies estimate that not more than 50 percent of those aged 18 to 20 who live in states where they have been granted the franchise have registered and voted.

Students who have previously engaged in protests against segregation meet with Ella Baker, executive secretary of the Southern Christian Leadership Conference, to establish the Student Nonviolent Coordinating Committee.

A group of 90 students meet with conservative commentator William F. Buckley Jr. to establish Young Americans for Freedom.

1961   Following ratification of the Twenty-Third Amendment granting the District of Columbia representation in the electoral college, President Kennedy recommends that the minimum voting age in the District be set at 18. However, the District establishes a minimum voting age of 21.

President Johnson accepts the report of the Commission on Voter Participation and Registration. The commission members express concern over the low voter turnout rate of citizens aged 21 to 30. They suggest that by the time young people reach the age of 21, they are far removed from the influence of formal education and their interest in public affairs has declined. The commission recommends that each state consider lowering the minimum voting age to 18.

F. A. "Baldy" Harper establishes the Institute for Humane Studies, an organization that engages in research and education projects related to the concept of freedom.

1962   Students for a Democratic Society (SDS) is formed as an outgrowth of the League for Industrial Society, a socialist organization. Sixty college students meet in Port Huron, Michigan, and adopt the Port Huron Statement, a document that advocates participatory democracy, a model of democratic governance in which individuals have the right and opportunity to participate in all decisions that affect their lives. Based on this notion of democracy, the statement criticizes major U.S. institutions, including corporations, political parties, labor unions, and the military establishment. By the end of the year, SDS membership has grown to 8,000.

1964   A Census Bureau survey following the presidential election indicates that approximately 39 percent of those aged 18 to 20 who live in states that have established a minimum voting age below 21 actually have voted in an election.

Students at the University of California at Berkeley organize to form the Free Speech Movement when the university administration institutes a new rule banning political groups from expressing their views at a public area on the campus. Thousands of students join the protest against the speech restriction, and the leadership, including Mario Savio, extend the movement to include criticisms of the entire university structure.

1965   In April, 25,000 people answer the call from Students for a Democratic Society (SDS) to meet in Washington, D.C., to protest U.S. involvement in Vietnam. Carl Oglesby, an SDS leader, associates U.S. involvement in Vietnam with the nation's support of undemocratic regimes in such countries as South Africa and Guatemala.

At the age of 25, Julian Bond, communications director for the Student Nonviolent Coordinating Committee (SNCC), is among eight African Americans elected to the Georgia house of representatives. Although the Georgia legislature refuses to seat Bond because he has publicly supported SNCC's criticism of U.S. involvement in Vietnam, the U.S. Supreme Court, in a 9–0 decision, rules that Bond must be given his seat in the legislature.

1966 The Black Panther Party, a radical African American organization, is founded in Oakland, California.

1967 An investigation of state legislatures indicates that 40 of them have established a minimum age of 21 for membership in the lower house of the legislature. Three states require a minimum age of 24, and 7 states have mandated an age of 25. For state senates, 15 states have a minimum age for membership of 18, 25 states mandate a minimum age of 25, and 1 state each requires the age of 24, 26, and 27. Seven states have established a minimum age of 30.

In October, an estimated 100,000 protestors meet at the Lincoln Memorial in Washington, D.C., to begin the march on the Pentagon in protest against the Vietnam War.

Timothy Leary, former Harvard University faculty member and advocate of the hallucinogen LSD, holds a "human be-in" in San Francisco. Leary advises the gathering of 20,000 young people to "turn on, tune in, drop out," certainly not the image of young people that advocates of youth political participation wish to convey.

1968 Those born following World War II, called the baby boomer generation, contribute their numbers to the 7 million students now attending college.

President Johnson, reversing his past resistance to extending the franchise to younger citizens, urges Congress to propose a constitutional amendment that will lower the minimum voting age to 18. Johnson's proposal is introduced into the House of Representatives in June.

Dennis Warren, a pre-law student at the University of the Pacific in Stockton, California, founds Let Us Vote (LUV) to campaign for the 18-year-old vote. The organization quickly expands nationwide, with chapters in more than 3,000 high schools and 400 colleges.

The Democratic Party platform advocates a constitutional amendment that would lower the minimum voting age to 18, while the Republican platform calls for individual state action to lower the voting age.

Tom Hayden, Abbie Hoffman, Jerry Rubin, and others organize anti–Vietnam War demonstrations at the Democratic National Convention in Chicago. The demonstrations lead to violent clashes between the demonstrators and police.

H. Rap Brown, the controversial chairman of the Student Nonviolent Coordinating Committee, signals a fundamental shift in philosophy, substituting "National" for "Nonviolent" in the organization's name.

1969   The Youth Franchise Coalition is established as an alliance of 23 civil rights and educational groups to work in support of the 18-year-old vote. The organization opens a Washington, D.C., office to coordinate the various groups across the nation. The coalition follows two strategies: lobbying state legislatures to lower the voting age and pushing for a national constitutional amendment.

The AFL-CIO executive council supports a constitutional amendment that would lower the minimum voting age to 18.

In an April survey of state governors, just five express their opposition to lowering the voting age at both the national and state levels.

In September, President Richard Nixon affirms his support for the 18-year-old vote. Stating that the younger generation is better educated and more knowledgeable than older people, the president comments that interest in elections and the quality of political debate would be improved.

The first selective service lottery drawing since 1942 is held in December to determine the order in which young men will be drafted.

1970   In February, President Richard M. Nixon becomes the third president to support passage of a constitutional amendment granting voting rights to those aged 18 to 20.

Supporters of reducing the minimum voting age express their belief that campus unrest associated with protests against the Vietnam War have led to a political backlash against efforts to win the franchise for young people.

On February 17, Deputy Attorney General Richard G. Kleindienst, testifying before the Senate Subcommittee on Constitutional Amendments, states that lowering the voting age will give young people responsibilities and hence can lower frustration attributed to their exclusion from the political realm. This frustration, Kleindienst suggests, could have contributed to the irresponsible actions of some youth.

On March 4, taking a statutory approach to voting age, Senate majority leader Mike Mansfield (D-MT) introduces an amendment to the Voting Rights Act of 1965 that would grant suffrage to 18-year-olds in federal, state, and local elections.

On March 5, Senator Edward M. Kennedy (D-MA), speaking in support of Senator Mansfield's amendment, provides written affirmations from well-known constitutional lawyers that Congress has the authority under the Constitution to lower the voting age.

On March 9, Senator Barry Goldwater (R-AZ), testifying before the Senate Subcommittee on Constitutional Amendments, suggests that if the 18-year-old vote is established by statute, the legislation should provide for direct appeal from any challenge in district court directly to the U.S. Supreme Court in order to avoid voting rights complications in the 1972 presidential election.

On March 10, Louis H. Pollack, dean of Yale Law School, testifies before the Senate Subcommittee on Constitutional Amendments that he doubts Congress has the constitutional authority to lower the voting age to 18 by statute rather than constitutional amendment.

Representative Emmanuel Celler, chairman of the House Judiciary Committee, continues his opposition to either legislation or a constitutional amendment that would lower the voting age.

In a letter, President Nixon informs U.S. House of Representatives speaker John McCormack and minority leader Gerald Ford that he doubts the constitutionality of legislation rather than a constitutional amendment to lower the voting age, but he states that he will sign the voting rights bill.

In May 26 balloting in Oregon, voters defeat a proposal to lower the voting age to 19. The defeat—despite aggressive voter canvassing efforts by Go–19, an affiliate of the Youth Franchise Coalition—is attributed in part to voter reaction to campus disruptions at the University of Oregon and Portland State University following President Nixon's decision to intervene militarily in Cambodia.

The young people who came to Washington to support lowering the voting age are contrasted with those youth associated with protest demonstrations. Supporters maintain that they have a cause but are far from rebellious.

The House of Representatives approves the voting age legislation, and on June 22, President Nixon signs the bill into law. Doubting the constitutionality of the legislation, the president urges Congress to proceed with proposing a constitutional amendment as a surer way to achieve the objective of lowering the voting age.

The day President Nixon signs the bill, a New York lawyer representing five state residents challenges provisions of the legislation extending the Voting Rights Act, including the one lowering the voting age to 18.

By June, 17 state legislatures have called for a referendum to be held in their states to lower the minimum voting age.

In an August 25th primary election, Alaskan voters approve a state constitutional amendment lowering the voting age to 18.

From 1943 to 1969, 15 states have held referenda to lower the voting age to 18, but the franchise efforts were successful in only two of them, Georgia and Kentucky. Past outcomes do not bode well for the November 3 general election. Despite extensive campaigning by youth groups, Connecticut voters reject a proposal to lower the voting age; Maine voters approve lowering the voting age to 20; Massachusetts voters approve a state constitutional amendment lowering the voting age to 19; New Jersey voters reject lowering the voting age; Michigan voters reject the 18-year-old vote; the Minnesota electorate narrowly approves a 19-year-old vote proposal; Nebraska voters pass a 20-year-old vote proposal; South Dakota voters for the third time defeat a youth suffrage measure; the Florida electorate reject an 18-year-old vote measure; Hawaiian voters reject a proposal to lower the voting age from 20 to 18, a decision that some attribute to reaction against campus disruptions; Washington state voters defeat a measure to establish a voting age of 19; a referendum in Colorado for the 19-year-old vote results in defeat of the proposal; Montana voters narrowly approve the 19-year-old vote; Wyoming voters reject a proposal to lower the voting age to 19. The general rejection of a lower voting age in state referenda is largely attributed to campus unrest as well as lack of voter concern given the recent passage of a federal law lowering the voting age to 18.

The U.S. Justice Department names Idaho and Arizona, states that have refused to comply with the 18-year-old vote provision in the Voting Rights Act, as defendants in a test the legislation's constitutionality.

In defending the new federal legislation lowering the voting age to 18, the government argues that there exists no compelling state interest that justifies retaining a minimum voting age of 21, that the Constitution authorizes Congress to pass laws to enforce the Fourteenth Amendment prohibition of state denial of equal protection of the law, and that state laws violate the equal protection clause of the Fourteenth Amendment by denying the vote to some people (those aged 18 to 21). Because there is no valid relationship between the minimum voting age of 21 and state interest in maintaining a responsible electoral system, Congress has the authority to lower the voting age.

In September, the Louis Harris polling agency reports that 57 percent of the population supports lowering the minimum voting age to 18.

On October 2, a federal district court three-judge panel rules in favor of the new law.

On December 15, in a special election to approve a new state constitution, Illinois voters reject a provision to lower the voting age to 18, thus making Illinois the last state to reject a voting age reduction measure.

On December 21, the U.S. Supreme Court, in *Oregon v. Mitchell*, issues a 5–4 decision that upholds the Voting Rights Act provision lowering the voting age to 18 in presidential and congressional elections but rules that the provision is unconstitutional when applied to state and local elections. The Court also upholds provisions that prohibit residency requirements longer than 30 days for voting in presidential elections and that prohibits literacy tests as a voter registration qualification. The decision creates a complex administrative problem for states, who in the 1972 election are mandated to allow those aged 18 through 20 to vote in the presidential and congressional contests, but are still prohibited by state age requirements to vote in elections for state and local offices. If not altered, the situation will require states to maintain separate registration lists and ballots for those less than, and those over, 21 years old. Jurisdictions using voting machines are faced with a virtually unsolvable predicament of determining how young voters can be allowed to vote in federal elections but be prevented from voting in state and local elections. The only workable strategy is to purchase a second set of machines, a very costly solution. State officials also perceive an ethical impasse with a policy that permits young voters to participate in federal elections but at the same time prohibit them from casting a ballot in state and local elections. Only three states—Georgia, Kentucky, and Alaska–which have instituted the

18-year-old vote, can avoid this inconsistency. The best solution to the quandary appears to be a constitutional amendment.

As of December 21, only nine states have age requirements for voters less than 21 (three states—Alaska, Georgia, and Kentucky—have a minimum age of 18; three—Montana, Minnesota, and Massachusetts—have established the age of 19; and three—Hawaii, Maine, and Nebraska—have stipulated the age of 20).

John Gardner establishes Common Cause, an organization dedicated to magnifying the voice of citizens, including young people, in government.

H. Rap Brown, facing legal difficulties, goes into hiding, and the organization he heads, the Student Nonviolent (now National) Coordinating Committee, soon disbands.

Plagued with divisions, Students for a Democratic Society, except for the Workers Student Alliance faction, ceases operations as a national organization.

1971   On January 17, President Nixon, speaking to a campus audience at the University of Nebraska, urges young people to exercise their newly acquired voting right in federal elections. He also invites young people to engage in voluntary service opportunities.

On January 25, Senator Jennings Randolph (D-WV) introduces a joint resolution to amend the Constitution to permit 18-year-olds to vote in state and local elections as well as federal elections. Because the 47 states that have not adopted the 18-year-old vote have complex state constitutional amendment procedures, a national constitutional amendment appears to be the surest way of avoiding serious voting difficulties in the 1972 election.

Senator James Eastland (D-MS), chairman of the Senate Judiciary Committee, opposes the 18-year-old vote, but agrees to report the amendment proposal from his committee.

Several youth organizations, led by the National Education Association's Project 18 youth group, begins intensive lobbying activity in support of the amendment. Meanwhile, 34 states have initiated proposals to lower the voting age to 18, a path not likely to avoid electoral dilemmas in 1972.

On March 2, the House Judiciary Committee, by a vote of 32–2, supports the proposed voting age amendment, which committee chairman Emmanuel Celler has sponsored.

On March 10, after tabling an amendment that Senator Edward Kennedy (D-MA) has proposed to grant congressional representation to the District of Columbia, the 94 senators present unanimously vote in favor of the resolution to submit a constitutional amendment to the states to lower the voting age to 18.

Youth group members nationwide are urged to call members of Congress to express their support for the proposed amendment.

On March 23, the U.S. House of Representatives, by a vote of 400–19, approves the constitutional amendment to lower the voting age to 18.

Project 18 leaders encourage supporters to lobby state legislatures in support of the proposed amendment and emphasize in their communications the crucial factor of avoiding the potential electoral predicament states face in the 1972 election. Sufficient state legislatures are expected to be in session or special session (ratification requires approval by at least 38 state legislatures) to ratify the amendment. Various groups, including Common Cause, the National Education Association, and Student NEA, engage in the effort to persuade state legislators to vote in favor of the amendment.

Residents in smaller university towns express concern over the proposed amendment, fearing that with 30-day residency requirements, students can control the election of local officials.

On March 23, at 3:14 p.m., the Minnesota house of representatives passes the proposed constitutional amendment that the state senate already approved earlier in the day, and thus Minnesota becomes the first state to ratify the amendment. Ultimately five states ratify the amendment on that day.

As the ratification process continues, Youth Franchise Coalition director Ian R. MacGowen and members of affiliated associations lobby state legislators to support the amendment.

On April 19, California becomes the 20th state to ratify the amendment.

By May 31, 30 states have ratified the proposed amendment and 15 state legislatures are still considering ratification.

In some state legislatures, opponents, fearful of municipal government takeovers by radical students, complicate matters by attempting to attach to ratification more restrictive residency requirements for students attempting to vote in university towns.

By June 18, the amendment is still 4 states short of the 38 necessary for ratification.

After the Illinois legislature's ratification on June 29, Alabama and North Carolina become the 36th and 37th states, respectively, to ratify on June 30.

Following strong lobbying efforts by the Ohio Democratic Party and the Young Democrats, on the evening of June 30, Ohio legislators make their state the 38th to ratify the amendment.

Informed of Ohio's ratification, President Nixon issues a statement urging those recently enfranchised to register and vote in each election.

On July 5, the Twenty-Sixth Amendment establishing 18 as the minimum voting age is officially certified at a White House gathering (although the president has no official role to play in the ratification process). This amendment achieves ratification just 100 days following congressional passage, thus becoming the most quickly ratified amendment to the constitution.

With ratification, 11.5 million young people gain the right to vote, and the United States joins 50 other nations that grant voting rights to 18-year-olds.

1972 Voter drives result in approximately 58 percent of those aged 18 to 20 being registered to vote. The voter turnout in the November election for this age group is 48.3 percent. The overall voter turnout rate is 63 percent, representing a nearly 6 percent decline from the 1968 turnout rate.

1973 The Selective Service Act is allowed to expire, ending compulsory military induction, the presence of which has been a key argument in favor of lowering the voting age. Voluntary recruitment replaces the draft.

1974 Approximately 62 percent of the voting age population are registered to vote, and in the November congressional elections, just 44.7 percent of registrants actually vote. The turnout rate for those 18 to 20 years old is estimated to be 20.8 percent.

Young Americans for Freedom and the American Conservative Union join forces to sponsor the first Conservative Political Action Conference (CPAC).

1976 In the November presidential election, while 59.2 percent of the voting age population turns out to vote, just 38 percent of those aged 18 to 20 do so.

1977 Conservative journalist M. Stanton Evans initiates the establishment of Young America's Foundation, an organization that recruits young people for political involvement.

1978 In the congressional election, approximately 46 percent of the voting age population turn out to vote, but the voting rate among those aged 18 to 20 is just over 20 percent.

Members of the National Student Association (NSA) and the National Student Lobby (NSL) meet to approve a merger of the two groups, forming the United States Student Association.

1979 Morton C. Blackwell, former executive director of the College Republican National Committee, establishes the Leadership Institute to train young conservatives for careers in politics, government, and the news media.

1980 The overall turnout rate in the presidential election remains at the 1976 level, but 18-to-20-year-old turnout falls to 35.7 percent.

1982   In the November congressional election, those aged 18 to 20 achieve a turnout rate of just 19.8 percent.

The Federalist Society is established to facilitate the participation of Conservatives and Libertarians—including law school students—in the public policy making process.

1983   Student Public Interest Research Groups (PIRGs) engage in a national student voter registration campaign, registering an estimated 1 million young people.

1985   The presidents of Brown, Georgetown, and Stanford universities join with the president of the Education Commission of the States to form Campus Compact, an organization dedicated to facilitating student civic engagement.

A youth organization representing young people adhering to communist ideology once again calls itself the Young Communist League. The organization in various forms has experienced a turbulent history dating back to the 1920s.

1986   Senator Tom Harkin (D-IA), radio commentator Jim Hightower, and former congressman Lane Evans (D-IL) establish 21st Century Democrats, an organization dedicated to preparing young people for political leadership in the new century.

Youth Service America is established to facilitate youth involvement in community service activities in the United States and other countries.

1988   The Student Environmental Action Coalition (SEAC) begins when students at the University of North Carolina at Chapel Hill invite fellow students around the nation to engage in activities relevant to the preservation of the environment.

1990   Rock the Vote begins get-out-the-vote efforts among young people and initiates efforts to persuade electoral candidates to address issues of concern to youth.

1998   The National Youth Rights Association is established to further the civil rights and liberties of young people.

A group of high school students meets to establish Young Politicians of America in order to increase young people's understanding of democracy and to increase political participation among youth.

2000   A political advertising study reports that 64 percent of television advertising during the election season was aimed at people over the age of 50, and just 14.2 percent of advertising was focused on those aged 18 to 34. This data adds credence to the conclusion that political campaigns tend to ignore younger people and suggests one reason why younger people have the lowest voter turnout rate of any age group.

2001   The Bus Project is established in Oregon to mobilize young people for political engagement.

The Pew Charitable Trusts provides funding to establish the Center for Information and Research on Civic Learning and Engagement to explore the condition of civic education and to provide assistance to organizations that offer services to youth.

2002   Responding to tuition increases, David B. Smith joins fellow students at the University of California at Berkeley to establish Mobilize.org.

Adam Fletcher founds the Free Child Project to offer workshops for youth, youth workers, teachers, foundation personnel, and government officials on engaging youth in social change.

2003   Billy Wimsatt establishes the League of Young Voters to encourage young people, especially those not attending college, to engage in electoral politics.

Deborah and Andy Rappaport establish Skyline Public Works to expand public service among young people by offering financial support to political entrepreneurs.

The Center for Progressive Leadership is established to train leaders who will support progressive political change.

Justin Krebs and Matthew O'Neill found Drinking Liberally in New York City as an outgrowth of Living

Liberally, a social networking organization for progressives. Drinking Liberally encourages young progressives to meet at local taverns and share political ideas.

2004   Andy Bernstein and Marc Brownstein establish Head Count, an organization that employs novel means of engaging young people in politics, including registering voters at music concerts.

Michael Connery establishes Music for America, an organization dedicated to encouraging youth political involvement.

Rosario Dawson and Maria Teresa Kumar establish Voto Latino, an organization dedicated to engaging young Latinos in the political process.

Hip Hop Caucus is established to involve young people in politics and policy making.

Trick or Treat begins in Portland, Oregon, as a get-out-the-vote campaign that organizes costumed volunteers to go door-to-door on Halloween distributing voter guides and generating publicity about the upcoming election.

People for the American Way Foundation begins the youth affiliate Young People For (YP4) to facilitate contact among young leaders and assist them in acquiring communication, organizing, and collaboration skills.

2005   Young People For, the League of Young Voters Education Fund, and the Movement Strategy Center collaborate to establish the Generational Alliance in order to coordinate the activities of youth organizations. Billy Wimsatt also takes part in creating the organization.

The New Leaders Council is established to offer young people the opportunity to train for positions in politics and industry.

2006   Andrew Gillam, with the assistance of People for the American Way Foundation, creates Young Elected Officials Network, which supports progressive elected officials who are 35 years of age or younger.

Twelve-year-old Alec Loorz establishes Kids vs. Global Warming to inform young people about the dangers of climate change and to engage them in politics.

Kevin DeAnna, a graduate student at American University, founds Youth for Western Civilization, an organization dedicated to educating college students in the values of Western civilization.

Jessica Rapchik and Pat Korte, two high school students, attempt to revive Students for a Democratic Society based once more on the principle of participatory democracy.

2007   Students for Liberty begins when four young people participating in the Institute for Humane Studies summer program join together to plan a Students for Liberty conference.

2008   The Census Bureau's Housing and Household Statistics Division reports that in the November presidential election, 49 percent of those aged 18 to 24 cast a ballot, compared to 47 percent in 2004. The report notes that older age cohorts still had higher rates of voting, with those aged 45 to 64 and 65 to 74 having turnout rates of 69 percent and 70 percent respectively. Among those 18 to 24 years old, African Americans have the highest turnout rate in this age group, reaching 55 percent, which is 8 percent higher than in 2004. The overall turnout rate of 64 percent is not statistically different from 2004 turnout.

Following Congressman Ron Paul's (R-TX) withdrawal from the Republican presidential nomination race, Jeff Frazee, Paul's national youth coordinator during the campaign, initiates, with Paul's blessing, the libertarian organization Young Americans for Liberty.

2010   The Tufts University Center for Information and Research on Civic Learning and Engagement (CIRCLE) estimates that the overall turnout rate of those aged 18 to 29 in the November congressional election was 20.5 percent, which amounts to a 3.5 percent decline from 2004. Voters in this age group represented 11 percent of all voters, while those aged 60 and older represented 34 percent.

2011   The national board of Young Americans for Freedom (YAF) expels U.S. Representative Ron Paul (R-TX) from the organization's national advisory board, citing Paul's opposition to U.S. military involvement in Iraq and Afghanistan. In 2008, Paul sanctioned the formation of Young Americans for Liberty, an organization that could be considered a rival to YAF.

Several state legislatures have passed, and many others are considering, bills that would require each voter to possess photo identification in order to cast a ballot. Opponents argue that such laws will disfranchise many people, including the elderly, the poor, and college students.

5

Biographical Sketches

The individuals covered here are either young people currently engaged in political activity, or individuals who were active in their youth and now participate in organizational efforts to engage young people politically. In addition, some contemporary politicians are profiled who became politically active and engaged in community service at a very young age and who have gained public office. These individuals are drawn from across the political spectrum, from liberal to conservative, and from both the Democratic and Republican parties. The profiles illustrate the many varied ways in which young people become involved in political activity and the ways in which they attempt to engage their peers in politics. Also included are some historical figures, such as Joseph Lash, Tom Haden, Mario Savio, and Ian MacGowan, who played important roles in organizing youth groups or protest movements in the early and mid-20th century and in the 1960s and 1970s, a time of especially active youth participation in the civil rights and antiwar movements.

Baker, Robert "Biko" (1978–)

In 2008, Robert "Biko" Baker became the executive director of the League of Young Voters (LYV), an organization dedicated to engaging young people in the political process. Baker has worked for the league since 2003, serving as national organizing director before succeeding Billy Wimsatt as executive director. He has contributed articles to *The Source*, a magazine that covers hip-hop music, culture, politics, sports, and entertainment. Baker received a BA degree in African American studies and political science from the University of Milwaukee in 2000 and a master of arts degree in African American studies from the University of California at Los Angeles. A native of Milwaukee, Wisconsin, Baker organized town hall meetings there to mobilize young people to participate in the political process, using popular culture and hip-hop music themes to attract young participants. In 2004 Baker helped to mobilize youth in Los Angeles to attend the first National Hip-Hop Political Convention. He also worked as the deputy publicity coordinator and young voter organizer for the Brown and Black Presidential Forum, and participated as an organizer for Slam Bush, a voter mobilization effort during the 2004 presidential campaign that was based on rap music and poetry. Also in 2004, he worked as the Milwaukee city director for the Young Voter Alliance to develop a voter outreach campaign that resulted in getting several thousand young people to vote in the November election. In 2006 Baker organized a training program for the LYV that is intended to prepare young people for local political organizing. He has served on the board of directors for the New Organizing Institute, an organization dedicated to engaging citizens in the democratic political process. In his capacity as a youth organizer, Baker was selected as a member of the advisory board for the Center for Information and Research on Civic Learning and Engagement (CIRCLE) and served as the city director for the Young Voter Alliance. He also has been active in the Campaign Against Violence, a project intended to lessen violent activity among youth in part by encouraging political engagement and particularly voting in elections. After the 2010 election, Baker commented that had the Democratic Party organization in his home state of Wisconsin adopted get-out-the-vote techniques developed by the League of Young Voters, including the use of art and social media, the Democratic turnout would have increased significantly.

Bernstein, Andy (1971–)

In 2004, Andy Bernstein helped to establish Head Count, an organization dedicated to engaging young people in politics, especially voting in elections. The organization introduces civic engagement at live musical events by offering fans the opportunity to register to vote at the concerts. Prior to becoming involved in youth politics, Bernstein wrote the popular book *The Pharmer's Almanac*, a treatment of the music group Phish. He manages Head Count's fund-raising efforts, coordinates the organization's relations with professional musicians, and takes part in planning the organization's activities. Bernstein received a BA degree from Brown University in 1993. A journalist for more than 10 years, Bernstein currently serves as U.S. vice president for the Canadian company Kangaroo TV, a firm that developed a handheld device that is used at sports events.

Emphasizing that Head Count is a nonpartisan organization, Bernstein notes that after the 2008 election, neither Democrats nor Republicans focused sufficient attention on attracting young voters, a consequence being that youth voter turnout declined from 23.5 percent in the 2006 midterm election to 20.4 percent in 2010. He speculates that had Republicans devoted more attention to activating young voters, they could have won an even greater victory by winning a majority in the U.S. Senate as well as the House of Representatives, and that Democrats, who attracted greater numbers of young voters in the 2008 presidential election than did the Republicans, failed to consolidate this success earlier in the 2010 campaign with get-out-the-vote efforts targeting youth. What was lacking in the 2010 campaign, Bernstein claims, was "something that would get young America talking about the election via social media." In order to continue the upward trend in youth voter turnout, Bernstein suggests, the voter turnout movement needs to develop more creative ways of attracting young people to politics; "out-of-the-box thinking" and "tech know-how," he insists, are the major factors in appealing to young voters. Bernstein has suggested a greater emphasis on issues rather than politics per se. Thus, in early 2010, Head Count initiated a campaign to encourage young people to contact public officials to present their views, whatever they may be, on the climate change issue as a way to keep youth interested in political participation.

Blackwell, Morton C. (1939–)

In his younger years, Morton Blackwell engaged in Republican Party youth organizations. He served on the Young Republican National Committee for more than 12 years, became national vice chairman at large of the Young Republican National Federation, and worked intermittently between 1965 and 1970 as the executive director of the College Republican National Committee. Blackwell established the Leadership Institute in 1979 to provide young conservatives training for participation in politics, government, and the news media. He continues to serve as the organization's president. The Leadership Institute conducts the Broadcast School of Journalism, a two-day seminar for those interested in a career in the mass media, and the Candidate Development School, a five-day training session to prepare attendees to run for public office. Among the graduates of the Institute's programs are Senate minority leader Mitch McConnell (R-KY); Grover Norquist, president of Americans for Tax Reform; and Ralph Reed, former director of the Christian Coalition. The institute has established and helped to fund conservative newspapers on many college campuses. Although Blackwell has called the Leadership Institute nonpartisan, he has worked for many years and in many capacities in the Republican Party. In 1964, Blackwell attended the Republican National Convention as the youngest elected delegate supporting Barry Goldwater for the presidential nomination. He attended the 1968 and 1976 conventions as an alternate delegate supporting Ronald Reagan. In 1980, he attended the Republican convention as a Reagan delegate, and during the 1980 election campaign he directed the Youth for Reagan activities. Following Reagan's victory in the 1980 presidential election, Blackwell served as a special assistant to the president from 1981 to 1984.

Blackwell served for eight years on the Louisiana Republican state central committee and worked for seven years with Richard Viguerie, the conservative activist noted for his direct mail campaigns. In 1988, he became Virginia's Republican National Committeeman, and in 2004, he was elected to the Republican National Committee's executive committee. Blackwell has disseminated a list of personally developed "laws" that can be beneficial to any youth organization or to any young person interested in politics. They include: "Give 'em a title and get 'em involved"; "Expand the leadership"; and "A prompt, generous letter of thanks can seal a commitment which otherwise might disappear when the going gets tough."

Cherny, Andrei (1975–)

The son of immigrants who left communist-dominated Czechoslovakia to settle in California, Andrei Cherny has been an active participant in politics and the Democratic Party since the 1990s. In 1996, at the age of 21, Cherny became a speech writer for Vice President Al Gore and worked in the Bill Clinton administration on policy efforts to balance the federal budget and encourage economic growth. In 2000, he shouldered the responsibility of negotiating the preparation of the Democratic Party platform. Cherny received his undergraduate degree from Harvard University and a JD degree from the University of California at Berkeley. Cherny has published two books, *The Next Deal: The Future of Public Life in the Information Age* (2001) and *The Candy Bombers: The Untold Story of the Berlin Airlift and America's Finest Hour* (2008). He also founded *Democracy*, a public policy journal dedicated to developing a renewed progressivism and to encourage novel approaches to the issues facing the nation. He has contributed articles to several periodicals, including the *New York Times* and the *Washington Post*.

In 2002, Cherny failed to win a seat in the California state assembly. Subsequently he worked as a senior aide in John Kerry's presidential campaign until April 2004. He then went to Harvard University, where he became a visiting fellow at the Belfer Center for Science and International Affairs at the Kennedy School of Government. From 2006 to 2009, he served as an assistant state attorney general in Arizona. In 2009, Cherny became the Democratic candidate for state treasurer of Arizona but lost the election to his Republican opponent. In 2011, the Arizona Democratic Party state committee elected Cherny to serve as the party's state chair.

Connery, Michael (1979–)

Michael Connery is an active supporter of youth political engagement. His book, *Youth to Power: How Today's Young Voters Are Building Tomorrow's Progressive Majority*, published in 2008, provides an account of the recent history of the movement to attract young people to political activity and offers advice for progressive activists about strategies to continue the trend toward increased youth political engagement in support of progressive Democratic candidates. In 2004, Connery established Music for America, an organization dedicated to youth political involvement. He served as the group's Web editor in 2003 and 2004 and also prepared a Web log for the organization Future Majority. After completing an MA degree in English at Indiana University in Bloomington, he became active in Howard Dean's 2004 campaign to gain the Democratic presidential nomination.

In *Youth to Power*, Connery focuses on the role that youth-led organizations played in the revival of youth political engagement. Connery notes that before 2003, youth activism had been low ever since the end of the protest movement of the 1960s and 1970s. However, he points to the increased participation of young people in the 2004 and 2006 elections as the crucial factor in deciding close races. Connery also notes that prior to 2003, there were few training and leadership programs for young progressives, but in more recent years, organizations such as Young People For, the Center for Progressive Leadership, the Movement Strategy Center, and the Young Elected Officials Network have arisen.

Connery observes that liberal organizations, unlike conservative groups, face serious funding problems and thus are unable to offer young people as much financial support. He also notes that conservative organizations have accumulated more experience with training programs than have progressive groups, which only recently have begun such educational endeavors. In order to compete with the more generously funded conservative groups, progressive organizations require sustained funding, and groups located in minority communities especially need assistance.

According to Connery, the Democratic Party's tendency to ignore the political importance of young people is associated with their unwillingness to support youth movements intended to politically activate young people. He argues that youth participation in voluntary causes is insufficient to engage them in political activity; a politically oriented youth movement is also required to encourage young people to take part in electoral politics. Young people's voice will be heard more clearly by politicians in Washington if youth organizations are successful in increasing youth voter turnout. Connery suggests that successful activity in such policy areas as climate change may depend on the ability of young people who support progressive causes to engage more forcefully in electoral politics.

Cranley, John (1974–)

John Cranley began his political career in 2000 at the age of 26 when he was appointed to fill a vacant seat on the Cincinnati, Ohio, city council. In 2001, he was elected as a Democrat to a full term on the council and was reelected in 2003, 2005, and 2007. From 2001 to 2008,

Cranley chaired the council's finance committee. Before graduating from St. Xavier High School in 1992, he took part in several community service activities, including a Jesuit-priest-sponsored summer mission trip to the Dominican Republic. Cranley received a BA degree in philosophy and political science from John Carroll University, a Catholic and Jesuit university in University Heights, Ohio. While a student there, he served two terms as student body president. In 1995, Cranley received a scholarship from the Harry S. Truman Scholarship Foundation, which awards financial support for further education to college juniors who demonstrate outstanding potential for leadership and who plan to follow a career in government, education, or a field in the public sector. In 2004, the foundation presented Cranley with a Distinguished Public Service Award.

Following graduation, Cranley attended Harvard Law School and received a JD degree in 1999. During his second and third years, he worked as a student attorney, providing legal counsel for those needing legal assistance. Cranley delivered the address for his graduating class at the commencement ceremony. In addition to the law degree, Cranley also received an MA degree in theological studies from Harvard Divinity School.

After completing his formal education, Cranley entered electoral politics, running unsuccessfully against the incumbent for a seat in the U.S. Congress in 2000 and 2006. He is the co-founder of the Ohio Innocence Project at the Rosenthal Institute for Justice at the University of Cincinnati Law School, where he served as administrative director from 2002 to 2006. The program conducts investigations leading to the exoneration of those who have been wrongly convicted of crimes. Most recently, Cranley joined City Lights Development, a project to revitalize the Incline District of East Price Hill, a neighborhood in southwest Cincinnati where Cranley resides.

Frazee, Jeff (1983–)

Jeff Frazee, a native of College Station, Texas, became the executive director of Young Americans for Liberty (YOL) after working as the national youth coordinator for U.S. Representative Ron Paul's (R-TX) 2008 unsuccessful bid for the Republican presidential nomination and Paul's subsequent reelection campaign for the U.S. House of Representatives. Before the 2008 campaign, Frazee worked as deputy campus services coordinator for the Leadership Institute and served as a congressional intern with Representative Paul's congressional office in summer 2005. In 2005, he received a BA degree in telecommunications and media studies with a minor in political science from Texas A&M University. After he raised more than $30,000 in 2007 for Paul's presidential bid, the campaign organization hired him as the national youth coordinator. In December 2007, Frazee organized a student effort called "Ron Paul's Christmas Vacation," a program that attracted several hundred students to Iowa to canvass for Paul before the January caucus.

Students for Ron Paul attracted 26,000 young people across the nation, who became the initial members of Young Americans for Liberty (YAL) after Paul discontinued his presidential bid. The organization's official inauguration occurred in December 2008. YOL remained closely associated with Paul and the congressman's political principles. Frazee envisaged YAL as an organization that would (like the Leadership Institute—where he previously worked as a deputy national field director) identify and train young conservatives to assume places in the mass media and in government. However, YAL would be a 501(c)(4) organization under the federal tax code and thus would be permitted to support and oppose political candidates.

Frazee shares Paul's libertarian views, such as opposing the federal government decision to assist the Wall Street bailout with the use of taxpayer funds. In September 2008, Frazee posted a sample letter on the Internet that organization members and voters in general were encouraged to send to senators and representatives demanding that the public officials refuse to support the government bailout. Frazee also developed a one-page flier that members distributed door-to-door that informed people about the economic situation and recommended an alternative solution. Frazee and Paul have commented that the purpose of YAL is similar to Young Americans for Freedom (YAF), but the new organization places greater emphasis on the political ideology of libertarianism.

Gillum, Andrew D. (1979–)

While the broad objective of youth-centered organizations has been to motivate young people to register to vote and cast a ballot in elections, Andrew Gillum has been a model for a young person who engages extensively in public affairs both as an activist and as a public official. In 2003, the voters of Tallahassee, Florida, elected Gillum, 23 years old and a student at the Florida Agricultural and Mechanical University (FAMU), to the five-member city commission, thus making him the youngest individual ever elected to that position. In 2004, the voters reelected him to a four-year term on the commission, and he was reelected again in 2008. In 2004, and again in 2008, his fellow city commissioners chose Gillum to serve a one-year term as mayor pro tempore. In 2005, the Capital Region Transportation Planning Agency, a joint organization of local and regional city and county commissioners, elected Gillum to a one-year term as the group's chairperson, and in 2008, he served for a year as chairperson of the Blueprint 2000 Intergovernmental Agency, a combined group of the Tallahassee city commission and Leon County commission.

When first elected to the city commission, Gillum became frustrated by the tendency of the other commission members to regard him solely as a spokesperson for the concerns of youth. Although accepting that role, he wished to broaden his participation to such areas as job creation, access to health care, and affordable housing. Wanting to be regarded as an equal member of the city commission and recognizing that other young office holders likely experience the same difficulties, in 2006, Gillum took part in establishing the Young Elected Officials Network. The network supports its members with leadership and development training, imparting the skills necessary to engage in public policy making.

Prior to his election to the Tallahassee city commission, Gillum took part in various school and community activities. At FAMU, he served as student government association president (2001–2002) and was selected to serve on the FAMU board of trustees as the first student member. Gillum also was a member of the Florida Higher Education Funding Advisory Board and the Leon County Civic Center Authority Board.

In 2002, as the Florida organizer for People for the American Way Foundation (PFAWF), Gillum oversaw an extensive get-out-the-vote campaign, called "Arrive with Five." Following the 2004 election, he became the PFAWF national deputy director of Young People For (YPF), a program to assist in the development of progressive leaders on college campuses. In 2009, PFAWF selected Gillum as the national director of youth leadership programs, which includes Young People For, Young Elected Officials Network, and the Young Professionals Activist Network. In addition, Gillum is a member of the board of directors for the Schott Foundation for Public Education, headquartered in Cambridge, Massachusetts, and works with the National Coalition on Black Civic Participation and its Youth Voter Coalition program.

Glenn, Dylan C. (1970–)

With a father who worked for the first Republican mayor of Columbus, Georgia, Dylan Glenn was introduced to political involvement at an early age, accompanying his father on outreach visits in the community. An African American, Glenn is a member of the Republican Party who has taken conservative economic and social positions, including support for limited government and opposition to abortion and gay marriage. Glenn graduated from Episcopal High School in Alexandria, Virginia, and received a BA degree in 1991 from Davidson College, an independent liberal arts college in Davidson, North Carolina. While at Davidson College, Glenn worked as a student intern on George H. W. Bush's presidential election campaign. Following graduation, he began work in Washington, D.C., as a public relations consultant. Glenn served on the board of directors of the Earth Conservation Corps, an initiative of the George H. W. Bush administration. The Corps provides opportunities for less privileged youth to become involved in environmental conservation efforts in the Washington, D.C., area. Glenn served as an adviser to the chairman of the Republican National Conventions of 1992 and 1996, and in 1996, he traveled with Republican vice presidential candidate Jack Kemp as a press aide. He also was a special adviser to the Commission on Minority Business Development and was active in the Republican National Committee.

Glenn returned to Georgia in 1997 and won the Republican nomination for U.S. representative from the second congressional district in 1998 and 2000, losing each time to the Democratic candidate. After the 1998 defeat, Glenn established the Georgia Economic Development Corporation, an organization to assist economic growth in the poorer parts of the state and to introduce innovative educational programs in the state's schools. When George W. Bush was elected president, Glenn served as a special assistant to the president on the National Economic Council and at the White House. In 2003, Glenn became the deputy chief of staff to Republican Governor Sonny Perdue of Georgia. In 2004, he entered electoral politics once again, campaigning in the Republican primary for the opportunity to run for an open seat in the U.S. House of Representatives from the eighth congressional district. He lost a runoff primary to the ultimate winner of the November general election, Lynn Westmoreland.

In January 2005, Glenn joined Guggenheim Advisors, a New York–based investment management company, and became the organization's senior vice president, directing the marketing and client services group. Glenn remained involved in politics, accompanying former U.S. representative and friend Harold J. Ford, Jr. (D-TN) on a trip to Buffalo, New York, in 2010, as Ford considered challenging Senator Kristen Gillibrand for the Democratic Party senatorial nomination that year.

Hayden, Thomas E. (Tom) (1939–)

In 1968, when Tom Hayden was 29 years old, he took part in organizing antiwar demonstrations at the Democratic National Convention in Chicago. He and seven others were indicted on conspiracy charges to incite a riot. When the judge separated one of the eight from the trial, the remaining defendants came to be known as the "Chicago Seven." Although Hayden and three other defendants initially were convicted of the charges, the convictions were overturned on appeal.

Hayden graduated from the University of Michigan in 1960. While a student, he joined the Student Nonviolent Coordinating Committee (SNCC) and engaged in civil rights work, including voter registration efforts, in the South. Subsequently Hayden helped to establish the Economic Research and Action Project in an attempt to mobilize poor people politically. Hayden's activist political involvement continued with his participation in writing the Port Huron Statement, a declaration of radical principles intended to guide Students for a Democratic Society (SDS). As part of his opposition to the Vietnam War in the 1960s, Hayden traveled twice to Hanoi, the capital of North Vietnam. As SDS's influence on young people's political engagement peeked, conflict among several factions within the organization contributed to its subsequent decline and ultimate disintegration. Meanwhile Hayden participated in other political activity, including support of People's Park in Berkeley, California.

In 1972, at the age of 32, Hayden decided to leave protest politics behind and joined George McGovern's presidential campaign. Four years later, Hayden ran in the Democratic primary for a U.S. Senate seat from California, losing the race with 40 percent of the vote. He subsequently established the Campaign for Economic Democracy (CED), and in 1982, he was elected to the California state assembly. As a member of the assembly from 1982 to 1991, Hayden pushed for educational reform and environmental protection. In 1992, Hayden won a seat in the California state senate, where he continued to pursue a progressive agenda. However, with political opponents emphasizing his activities as a young activist, he failed to achieve many of his policy goals. In 1994, Hayden lost the Democratic primary for the governorship of California, and in 1997, he lost the election for mayor of Los Angeles.

Adding to his celebrity status, in 1973, Hayden married Jane Fonda, the well-known movie star who also engaged in radical political causes. Hayden and Fonda ultimately divorced in 1989. Hayden's early political views and activities undoubtedly reflected the political era in which he lived, but as he grew older and the issues facing society changed, the former radical activist appeared to moderate his political beliefs in order to gain some success in mainstream electoral politics. He presently serves as a member of the advisory board of Progressive Democrats of America, an organization dedicated to furthering the cause of progressives in the Democratic Party.

Howell, Zach (1987–)

In 2009, Zach Howell was elected chairman of the College Republican National Committee (CRNC). He received a BA degree from the University of Utah in 2010. Although, as Howell noted during the 2010 election campaign, 66 percent of voters aged 18 to 29 voted for Barack Obama in the 2008 presidential election, he argued that young voters disliked the policies pursued by big government and hence would express their displeasure by voting for Republican candidates in 2010. He claimed that President Obama had broken his campaign promises to cut taxes, eliminate corruption, and restore fiscal responsibility. Howell's predictions about the 2010 election appear to have come true; however, the turnout among the youngest age cohort was much lower in 2010 than in 2008, thus suggesting that the election results were as much a result of low turnout as of youth switching political party preference. Nonetheless, Howell expressed the Republican argument for becoming politically engaged in support of conservative political ideals, and during the 2010 election campaign, he presided over the strategic use of 27,000 young volunteers in six states.

Howell certainly did not need very much outside encouragement to become politically engaged. A native of Sandy, Utah, he first volunteered to work in a campaign at the age of 13. While still a high school student, he first became involved with College Republicans by helping to organize a get-out-the-vote campaign among high school and college students in support of a Republican congressional candidate. In 2005, at the end of his freshman year in college, Howell won a campaign for state chairperson of the Utah Federation of College Republicans and was reelected the following year. The CRNC named Howell the "Best State Chairman" of 2006, noting that during Howell's chairmanship, the number of College Republicans in the state doubled. In 2005 and 2006, the Utah Federation sent hundreds of volunteers to campaign for Republican candidates. In 2007, Howell became vice chairman for the western region, helping to establish new state federations. He also became a White House and congressional intern, and worked in several election campaigns. In the off-year elections of 2009, Howell visited Virginia and New Jersey, where he assisted hundreds of College Republican volunteers in successful efforts to assist Republican candidates.

Kimball, Richard (1949–)

Concerned about the general lack of knowledge that voters have about candidates for public office, Richard Kimball founded Project Vote Smart (PVS) in 1992, a nonpartisan and nonprofit voter education organization that, with the assistance of high school and college students, collects information about political candidates nationwide and makes the information available to voters. Kimball serves as the organization's president. While a college student, he became active in politics, participating in anti–Vietnam War demonstrations. In 1986, after serving in the Arizona legislature and on the state's corporation commission, Kimball became the Democratic nominee for the U.S. Senate. John McCain, who was running for the first time for a Senate seat, was his Republican opponent. Both the Kimball and McCain campaigns employed negative campaign tactics. For instance, the Kimball campaign accused McCain of being a special pleader for the defense and utility industries. For their part, the McCain people mentioned that Kimball, in contrast to McCain's sterling military record, never served in the military, and commented that he "flunked ROTC." Kimball, who did not amount to a major threat to a McCain victory, concluded after the election that both sides, in using shallow campaign tactics, had failed to engage the public in serious issue debates.

The 1986 campaign convinced Kimball that an effort needed to be made to educate voters about the background of political candidates and their positions on political issues. This concern led to the formation of PVS. Kimball succeeded in having various universities serve as the organization's headquarters, and beginning in 1999, PVS also established a headquarters at the Great Divide Ranch near Philipsburg, Montana, where student interns could take part in gathering information about political candidates. Following the 2010 election, Kimball publically criticized office seekers who declined to return the candidate questionnaire that PVS had submitted to them. He called the low response rate (about 25 percent) a measure of "each congressional candidate's bravado, tenacity and eagerness to avoid public scrutiny." When candidates refuse to provide the requested information, PVS volunteers gather information from various sources to determine their political background and issue positions. In 2011, PVS reached a collaboration agreement with the University of Southern California in Pasadena, where student interns began to assist in gathering candidate information to help voters make more informed decisions.

Kleeb, Jane Fleming (1973–)

Jane Fleming Kleeb has been a major participant in efforts to encourage youth political participation. Kleeb received a BA degree in religious studies from Stetson University in 1995, and an MA degree in international training and education, and nonprofit management from American University in 2002. As executive director of Young Voter PAC (2007–2008), she assisted Democratic candidates and state party organizations to attract the votes of those aged 18 to 35. As executive director of the Young Democrats of America (YDA) from 2005 to 2007, Kleeb instituted a strategy for engaging youth that involves YDA members directly contacting young people to stimulate political engagement. While executive director, she engaged in fund-raising to ensure the financial stability of the organization. In 2009, Kleeb left Young Voter PAC to work for the Service Employees International Union as the director of the Change That Works project. Kleeb also has served as a consultant to the Campus Outreach Opportunity League (2000–2001) and as co-chair of the Democratic National Committee's Youth Council, beginning in 2007. She has appeared on FOX News and MSNBC television networks to discuss youth political participation.

Recognizing that young people began to vote in larger numbers in the 2004, 2006, and 2008 elections, Kleeb suggested a plan to maintain and further increase youth voter turnout in subsequent elections. Although recognizing that such media tools as Facebook, blog posts, text messaging, and online debates have a role to play in attracting young people's interest in politics, she has emphasized that the sophisticated use of the media alone must be combined with greater attention to the interests of young people and efforts to contact them directly at their homes and where they meet publicly. Campaigns should target young people as genuine constituents and use the results of voting behavior research to gain their loyalty.

Unfortunately, Kleeb notes, in the past most campaigns failed to acknowledge young people as a voting group, and consequently voter turnout among youth lagged far behind other age cohorts. Many young people, she argues, avoided the voting booth as a means of achieving their goals and instead engaged in fundamentally nonpolitical community service activities. Kleeb mentions early successes from the 2006 congressional election, when some candidates developed campaign plans that specifically targeted young people. Candidates relied on both the mass media and youth groups to get young voters to the polls. She claims that youth voter turnout provided the margin of victory for representatives Patrick J. Murphy (D-PA) and Harry E. Mitchell (D-AZ) as well as Senator Jon Tester (D-MT). Kleeb has urged candidates to "target young voters, listen to them, talk with them about issues they care about and treat them like any other constituency group they are trying to secure to help them win," which will result in youth providing not only their votes but also monetary contributions and volunteer time.

Kumar, Maria Teresa Petersen (1975–)

Maria Teresa Kumar is the executive director and cofounder of Voto Latino (VL), an organization committed to engaging Latino youth in the political process. Kumar received a BA degree in international economics from the University of California at Davis in 1997 and an MA degree from the Kennedy School of Government at Harvard University in 2001. She served as a legislative aide to then Congressman Vic Fazio (D-CA). Prior to joining VL, Kumar served as associate director for new business development at Advisory Board Company and also established the political consulting firm Petersen Advisory. Kumar, along with Rosario Dawson, established VL in 2004 initially as a public service announcement campaign. Kumar developed VL into an organization that mobilizes Latino voters and facilitates civic participation. During the 2008 presidential campaign, VL registered more than 30,000 voters in five states and used media tools such as MySpace, YouTube, and MTV to reach youth organizations and to encourage voter turnout.

Kumar has appeared frequently as a political commentator on news programs, including MSNBC, CNN, and Fox. She is a member of the board of directors of PODER (power) PAC, an organization working to increase the number of Hispanic women elected to government positions at all levels. Kumar is a Woodrow Wilson Public Policy International Affairs fellow and a Women's Media Center fellow, and she received a fellowship from the Ambassador Swanee Hunt Fund, Prime Mover: Cultivating Social Capital for her accomplishments and promise as a social movement leader.

Lash, Joseph P. (1909–1987)

Joseph Lash became a prominent student leader during the Great Depression era. He served as executive secretary of the American Student Union and was a member of the American Youth Congress. While a student at the City College of New York, Lash wrote for the campus newspaper, became involved in a campus socialist group, and joined the Socialist Party of America. Lash received a BA degree from City College in 1931 and an MA degree from Columbia University in 1932. After graduation, he worked for the League for Industrial Democracy and from 1933 to 1935 was the leader of the Student League for Industrial Democracy. In 1935, Lash became executive secretary of the American Student Union, serving in that position until 1939.

Lash campaigned against mandatory military service, and from 1934 to 1941, he organized antiwar demonstrations on college campuses. Suggestive of the antiwar campus disruptions of the 1960s, students refused to attend one class period as a protest against military service. In 1937, Lash traveled to Spain during that country's civil war and addressed youth groups in support of the Loyalist side. He returned to the United States, where he continued to champion the Loyalist cause at student group meetings. In 1939, because of the apparent relationship between student groups and the Communist party, Lash was subpoenaed to testify before the House Un-American Activities Committee about his association with the American Student Union and the American Youth Congress. He already had resigned from the Socialist Party and opposed the signing of a nonaggression pack by the Soviet Union and Nazi Germany. First Lady Eleanor Roosevelt, who first met Lash in 1939, came to his defense. She involved Lash in Franklin Roosevelt's 1940 reelection campaign as the director of the Democratic National Committee's youth committee. Lash established the International Student Service and led the organization until 1942, when he enlisted in the army. Following World War II, Lash, along with Eleanor Roosevelt and other liberal Democrats, established Americans for Democratic Action. Lash remained a lifelong friend of Eleanor Roosevelt, and following her death in 1962, he became her biographer, publishing a two-volume work in 1971 titled *Eleanor and Franklin*, for which he won the Pulitzer Prize for biography.

Loorz, Alec (1995–)

When he was 12 years old, Alec Loorz attended a showing of former vice president Al Gore's *An Inconvenient Truth*, a film documenting the phenomenon of global warming and the role that human activity has played in creating the environmental crisis. Loorz applied to the Climate Project, a program supported by Gore's Alliance for Climate Protection, requesting to be accepted as a presenter. When the project declined his request, Loorz developed his own presentation. After making more than 30 presentations, Loorz came to the attention of the Gore organization, and he was invited to take part in the next training session in October 2008. Thus Loorz became the project's youngest presenter.

Loorz established Kids vs. Global Warming, an organization that works to educate students about the science of global warming and to assist young people in taking action to ameliorate the problem. A student at El Camino High School in Ventura, California, Loorz has spoken to well over 25,000 people via formal presentations, keynote addresses, and panel participation. He aims his presentation at young people and includes videos, animation, scientific explanations, and a motivational talk to encourage youth to become involved in the campaign. Among the points he emphasizes, Loorz notes the greatly increased carbon dioxide emissions in the last several decades and their relationship to global warming, and discusses what actions young people can take to "make a difference." He initiated the iMatter campaign, also known as the Million Kid March, that involved events organized by young teenagers in the United States and 24 other countries, targeted for May 7–14, 2011, in order to bring attention to climate and energy issues. The campaign included a mobile phone application intended to unite young activists around the world. Available through the iTunes App store, it allows users to upload projects and personal reflections related to the issue of global warming. Loorz is a member of various youth advisory boards, including the Alliance for Climate Education, the Ventura County School District, and the Rainforest Action Network Youth Sustaining the Earth.

Lopez, Marco Antonio (1978–)

Marco Lopez is an archetype of a young person who succeeds in becoming engaged in politics early on as an elected and appointed public official. In 2009, National Security Secretary Janet Napolitano appointed Lopez, 30 years old, as the senior adviser to the commissioner of U.S. Customs and Border Protection (CBP) to assist in the transition of president-elect Barack Obama's administration. Lopez then was appointed to serve as the chief of staff of CBP. Lopez's political career began in 2000 when he was elected mayor of Nogales, Arizona, at the age of 22, thus becoming one of the nation's youngest mayors. In 2002, he was elected to a second term. Born in Nogales, Sonora, Mexico, Lopez came to the United States with his parents and settled in Nogales, Arizona. In 1994, at the age of 16, Lopez served as a congressional page in Washington, D.C., working for Representative Ed Pastor (D-AZ). In 1998, Lopez worked for Vice President Al Gore's advance preparation for the 2000 presidential race. He earned a BA degree in liberal studies and political science from the University of Arizona in 2000, and soon after entered the race for mayor of Nogales. In December 2003, Lopez resigned his position as mayor when Napolitano, then governor of Arizona, appointed him to serve as the executive director of the Arizona-Mexico Commission, a state government agency intended to improve the mutual economic base of Arizona and the state of Sonora, Mexico. Subsequently Lopez was named Arizona's policy adviser for Latin America. In 2006, Napolitano chose Lopez to be her senior adviser on the state's various interactions with other nations, and in 2008, the governor appointed him to the position of director of Arizona's Department of Commerce. When Barack Obama won the 2008 presidential election, he appointed Janet Napolitano to his cabinet, and Lopez, who had worked in her Arizona administration for five years, received the position in the Department of Homeland Security.

MacGowan, Ian (1940–)

In 1969, Ian MacGowan, a 29-year-old attorney who had lobbied for insurance companies, became executive director of the Youth Franchise Coalition (YFC), the leading organization working to have state legislatures and Congress lower the minimum voting age to 18. His major responsibility was to communicate with member organizations and affiliated groups and to facilitate the groups' political strategies and activities toward the final goal of youth enfranchisement. At a conference of the National Association for the Advancement of Colored People (NAACP) in April 1969, MacGowan outlined the role that the YFC would play and the strategy that the organization would follow, which included distributing information, facilitating coordination among coalition members, and constructing a network for future lobbying. He defended the prominence of 18 as the minimum voting age, stating that at that age most people had graduated from high school and become adult members of society.

In his leadership role, MacGowan differed significantly from the activists in the counterculture and antiwar movements of the 1960s and early 1970s. He had a definitely mainstream goal of bringing those aged 18 to 20 into traditional U.S. politics, where campaigns, elections, and interest group politics play a major role. MacGowan noted that campus protests had for a time stalled the franchise effort when some public officials questioned granting the right to vote to a generation represented by college activists. However, arguably youth protests and demonstrations ultimately contributed to the final decision to grant the right to vote to young people, who would then be expected to follow traditional channels of political participation. MacGowan also conceded that the struggle for the vote did not hold the same appeal as did opposition to the Vietnam War, which, with the military draft still in place, young people could consider a life-or-death issue. The franchise campaign did not attract the same level of commitment from activist youth. In 1971, MacGowan joined the public interest group Common Cause as a lobbyist and coordinated the lobbying of state legislators to vote for ratification of the Twenty-Sixth Amendment.

Marks, Jordan (1984–)

Jordan Marks is the senior national director of Young Americans for Freedom and the publisher of the organization's *New Guard Magazine*. In that capacity, Marks engages in training young people for conservative political activism and frequently serves as a guest lecturer at political meetings, including the Conservative Political Action Conference and the Tea Party National Convention, on the topics of student recruitment and youth activism. He also has appeared on news programs, including CNN, Fox News, and National Public Radio as a commentator on youth activism and the Tea Party movement. Marks received a BA degree in political science from the University of California at Los Angeles in 2006 and a JD degree from the State University of New York at Buffalo with a certificate in finance transactions in 2009. In summer 2007, he interned with the New York State Supreme Court, and in 2008, he was a visiting student at the Georgetown University Law Center, where he clerked for the U.S. House of Representatives Financial Services Committee. Marks has worked on several campaigns, including the presidential campaigns of Steve Forbes and Fred Thompson, and the congressional campaign of Duncan Hunter.

In February 2011, Marks joined the other members of YAF's national board in expelling U.S. Representative Ron Paul (R-TX) from the organization's national advisory board. Paul previously had been presented with YAF's Guardian of Freedom award, the organization's highest honor. Marks and other YAF members cited what they considered Paul's "refusal to support our nation's military and national security interests," referring to the congressman's opposition to U.S. involvement in Iraq and Afghanistan and failure to provide a sufficiently forceful condemnation of radical Islam. Marks commented further that Paul "cares more about a doomed presidential run than he does our country." Jessie Benton, Paul's political director, minimized the importance of YAF, suggesting that the organization was "defunct." Some suggested that Marks and other members of YAF were reacting to Paul's support of Young Americans for Liberty, a potential rival to YAF.

Morales, Eddy (1984–)

Eddy Morales has been active in several organizations that encourage youth political engagement. A graduate of the University of Oregon, Morales served as president of the U.S. Student Association, where he led efforts to block reductions in expenditures for education programs. He also succeeded in raising funds for the organization and worked to increase the visibility of youth concerns among public officials. Morales has served as the deputy director of leadership development for the Center for Community Change, managing voter-engagement programs principally in low-income communities. He played a major role in the development of Generation Change, the organization's program to mobilize and train young people to become community leaders, especially in low-income and minority areas. Morales has been involved in efforts to register and turn out voters, especially in minority communities; has provided assistance to youth organizations attempting to increase community engagement; and has served as a consultant to political candidates. He has served on the boards of directors of several youth organizations, including Choice USA and the United States Student Association. Morales is national field director for Voto Latino, an organization that encourages political engagement among young Latinos. He is the organization's national youth leader.

Powell, William (1949–)

Although not as noted as other 1960s activist figures such as Tom Haden, Abbie Hoffman, and Jerry Rubin, William Powell achieved a level of notoriety as the author of *The Anarchist Cookbook*, a terrorist manual that provides tactical advice for would-be revolutionaries.

Powell's father was a United Nations press officer, and Powell lived in London during his early childhood. In the late 1960s, Powell, who left high school in 1968, became involved in the anti–Vietnam War movement and engaged in various peace rallies and demonstrations. He decided to express his anger and disaffection with a government that could draft him into the military and send him to Southeast Asia to fight in a war he vehemently opposed by writing what amounted to a terrorist manual. Powell wrote the manuscript in 1968 and 1969, which was published in 1970. In the book, he gave the false impression that he was providing information from practical experience. In fact, Powell, who was not a member of any radical group, used material from military and special forces manuals that he found at the New York City Public Library as well as electronics catalogs and little-known pamphlets on revolutionary tactics. Powell called violence an acceptable way to achieve political change and offered advice about such topics as making a hand grenade, engaging in sabotage and hand-to-hand combat, and demolition methods. In the introduction, Powell commented that he hoped the book would be more than a theoretical commentary and would serve as a practical guide to action. Terrorist bombings increased significantly in the 12 months following publication, a phenomenon that many blamed directly on the material Powell presented in the book. Publishers ultimately sold more than 2 million copies, and with the development of the Internet, various Web sites appeared that publicized the book.

Subsequent to the book's publication, Powell attended college, completed an MS degree in English, married, began a teaching career, and in 1976 became an Anglican Christian. No longer believing in the message his book delivered, Powell became an educator in various locations around the world, including Dar es Salaam, Jakarta, and Kuala Lumpur. In 2011, he received a lifetime achievement award from the Association for the Advancement of International Education. Powell has repudiated the *Cookbook*, stating that he considers it "a misguided and potentially dangerous publication which should be taken out of print." However, publishers, who own the copyright, have refused Powell's request to cease publication.

Robinson, Ron (1956–)

Ron Robinson has served for more than 30 years as president of Young America's Foundation (YAF), a conservative organization dedicated to supporting student rights and to disseminating the conservative cause among college students. He has directed YAF's efforts to organize various programs on college campuses and to defend the interests of conservative campus organizations. Robinson earned a BA degree in political science from Canisius College in Buffalo, New York, and a JD degree from the Catholic University of America. Robinson served as executive director of Young Americans for Freedom (1977–1979) and as president of the United States Youth Council (1983–1985). In 1983 and 1984, he was president of the International Youth Year Commission, and during the Ronald Reagan administration (1981–1989), Robinson was an adviser to the U.S. Department of Education.

Among his various activities, Robinson is a director of the American Conservative Union; a board member of Citizens United, an organization dedicated to traditional values, limited government, and free enterprise; and the vice president of the Free Speech Defense and Education Fund. He began the National Conservative Student Conference and the National High School Leadership Conference, which meet annually in Washington, D.C. Robinson, along with Nicole Hoplin, authored *Funding Fathers: The Unsung Heroes of the Conservative Movement* (2008), an historical examination of the people who contributed financially to the conservative movement. Although no longer a "Young American" himself, Robinson has acquired significant organizational knowledge and continues to provide support through the YAF for conservative students on college campuses.

Rubin, Jerry C. (1938–1994)

Along with Abbie Hoffman, Jerry Rubin became a notorious participant in many of the more outrageous protest events of the 1960s, attracting thousands of young people to the anti–Vietnam War movement. Rubin's activist politics undoubtedly originated from his father, who was a high school dropout who became a bread delivery truck driver in Cincinnati, Ohio, and a Teamsters Union representative. After one year at Oberlin College, Rubin transferred to the University of Cincinnati and worked in journalism. When both of his parents died, he assumed responsibility for his 13-year-old brother. He and his brother traveled to Israel, where Rubin enrolled as a sociology major at Hebrew University. In 1964, after a short stay as a graduate student at the University of California at

Berkeley, Rubin became engaged in social activism. Despite U.S. State Department restrictions, he traveled to Cuba and was able to interview Che Guevara, one of the heroes of the Cuban revolution that brought Fidel Castro to power a few years earlier.

In 1965, Rubin organized protests against the Vietnam War and established the Vietnam Day Committee, which provided information to young people on a wide variety of subjects related to social and political protest. Rubin's antiwar activities led the U.S. House Un-American Activities Committee (HUAC) to subpoena him to appear before the committee. His appearance presaged Rubin's future theatrical approach to politics when he arrived dressed as a Revolutionary War soldier. In 1967, Rubin, along with Abbie Hoffman and other confederates, gained entrance to the balcony of the New York Stock Exchange, where Rubin gave a brief speech on the war and then he and the rest of the group threw money down to the stock brokers, some of whom ran after the bills. In 1968, Rubin took part in organizing a march on the Pentagon, where he and thousands of protesters conducted an "exorcism" in a theatrical attempt to levitate the building. Rubin was arrested and received a 30-day sentence for trespassing.

In early 1968, Rubin and Hoffman established the Youth International Party, or "Yippies," the primary purpose of which was to organize a demonstration that summer at the Democratic National Convention in Chicago. After thousands of demonstrators clashed with police on the streets of Chicago, Rubin and seven others, including Tom Haden and Abbie Hoffman, were arrested and charged with conspiracy and rioting. The defendants used the trial to continue a display of outrageous behavior (for instance, at one point Rubin strutted in front of Judge Julius Hoffman, giving the Nazi salute and yelling "Fascist" and "Tyrant"). Rubin ultimately received a five-year sentence, but the convictions were overturned on appeal. When the Vietnam War ended, Rubin faded from the limelight and ironically became a successful business entrepreneur. He died in November 1994 in Los Angeles after being struck by an automobile as he was jaywalking.

Savio, Mario (1943–1996)

Born into a working-class family in New York City, Mario Savio became a leader in the Free Speech Movement at the University of California at Berkeley in the early 1960s. Savio graduated first in his class at Martin Van Buren High School in Queens and attended Manhattan College and Queens College before enrolling at Berkeley in 1963 as a philosophy major. Circumstances, specifically the civil rights movement and the war in Vietnam, contributed to Savio's political activism. In summer 1964, he took part in civil rights activities in Mississippi. When he returned to Berkeley, Savio discovered that the administration had established new regulations that placed limitations on campus political activities. He joined in the protests against what students considered restrictions on their right of free speech. On December 2, 1964, Savio made an inspiring presentation in Sproul Hall Plaza to student protestors, thus giving momentum to the movement that engaged in three months of campus disruption. The Berkeley demonstrations became the archetype for protest movements and student sit-ins on college campuses over the next 10 years. As the result of participating in one demonstration, Savio was sentenced to four months in jail, and he was suspended from the university.

Savio's public role in political activity subsided after the Free Speech Movement. He ultimately received a BA degree in physics from San Francisco State University in 1984, where he subsequently received an MA degree, also in physics. Savio taught at Modesto Junior College in California before taking a position at Sonoma State University teaching mathematics and philosophy. Although out of the limelight, Savio continued to be politically active, speaking and organizing in support of immigrant rights and affirmative action and in opposition to U.S. policy in Central America. Savio, who had a history of heart trouble, died in 1996 at the age of 53.

Schock, Aaron (1981–)

Congressman Aaron Schock (R-IL) was first elected to the U.S. House of Representatives in 2008 at the age of 27. When reelected in 2010 at the age of 29, Schock was still the youngest member of Congress. When Schock was 9 years old, he moved with his family from Minnesota to Peoria, Illinois. He became involved in student government and in 1995, at the age of 15, was elected to serve on the executive board of the Illinois Association of Junior High School Student Councils. In 2000, following high school graduation, Schock, then 19 years old, ran as a write-in candidate for a position on the local school board and defeated the incumbent. In 2003, the other members elected him the board's president. In

2002, Schock graduated with a BS degree in finance from Bradley University in Peoria. Because he had completed college credit while still a high school student, Schock was able to complete the BS degree in two years. In 2004, at the age of 23, he narrowly won a seat in the house of representatives of the Illinois General Assembly, making him the youngest member of the state legislature in the history of Illinois. He served four years in the legislature before campaigning for an open seat in the U.S. House of Representatives, winning the Republican primary and the general election. Schock became the first member of the U.S. Congress to be born in the 1980s.

The Republican Party selected Schock to give a speech at the 2008 Republican National Convention, and in 2011, he was chosen to chair the Ronald Reagan centennial birthday celebration. In 2011, with Republicans gaining a majority in the House of Representatives, Schock gained a seat on the influential Ways and Means Committee. Along with other representatives, he introduced legislation to establish a Federal Program Sunset Commission that would be composed of former House and Senate members as well as financial professionals. The commission would have the responsibility of ending federal programs judged to be "duplicative, unnecessary, inefficient, or [that] don't meet specific performance standards."

Snyder, Rod (1980–)

In July 2010, Rod Snyder became the 39th president of Young Democrats of America (YDA). He works as a lobbyist in Washington, D.C., as the public policy director for the National Corn Growers Association. In 2002, Snyder received a BA degree in political science from Eastern University, a private Christian school located near Philadelphia, Pennsylvania. While at Eastern University, Snyder served as student body president. Before becoming YDA president, he served in several political positions, including president of the Jefferson County, West Virginia, Young Democrats (2004–2005), West Virginia Young Democrats national committeeman (2005–2007), president of West Virginia Young Democrats (2007–2009), YDA Mid-Atlantic Region director (2007–2009), and YDA executive vice president (2009–2010). In 2004, Snyder ran unsuccessfully for a seat in the West Virginia House of Delegates, and in 2008, he managed three successful campaigns in West Virginia, including Tiffany Lawrence's race for the House of Delegates. Lawrence became the youngest woman ever to be elected to the West Virginia legislature. In 2008, Snyder joined Barack Obama's presidential campaign as a member of the Agriculture and Rural Policy Advisory Committee.

While in West Virginia, Snyder focused on developing high school programs and providing opportunities for leadership development to members of YDA. As regional director, he developed greater interaction among local organizations. When Liberty University in Lynchburg, Virginia, withdrew recognition from the campus College Democrats in 2009, Snyder defended the organization, objecting to the action in letters to the university's vice president of student affairs and university president Jerry Falwell. In September 2010, the *New York Times* published Snyder's letter to the editor in which he claimed that, difficult economic times notwithstanding, young people still preferred the Democratic Party to the Republican Party by a wide margin. However, the results of the 2010 election indicated that, regardless of political party preference, a smaller proportion of young people participated than did so in the 2008 presidential election.

Stickan, Lisa Marie (1977–)

In May 2010, when Young Republican National Federation (YRNF) chairperson Audra Shay resigned from her position, co-chair Lisa Stickan became the organization's new chairperson. Stickan previously had served as chair of the Ohio Young Republicans, president of the Greater Cleveland Young Republicans, and vice chair of the Midwest Regional YRNF. Explaining her resignation, Shay mentioned the lack of a salary and the stress caused by absence of a full-time staff. Others referred to divisions within the YRNF resulting from the 2009 chair campaign and election. Stickan served as president of the Greater Cleveland, Ohio, Young Republicans (2003–2007), chairperson of the Ohio Young Republicans (2007–2009), and YRNF Midwest regional chair (2007–2009), and has engaged in several election campaigns in Ohio. In 2009, Stickan, an assistant Cuyahoga County prosecutor, was elected to the Highland Heights city council. At the YRNF bi-annual conference in 2007, the Greater Cleveland Young Republicans were selected as the "Best Large Young Republican Organization in the United States." In becoming the YRNF chairperson, Stickan assumed the responsibility of providing leadership that would heal any remaining discord among organization members.

In September 2010, Stickan stated that the YRNF welcomed "new, young voices to the Republican Party." She claimed that Young Republican organizations nationally had experienced large increases in membership and that many current members were running for public office. Given the large proportion of young people who voted for Barack Obama in the 2008 presidential election, Stickan's emphasis on gaining greater youth support for the Republican Party was especially important for the organization. She strongly supported Rob Portman's (R-OH) successful 2010 U.S. Senate campaign. Following the Republican victories in the 2010 election, Stickan announced that the organization would attempt to build on those successes in the next election cycle, emphasizing the need to attract active supporters among those aged 18 to 40.

Wimsatt, William (Billy) (1972–)

Billy Wimsatt, who admits that he did not vote until he was 27 years old, is a political and social organizer and a journalist. He established the League of Young Voters (LYV) in 2003 and served as the organization's director from 2003 to 2008. In 2005, he co-founded Generational Alliance, a coalition of groups concerned with racial and social justice and with encouraging political engagement. He also has been involved in Power Vote, an organization that focuses on climate change. He is the author of *Please Don't Bomb the Suburbs: A Midterm Report on My Generation, and the Future of Our Super Movement* (2010), in which he presents a personal account of the development of cultural and political movements from 1985 to 2010 and speculates about the future of political movements. The LYV organized more than 3,000 young people to prepare more than 300 voter guides to influence 29 state and local elections. In 2008, Wimsatt established Ohio Youth Corps, which trained 50 individuals to work for the Ohio Democratic Party and the Barack Obama presidential campaign that year.

As a high school student in Chicago, Wimsatt took part in organizing a student walk-out to protest the state of public education in the city. He has worked for such organizations as Rock the Vote, MoveOn.org., the Funders' Collaborative on Youth Organizing, and Vote Again 2010. Wimsatt claims that, as a fund raiser, he has helped bring in more than $8 million in donations for progressive causes.

In 2010, he was a fellow at the Movement Strategy Center, where he developed the Field 3.0 Project to anticipate social and political change and contribute to movement building and field organizing. During the last three months before the 2010 election, Wimsatt, as chief executive officer of the All Hands On Deck consulting firm, participated in organizing the 12 Week Plan to assist associated organizations engage volunteers to bring unlikely voters to the polls.

Yearwood, Lennox, Jr. (1974–)

Lennox Yearwood, an ordained minister of the Church of God in Christ (COGIC), serves as president of the Washington, D.C.–based Hip Hop Caucus (H2C), an organization that encourages political engagement among young people. Born in Shreveport, Louisiana, Yearwood received a BA degree from the University of the District of Columbia in 1998 and a master of divinity degree from Howard University in 2002. He served as student government president at both universities. During the Bill Clinton administration, Yearwood served as a White House intern. Yearwood has recruited celebrities, popular music stars, and athletes to participate in the engagement of youth in political activity. In 2004, he and Sean "Diddy" Combs established the Vote or Die campaign to increase the number of young voters. In 2003 and 2004, Yearwood served as political and grassroots director of the Hip Hop Summit Action Network.

Yearwood is chairman of the board of E.G.O.S. (Education, Goals, Opportunities, and Sports) United and also Helping the Homeless of the World, and serves on the board of directors of Progressive Democrats of America and of United Progressives for Democracy. He also organized Respect My Vote!, a voter mobilization campaign to register young people aged 18 to 39. The campaign has focused primarily on racial minorities, particularly those who live in urban areas, are not college students, or attend historically black colleges. In 2005, Yearwood became active in supporting the rights of Louisiana residents affected by Hurricane Katrina. An opponent of U.S. involvement in Iraq, Yearwood organized a national bus tour in 2007 called Make Hip Hop Not War, as a way to involve young people in a campaign for peace. In 2009, Lennox participated in the effort to enact health care reform, and he has also engaged in publicizing the issue of climate change, adding the hip-hop theme to the environmental movement.

6

Data and Documents

This chapter includes two principal topics: the political attitudes and participation of those aged 18 to 29 compared to those aged 30 and older (as presented in General Social Survey data); and an examination of current college textbooks in American government and politics. The survey data are used to compare attitudes of the two age cohorts on specific issues. The differences between the two age cohorts may have potential influence on U.S. politics, especially given that until recently, youth voter turnout has lagged far behind older age cohorts. The outcome of public policy debates could vary significantly depending on how successful efforts are to engage young people, who have different views on some policy issues than do their elders.

Data Overview of Political Attitudes and Behavior

Table 6.1 presents the reported voting behavior of respondents in a sample survey.

With the proviso that self-reported voting behavior tends to inflate the actual level of turnout, these results correspond to those of previous studies indicating that the youngest voters have the lowest voter turnout rate. While more than 73 percent of those aged 30 and over reported having voted in the 2004 presidential election, just 46 percent of those 18 to 29 reported that they had done so. Table 6.1 also shows the obvious consequence that the voter turnout rate for the total sample is negatively affected by the

TABLE 6.1
Reported Voting in the 2004 Election among Those Eligible to Vote (percentage)

| | Age | | |
	18–29	30+	Total Sample
Voted	46.03	73.67	69.76
Didn't vote	53.97	26.33	30.24
Total	100 (n = 252)	100 (n = 1,527)	100 (n = 1,779)

Source: General Social Survey, 2008. *Question:* In 2004, you remember that [John] Kerry ran for president on the Democratic ticket against [George W.] Bush for the Republicans. Do you remember for sure whether you voted in that election?

low turnout rate among younger people. For various reasons mentioned in the first two chapters, young people have not engaged in electoral politics in as high a proportion as older citizens.

Table 6.2 presents the level of educational attainment reported by respondents.

Respondents in the younger age cohort show more than a 9 percentage point advantage in completing high school, and a roughly equal proportion of both age groups completed junior college. The widening difference for those completing a BA degree and graduate degree to some extent reflects the fact that the younger age cohort has not had the opportunity to complete these degrees. The higher completion rate for high school graduation coincides with the findings of researchers, who note that although education levels have been increasing, the political participation rate among young people has not grown apace.

Table 6.3 presents various levels of stated political party affiliation by the two age cohorts 18 to 29, and over 30 years old. Combining the three levels of party affiliation (strong, weak, and independent but leaning toward a party), the Democratic Party in this survey enjoys a two-to-one advantage over the Republican Party among those less that 30 years old (51 percent for Democrats and 24.7 percent for Republicans). The Democratic Party has a less commanding advantage in party affiliation among those 30 years old and older: roughly 49 percent for Democrats versus 35 percent for Republicans.

TABLE 6.2
Level of Education Measured by Report of Highest Degree (percentage)

	Age		
	18–29	30+	Total Sample
Some high school	17.83	14.10	14.76
High school	57.66	48.09	49.80
Junior college	7.52	8.59	8.40
Bachelor	15.04	17.97	17.45
Graduate	1.95	11.25	9.59
Total	100 (n = 359)	100 (n = 1,653)	100 (n = 2,012)

Source: General Social Survey, 2008.

TABLE 6.3
Political Party Affiliation by Age (percentage)

	Age		
	18–29	30+	Total Sample
Strong Democrat	14.48	20.40	19.34
Weak Democrat	19.78	15.78	16.49
Independent, lean Democrat	16.71	12.30	13.09
Independent	20.89	14.92	15.99
Independent, lean Republican	6.13	8.53	8.10
Weak Republican	12.54	15.65	15.09
Strong Republican	6.13	10.96	10.10
Other party	3.34	1.46	1.80
Total	100 (n = 359)	100 (n = 1,642)	100 (n = 2,001)

Source: General Social Survey, 2008. *Question*: Generally speaking, do you usually think of yourself as a Republican, Democrat, Independent, or what?

The Democratic Party also has an advantage among those who express a strong party identification—14.5 percent among those aged 18 to 29 and 20.4 percent among those aged 30 and older, versus 6.1 percent and 10.9 percent respectively for the Republican Party. Much of the support for the Democratic Party among the younger cohort falls into the weak and leaning categories, suggesting that younger voters have a weaker attachment to a political party and perhaps are more willing to abandon party loyalty and support candidates of the competing party. The same may be true for Republican identifiers; the modal category of party identification for younger respondents is weak for both Democrats (19.8 percent) as well as Republicans (12.5 percent). The percentage of younger respondents adhering to a political preference completely independent of either major party (20.9 percent) also exceeds that of older respondents (14.9 percent). There is also somewhat more support for other parties among the younger cohort (3.4 percent) than older respondents (1.5 percent). Given the small percentages and small difference, no confident conclusions can be drawn, but the result at least hints at the possibility that younger people are more willing to abandon both of the major political parties to support a third party. However, the single-member district plurality system of electing representatives, which dominates in U.S. politics, has until now militated against (but, as the English three-party system demonstrates, does not absolutely preclude) the success of third parties in gaining legislative seats. The weaker party identification among younger people, in addition to the single-member district system, may contribute to lower voter turnout among this age cohort. Organizations dedicated to attracting young people to the polls have the task of overcoming this combination of factors militating against youth voter turnout. The low levels of competition between the two major political parties in the vast majority of legislative districts, due in part to partisan gerrymander, also may discourage voter turnout, especially if party identification is weak.

The survey results presented in Table 6.4 indicate that the percentage of those in the sample aged 18 to 29 and 30 and over that labeled themselves very liberal is virtually the same (3.2 percent and 3.6 percent respectively). Likewise, there is only a slight difference in the percentage categorizing themselves very conservative (2.1 percent versus 3.8 percent).

A more substantial difference occurs when all three categories each of liberal and of conservative are combined. While 35.6 percent of those aged 18 to 29 regard themselves as very liberal, liberal, or slightly liberal, 25.8 percent of the older age cohort select one of the three liberal categories. Correspondingly, 27.6 percent of the younger age group place themselves in one of the three conservative categories while 35.8 percent of the older age cohort identify themselves as in some degree conservative. There is little difference in the percentage of each age group that categorize themselves as politically moderate (36.8 percent for the 18 to 29-year-olds and 38.4 percent for those 30 and over). To the extent that these survey findings accurately present the ideological self-identification of the population, Democrats once again can find reason for optimism about the future voting preferences of young people, assuming that the party can make use of effective political engagement strategies.

For several decades gun control policy has been a key issue in U.S. politics. However, the survey results presented in Table 6.5 indicate that a large majority of those interviewed in both age cohorts support the requirement that individuals should have a permit before possessing a firearm.

TABLE 6.4
Ideological Self-Identification (percentage)

	Age		Total Sample
	18–29	30+	
Very liberal	3.24	3.60	3.54
Liberal	15.29	11.88	12.48
Slightly liberal	17.06	11.30	11.49
Moderate	36.76	38.41	38.12
Slightly conservative	12.65	14.21	13.94
Conservative	12.94	17.75	16.90
Very conservative	2.06	3.85	3.53
Total	100 ($n = 340$)	100 ($n = 1,583$)	100 ($n = 1,923$)

Source: General Social Survey 2008. *Question*: We hear a lot of talk these days about liberals and conservatives. I'm going to show you a seven-point scale on which the political views that people might hold are arranged from extremely liberal (point one) to extremely conservative (point 7). Where do you place yourself on this scale?

TABLE 6.5
Favor or Oppose Gun Permits (percentage)

	Age		Total
	18–29	30+	
Favor	78.19	78.82	78.71
Oppose	21.81	21.18	21.29
Total	100 ($n = 83$)	100 ($n = 1,046$)	100 ($n = 1,329$)

Source: General Social Survey, 2008. *Question*: Would you favor or oppose a law that would require a person to obtain a police permit before he or she could buy a gun?

Table 6.6 presents results from a survey conducted following the September 11, 2001, terrorist attacks on the World Trade Center in New York and on the Pentagon in Washington, D.C. The survey shows that an overwhelming majority (nearly 82 percent) of the total sample supported passage of stricter gun control laws. A slightly higher percentage of respondents (nearly 87 percent) in the younger age cohort supported stricter laws.

Survey results in Table 6.7 indicate that younger respondents reported a considerably lower level of gun ownership than the older cohort. Also, just 33 percent of the total sample reported firearm ownership. Given that in the long term firearm ownership has declined, especially among young people, members of the younger cohort might be inclined to support, or not strongly oppose, greater limitations on firearm ownership, at least within the limits set by the Second Amendment to the U.S. Constitution.

TABLE 6.6
Should Gun Control Laws Be Stricter After 9/11? (percentage)

	Age		Total
	18–29	30+	
Should be stricter	86.73	81.02	81.99
Should be less strict	13.27	18.98	18.01
Total	100 ($n = 211$)	100 ($n = 1,249$)	100 ($n = 1,460$)

Source: General Social Survey, 2006. *Question:* As a result of the 9/11 terrorist attacks, do you think that gun control laws should be stricter, making it harder for people to purchase firearms or that gun control laws should be less strict, making it easier for people to purchase firearms?

TABLE 6.7
Do You Have a Gun in the Home? (percentage)

	Age		Total
	18–29	30+	
Yes	19.55	36.15	33.22
No	80.17	62.14	65.33
Refused	0.28	1.70	1.45
Total	100 ($n = 353$)	100 ($n = 1,643$)	100 ($n = 1,996$)

Source: General Social Survey, 2006. *Question:* Do you happen to have in your home (IF HOUSE: or garage) any guns or revolvers?

A major factor in the controversial nature of the gun control issue involves the intense attitudes especially of those who oppose restrictions on the ownership of firearms. Those who are willing to accept greater restrictions are not as well organized as gun rights groups, and such groups, especially the National Rifle Association, play a crucial role in election campaigns, supporting candidates who oppose gun control measures and opposing candidates who advocate further gun control measures. Interestingly, the General Social Survey included a refusal category to this question, which shows that some respondents declined to answer the question. The relatively small difference between the younger (0.28 percent) and older respondents (1.70 percent) suggests that, with a greater commitment to gun rights, more older respondents consider the question to be no one's affair but their own.

Social Security spending, although applicable to young people in certain circumstances, applies primarily to older people. The survey results presented in Table 6.8 indicate that although support for greater spending for Social Security is lower among those aged 18 to 29 (59.88 percent) than among those aged 30 and older (64.96 percent), a large majority in both groups support greater spending. Just 8 percent and 4 percent among the younger and older age cohorts respectively state that too much is being spent.

Some have argued that the greater political participation among older citizens helps to explain why programs to aid the elderly tend to be funded at greater levels than competing programs for younger people. However, these results suggest that even if those aged 18 to 29 participated in greater numbers, the emphasis on Social Security programs likely would not change

TABLE 6.8
Spending on Social Security (percentage)

	Age		Total
	18–29	30+	
Too little	59.88	64.96	64.09
About right	31.98	30.90	31.08
Too much	8.15	4.14	4.83
Total	100 (n = 491)	100 (n = 2,366)	100 (n = 2,857)

Source: General Social Survey, 2006. Question: We are faced with many problems in this country, none of which can be solved easily or inexpensively. I'm going to name some of these problems, and for each one I'd like you to tell me whether you think we're spending too much money on it, too little money, or about the right amount.

greatly. Nonetheless, given the reported projection of shortfalls in Social Security funding, those reaching voting age in the coming years may exercise greater influence in public policy making areas that affect the ability of government to respond to their more immediate wishes.

The government's role in providing health care has become a major political issue, especially with passage of the 2010 health care bill. Table 6.9, presenting survey results from 2006, indicates the preferences of respondents by age.

A very small percentage of both age cohorts responded that people themselves should be exclusively responsible for providing for their health care independent of the federal government. Roughly a third of respondents in both age groups indicated that government should play an important role, and 59 percent of young respondents and 51 percent of older respondents chose the first two categories, indicating an overall preference for government involvement, compared to 12 percent of young respondents and approximately 16 percent of older respondents who expressed a preference for individual responsibility. This is a complex issue in which age can play a significant role (for instance, younger people on the whole tend to require less medical attention than do older people), and as the debate continues, the preferences of people in both age groups can shift. The issue of federal and state budget deficits and the increasing national debt may alter people's inclination to support additional government

TABLE 6.9
Should Government Help Pay for Medical Care? (percentage)

	Age		
	18–29	30+	Total Sample
Government should help	35.77	33.42	33.84
Scale Score 2	22.82	17.77	18.68
Both	29.30	32.92	32.26
Scale Score 4	7.61	8.67	8.47
People should help themselves	4.51	7.23	6.74
Total	100 ($n = 355$)	100 ($n = 1,604$)	100 ($n = 1,959$)

Source: General Social Survey, 2006. Question: In general, some people think that it is the responsibility of the government in Washington to see to it that people have help in paying for doctors and hospital bills. Others think that these matters are not the responsibility of the federal government and that people should take care of these things themselves. Where would you place yourself on this [5-point] scale?

spending, especially when younger generations are perceived as being those who will suffer the consequences of current spending levels.

A central issue in U.S. politics, especially since the 1973 U.S. Supreme Court decision in which the majority of justices legalized the medical procedure throughout the country, has been abortion. One measure of support and opposition to abortion is the extent to which people are willing to accept the right of a woman to have an abortion for any reason. Table 6.10 presents survey results by age.

Allowing an abortion for any reason results in the lowest level of approval in attitude surveys. Respondents generally are willing to support a woman's right to an abortion under certain circumstances, such as when the health of the woman is endangered by continuing the pregnancy or when the pregnancy resulted from rape. The results in Table 6.10 indicate that although less than a majority approve of abortion for any reason, those approving are a substantial minority: nearly 38 percent for the younger age category and 41 percent for older respondents. Although a smaller percentage of younger respondents approve of abortion in this more lenient category, the levels of approval and disapproval of the two age groups do not differ substantially.

Recent political events, such as the federal bailout of financial institutions, government deficits, and the increasing national debt, suggest that confidence in the federal government, and government in general, has declined. The 2006 survey results presented in Table 6.11 suggest that a significant proportion of the population already had low confidence in the executive branch of the federal government undoubtedly due in part to the unpopular military involvement in Iraq and Afghanistan.

TABLE 6.10
Approve Abortion for Any Reason (percentage)

	Age		Total Sample
	18–29	30+	
Yes	37.50	40.92	40.31
No	62.50	59.08	59.69
Total	100 ($n = 344$)	100 ($n = 1,591$)	100 ($n = 1,935$)

Source: General Social Survey, 2006. *Question:* Please tell me whether you think it should be possible for a pregnant woman to obtain a legal abortion if the woman wants it for any reason.

TABLE 6.11
Confidence in the Executive Branch of the Federal Government (percentage)

	Age		
	18–29	30+	Total Sample
A great deal	21.20	13.04	14.51
Only some	46.42	44.42	44.78
Hardly any	32.38	42.53	40.70
Total	100 (n = 349)	100 (n = 1,587)	100 (n = 1,936)

Source: General Social Survey, 2006. Question: I am going to name some institutions in this country. As far as the people running these institutions are concerned, would you say you have a great deal of confidence, only some confidence, or hardly any confidence at all in them?

In the sample, among those aged 18 to 29, 78.80 percent registered only some, or hardly any, confidence in the executive branch of the federal government, and among those aged 30 and over, the percentage is even greater: 86.95 percent. Examining the results differently, 67.62 percent of those aged 18 to 29 have at least some confidence in the executive branch, while among those aged 30 and above, 57.46 percent register such confidence. Roughly 10 percent more of the younger cohort express confidence in the executive branch. The difference, to the extent that it is statistically significant, might be explained by a number of factors, including a possibly greater positive political socialization of young people to the general political system and institutions of U.S. government. In addition, if, as discussed in chapter 2, young people generally are less informed about politics, the issues, such as U.S. military involvement, although leading to an overall lower level of confidence in the government, nonetheless are brought to bear more heavily on older than on younger citizens.

Overall, confidence in the U.S. Supreme Court surpasses that of the president for both age cohorts (see Table 6.12). While 87.54 percent of the younger cohort expressed a great deal or some confidence, 83.20 percent of the older cohort registered those levels of support. However, the great deal of confidence category for the older group is 10 percentage points lower than the younger group.

Examining the results differently, about 59 percent of the young cohort expressed only some or hardly any confidence, while 68 percent of the older cohort expressed those views. As with attitudes toward the executive branch shown in Table 6.11, the difference might result from the more recent positive political socialization among the younger cohort, and also less exposure to past Supreme Court decisions with which older respondents may have disagreed. Although the Supreme Court can be considered the least democratic institution in the federal government, with its nine members being appointed by the president (with Senate approval) for life ("during good behavior"), the Court's legal status nonetheless is established in the U.S. Constitution, a document that citizens generally hold in high regard.

Expressions of confidence in Congress follow the trend found with the other two branches of the federal government but follow more closely the attitudes toward the executive branch (see Table 6.13). While more than 20 percent of the young cohort

TABLE 6.12
Confidence in the U.S. Supreme Court (percentage)

	Age		Total Sample
	18–29	30+	
A great deal	41.45	31.16	33.02
Only some	46.09	52.04	50.97
Hardly any	12.46	16.79	16.01
Total	100 (*n* = 345)	100 (*n* = 1,566)	100 (*n* = 1,911)

Source: General Social Survey, 2006. *Question*: I am going to name some institutions in this country. As far as the people running these institutions are concerned, would you say you have a great deal of confidence, only some confidence, or hardly any confidence at all in them?

TABLE 6.13
Confidence in Congress (percentage)

	Age		Total Sample
	18–29	30+	
A great deal	20.29	8.72	10.81
Only some	55.14	52.43	52.92
Hardly any	24.57	38.85	36.26
Total	100 (*n* = 350)	100 (*n* = 1,583)	100 (*n* = 1,933)

Source: General Social Survey, 2006. *Question*: I am going to name some institutions in this country. As far as the people running these institutions are concerned, would you say you have a great deal of confidence, only some confidence, or hardly any confidence at all in them?

express a great deal of confidence in Congress, less than 9 percent of the older group do so.

The percentage expressing only some confidence is very close in both groups, but nearly 39 percent of the older group express hardly any confidence, as opposed to less than 25 percent in the younger group. Once again, the younger respondents expressed greater confidence in the Congress, which, as with the executive branch and the Supreme Court, may be a consequence of differing factors, including political socialization, lack of experience with politics, lack of knowledge about political events, and perhaps disinterest in the political realm.

As discussed in chapter 1, knowledge of politics is related to inclination to engage in political activity. The survey results presented in Table 6.14 indicate that a plurality of all respondents categorize themselves as "somewhat informed" about U.S. foreign policy. Whereas 46.20 percent of younger respondents categorize themselves as "very informed" or "somewhat informed," 54.83 percent of older respondents do so. The difference between the two groups is not very pronounced, especially when it is recognized that the information is based on self-evaluation of knowledge level.

Related to respondents' report of how informed they consider themselves to be about politics, Table 6.15 presents survey results of respondents' level of agreement or disagreement with the statement that the average person can influence politicians.

TABLE 6.14
Level of Information about Foreign Policy (percentage)

	Age		
	18–29	30+	Total Sample
Very informed	6.08	8.39	7.98
Somewhat informed	40.12	46.44	45.30
Neither	20.97	15.39	16.39
Somewhat informed	16.41	15.72	15.85
Very uninformed	16.41	14.06	14.48
Total	100 (*n* = 329)	100 (*n* = 1,501)	100 (*n* = 1,830)

Source: General Social Survey, 2006. *Question:* We want to ask about how much information you have on various topics. Please look at [this card]. For each of the following areas, please indicate whether you are very informed, somewhat informed, neither informed nor uninformed, somewhat uniformed, or very uninformed about the issues.

TABLE 6.15
Can the Average Person Influence Politicians? (percentage)

	Age		
	18–29	30+	Total Sample
Agree or strongly agree	7.63	6.92	7.03
Agree	32.20	25.91	26.91
Neither agree nor disagree	16.53	16.06	16.13
Disagree	33.05	35.06	34.74
Strongly disagree	10.59	16.06	15.19
Total	100 (*n* = 236)	100 (*n* = 1,258)	100 (*n* = 1,494)

Source: General Social Survey, 2006. *Question*: Please indicate whether you agree or disagree with the following statement: the average citizen has considerable influence on politics.

While a majority of those at least 30 years old (51 percent) either disagree or strongly disagree with the statement about the average person's ability to influence politicians, a plurality (nearly 44 percent) of those aged 29 and under disagree or strongly disagree. Those either agreeing or strongly agreeing with the statement are approximately 40 percent and 33 percent respectively for younger and older respondents (with roughly equal percentages of each age group expressing no opinion). The result that younger respondents were at least as willing to agree with the statement is especially interesting, given the often-expressed observation that politicians traditionally have ignored the interests of young people. Once again, positive political socialization may be a factor in how young people view the political process: politicians are *expected* to listen to the average person, which may not be an accurate assessment.

A key factor in whether people participate in politics is the level of interest they have in the political realm. Table 6.16 presents the responses of survey respondents to a question regarding their level of interest in politics.

Combining the three categories that express a great deal of interest to at least some interest, approximately 60 percent of young people, as opposed to more than 74 percent of older people, express interest in politics. Correspondingly, more than 40 percent of young respondents compared to less than 28 percent of older respondents said they were either not very interested or not interested at all in politics. If the percentage of those young respondents who said they were only somewhat interested in politics

TABLE 6.16
Level of Interest in Politics (percentage)

	Age		
	18–29	30+	Total Sample
Very interested	13.87	19.24	18.39
Fairly interested	19.75	24.61	23.84
Somewhat interested	26.05	28.47	28.09
Not very interested	21.43	14.43	15.54
Not at all interested	18.91	13.25	14.14
Total	100 (n = 238)	100 (n = 1,268)	100 (n = 1,506)

Source: General Social Survey, 2006. *Question:* How interested would you say you personally are in politics?

(however that may be interpreted) is added to those who expressed some level of disinterest, the total percentage increases to more than 66 percent (the corresponding proportion for older respondents is just over 56 percent). Great interest in politics generally is fairly low, and particularly low among the younger age cohort. Undoubtedly, lower political participation rates among young people can be attributed in part to lower levels of interest in politics.

A measure of cynicism about politics is the extent to which persons do not believe that they have any influence on the decisions that government officials make. Table 6.17 presents the results of a question asking survey respondents to state whether they agree or disagree with the statement that they do not have any say about what government does.

A plurality of both the younger and older age cohorts (45.6 percent and 46.9 percent respectively) either agreed or strongly agreed with the statement. A slightly higher percentage of the younger age cohort (41.4 percent) than the older age cohort (37.8 percent) disagreed with the statement about influencing government. Except for the percentage of those in the younger age group expressing some level of disagreement, the results for the two age cohorts are very similar. A relatively small minority of both age cohorts (13.92 percent of younger respondents and 9.93 percent of older respondents) strongly disagreed with the statement, hence indicating that they thought they did have a say in government decisions and actions. The results suggest one reason why the level of voter participation in the United States is relatively low for both age cohorts: cynicism about politics.

Another survey question that relates to level of cynicism about politics is the extent to which respondents believed that members of Congress keep promises made during the election. Table 6.18 presents the survey results.

The responses of the two age cohorts closely correspond, with 22.6 percent of younger respondents and 21.8 percent of the older respondents either strongly agreeing or agreeing with the statement about keeping promises. The proportion of those disagreeing and strongly disagreeing (56.6 percent among the younger group and 58.4 percent among the older group) suggests a high level of skepticism among the overall sample of respondents. The

TABLE 6.17
Does the Respondent Have Any Say about What Government Does? (percentage)

| | Age | | |
	18–29	30+	Total Sample
Strongly agree	18.99	20.89	20.59
Agree	26.58	25.97	26.07
Neither agree or disagree	13.08	15.33	14.97
Disagree	27.43	27.88	27.81
Strongly disagree	13.92	9.93	10.56
Total	100 (n = 237)	100 (n = 1,259)	100 (n = 1,496)

Source: General Social Survey, 2006. Question: How much do you agree or disagree with the following statement: People like me don't have any say about what the government does?

TABLE 6.18
People Elected to Congress Try to Keep Promises (percentage)

| | Age | | |
	18–29	30+	Total Sample
Strongly agree	2.98	2.07	2.22
Agree	19.57	19.70	19.68
Neither agree nor disagree	20.85	19.86	20.01
Disagree	40.00	35.09	35.86
Strongly disagree	16.60	23.29	22.23
Total	100 (n = 235)	100 (n = 1,254)	100 (n = 1,489)

Source: General Social Survey, 2006. Question: How much do you agree or disagree with the following statement: people we elect to Congress try to keep the promises they have made during the election?

two age cohorts do not differ significantly, indicating that the large majority of both age groups do not find campaign promises a particularly relevant factor in vote decisions or the decision to vote in the first place.

Turning to instruction in U.S. government and politics, several textbooks are examined to determine the topics covered (which overall are fairly standard in all texts) and the pedagogical tools used to engage students in the subject and ultimately to interest students sufficiently in politics that they will become active participants.

American Government and Politics Textbooks

In the mid-20th century, American government textbooks tended to emphasize primarily an understanding of the U.S. Constitution; the operation of the three branches of the national government; the relationship between Washington, D.C., and the state capitals; public policy making; interest groups and political parties; and campaigns and elections. Most students at that time who took such courses in their freshman or sophomore years could not yet vote. The suffrage right for them was still one to three years away. The textbooks did not place major stress on student participation in the political process. In addition to the age disqualification of most students participating in electoral politics, many political scientists were still influenced by post–World War II research that concluded that the health of democracy may depend on the nonparticipation of the fairly large portion of the population that was uninformed about politics and that was not committed to democratic values. Students gained basic knowledge of the workings of U.S. politics and government, but if they were to become active politically, that generally would be due to factors other than encouragement from formal education classes. If certain youth engaged in student political activities, they were self-starters, and the rest of the student body remained relatively passive, except for participation in student government elections. The key exceptions during the 1960s were the civil rights and the anti–Vietnam War movements, which motivated large numbers of students to political activity.

With the rise in student engagement during the civil rights movement and protests against the Vietnam War, followed by ratification in 1971 of the Twenty-Sixth Amendment lowering the minimum voting age to 18, political scientists exhibited greater concern for students' level of political knowledge, understanding of political participation, and commitment to democratic values. This concern was fueled in part by the reported low voter participation rates among the youngest citizens. Textbook authors focused not only on the transfer of information about the institutions of government but also on the undergraduate's own potential role in the political realm. In order to encourage participation, textbook authors needed to convince students that politics was relevant to their lives and that students could influence the outcomes of the policy making process. In more recent years, the development of new media technology led to novel techniques of conveying knowledge and understanding as well as providing training in political engagement. This section examines a series of recent college textbooks to identify the extent to which, and how, they encourage political participation. As the summaries indicate, authors and publishers supplement contemporary textbooks with a wealth of material intended to engage students' interest in the subject and ultimately in political participation.

Current textbook authors, as did those of the mid-20th century, tend to include uniform topics presented in separate chapters: the U.S. Constitution; Federalism; civil liberties; civil rights; public opinion; the mass media; interest groups; political parties; campaigns and elections; Congress; the presidency; the bureaucracy; public policy; and the federal court system.

The publishers of most of the textbooks summarized here prepare editions that include chapters on state-specific government and politics that separate authors have written (in these cases, Texas editions have been consulted). However, the state government portions of the textbooks have not been reviewed.

America's Politics: A Diverse Country in a Globalizing World, first edition

Author:	John T. Rourke
Publisher:	Paradigm, 2011
Major theme:	Globalization and diversity; the author discusses the U.S. political system in the context of international and comparative politics.

Key features

- "You Decide" boxes invite students to present their own thoughts on issues.
- "A World of Difference" boxes place the discussion of U.S. politics in a global context.
- "American Diversity" boxes emphasize the culturally diverse U.S. population.
- Insets focus on leading examples from the text.

Additional materials

- Instructor's manual and test bank.
- PowerPoint slides.
- Full-text glossary.
- Occasional updates.

American Democracy Now

Authors:	Brigid Callahan Harrison and Jean Wahl Harris
Publisher:	McGraw Hill, 2011
Major theme:	Students are encouraged to develop critical thinking skills, apply them to U.S. government and politics, and use them as a basis for political participation; and to employ communication technologies—including Facebook, YouTube, and Twitter—as helpful tools for political engagement.

Key features

- "Then, Now, Next": Presents historical contexts and precedents to encourage students to examine current political events in light of past actions, to form informed judgments, and to consider how the past and the present may influence the future.
- "Thinking Critically About Democracy": Presents differing sides of political issues to encourage students to consider various approaches and to develop well-reasoned opinions.
- "Political Inquiry": Involves the analysis of data and figures.

Additional materials

- Online Learning Center
  - Instructor's manual includes chapter summaries and outlines; lecture summaries with PowerPoint presentations and suggested class activities.
  - Create: An instructor's tool to organize the course material individually.
  - Coursesmart e-textbook: The textbook can be viewed online or downloaded to a computer.
  - Blackboard: Integration of textbook materials with the Blackboard instructional system.

American Government: Political Development and Institutional Change, sixth edition

Author:	Cal Jillson
Publisher:	Routledge, 2011
Major theme:	How U.S. government and politics have evolved over time from the founding principles to contemporary practices, and how U.S. democracy might be reformed.

Key features

- Chapter introductions that emphasize how the U.S. Constitution directs political change and how the document is constantly reinterpreted.
- "Focus Questions" that stress the main learning objectives are presented at the beginning of and throughout each chapter to facilitate applicable discussion.
- "Let's Compare" boxes analyze the way governmental functions and political participation work in other countries.
- "Pro and Con" boxes introduce a pivotal debate, such as campaign finance, media bias, and judicial activism and restraint.
- Time lines in each chapter provide a reference for the stages of political development.

Additional materials

- For instructors:
  - Instructor's manual including such items as sample answers to Focus Questions; suggested projects,

exercises, and activities; and references to additional
print and online resources.
- PowerPoint lecture slides.
- Test bank.
- Links to further audio and video resources.
- For students:
  - Chapter summaries.
  - Flash cards.
  - Practice quizzes.
  - Participation activities providing opportunities for
    further study of themes introduced in the textbook.
  - Interactive time lines.
  - Links to further resources.

American Government and Politics: Deliberation, Democracy, and Citizenship, first edition

Authors: Joseph M. Bessetter and John J. Pitney Jr.
Publisher: Wadsworth, 2012
Major theme: U.S. citizens are politically motivated not
              only by self-interest, but by ideals, particu-
              larly the principles of freedom and equality.

Key features

- "Pledges and Promises" boxes emphasize that the
  United States relies on individual commitment to
  governing principles.
- "Myths and Misinformation" boxes reveal the untruth of
  often widely held beliefs.
- "International Perspectives" boxes compare the United
  States with other countries and the viewpoints of people
  in other countries with those of U.S. residents.
- "Deliberation, Citizenship, and You" boxes: At the
  end of each chapter, these items challenge students to
  analyze a significant issue and discover ways to engage
  in civic life; for instance, students are asked to consider
  the possibilities and potential problems of Internet
  activism.
- Photo essays present a number of people who epitomize
  a major theme of a chapter.

Additional materials

- For instructors:
  - Interactive PowerPoint lectures for each chapter.
  - Computerized test bank.
  - Instructor's manual that includes learning objectives, chapter outlines, suggestions for stimulating class activities and projects, recommendations for including media sources in class, and "Join In," which offers "clicker" questions to be used in class to engage students.
- For students:
  - CourseMate: A supplement for students and instructors that provides various online learning resources such as NewsNow, which includes weekly news stories, videos, and photos intended to engage students in current events.
  - WebTutor: A Web-based teaching and learning tool that offers interactive tutorials and simulations, practice quizzes, and Web links.
  - Latino American Politics Supplement: Fernando Piñon (San Antonio College) prepared this booklet that focuses on the political behavior of Latino Americans.
  - The Obama Presidency–Year One Supplement. Kenneth Janda, Jeffrey Berry, and Jerry Goldman prepared this booklet that analyzes such topics as health care, the economy, the U.S. Supreme Court, and foreign affairs.

Keeping the Republic: Power and Citizenship in American Politics, fourth edition

Authors:	Christine Barbour and Gerald C. Wright
Publisher:	CQ Press, 2011
Major theme:	Politics is a competition to achieve limited power and resources; students are offered ways in which they as citizens can evaluate the performance of the political system.

Key features

- Primary goal: "To get students to think critically and be skeptical of received opinion."
- "What at Stake?–What at Stake Revisited" items begin and end each chapter to encourage students to consider what people are trying to get from politics and how rules influence the outcome of the political process.
- "Consider the Source" examines different sources of information to determine possible bias, present arguments, and uncover sources of information, and considers possible political consequences.
- "Who Are We?" presents demographic data in graphs, figures, and maps, and asks students to examine the effect of diversity on an understanding of government's role in people's lives.
- "Profiles in Citizenship": Prominent figures in politics offer advice about ways that students may engage effectively in public life.
- "Who, What, How, and When": Time lines follow the progression of major issues through history.

Additional materials

- Online ancillaries
  - Chapter summaries.
  - Review questions.
  - Key-term flash cards.
  - Crossword puzzles.
  - Practice quizzes.
  - KTRBlog: Author Christine Barbour regularly updates the blog, which relates news events to themes presented in the textbook.

Politics in America, ninth edition

Author:	Thomas R. Dye
Publisher:	Longman, 2011
Major theme:	Politics is the struggle for power that results in various expressions of conflict and controversy; several controversial issues are presented as examples.

Key features

- "What Do You Think?" boxes ask students to take sides on controversial questions.
- "Controversy" boxes present some of the "more vexing" questions in contemporary U.S. politics.
- "A Conflicting View" boxes challenge students of "rethink conventional wisdom" in U.S. politics.
- "People in Politics" boxes examine the early education of major political actors and their entrance into politics.
- "Politics Up Close" boxes offer students examples of political issues, organizations, and events.
- "Compared to What?" boxes present comparisons between key features of the U.S. political system with those of other countries.

Additional materials

- MyPoliSciLab, an online teaching and learning Web site
  - Study helps
    - Pretests: Personalized study plans following learning objectives.
    - Pearson e-Text: Identical to the print book.
    - Flashcards: Learning key terms.
    - Posttests.
    - Chapter exams test the knowledge obtained from each chapter.
  - Participation
    - News Review: Analysis of major news stories.
    - Associated Press Newsfeeds: Political news from the United States and internationally.
    - Weekly Quiz: Review of current events.
    - Weekly Poll of political attitudes.
    - Voter Registration emphasizes voting as a right and responsibility.
    - Citizenship Test presents questions used in naturalized citizen tests.
  - Applications
    - Videos: Streaming videos from the Associated Press and ABC News.
    - Simulations: Practice of hypothetical political experiences.

- Comparative Exercises encourages critical examinations of comparisons between features of U.S. politics and that of other nations.
- Time lines that place political issues in historical perspective.
- Visual Literacy Exercises: How to interpret data presented in figures and tables.
- MyPoliSciLibrary: Historical and contemporary full-text primary source documents.
- Course management
  - Grade Tracker: Assessment of MyPoliSciLab materials.
  - Instructor Resources: Downloadable supplements for instructors.
  - Sample Syllabus: Suggestions for inclusion in the course syllabus.
  - MyClassPrep: Downloadable lecture resources.

We the People: An Introduction to American Politics

Authors:	Benjamin Ginsberg, Theodore J. Lowi, and Margaret Weir
Publisher:	W. W. Norton, 2011
Major theme:	The authors attempt to provide a response to the question, "Why should we be engaged with government and politics?"

Key features

- Chapter introductions: "What Government Does and Why It Matters."
- "Get Involved" units that present ways to participate in the political process.
- "Politics and Popular Culture" boxes relating politics to subjects in which students are interested; for instance, media examples drawn from television, film, music, cartoons, and the Internet.

Additional materials

- Coursepacks: Prepared assignments for instructors using course management systems such as WebCT and

Blackboard for online courses and hybrid courses with in-class and online components.

- Instructor's resource disc contains figures drawn from the textbook and selected photographs in PowerPoint format.
- Instructor's Resource Site contains instructional content available for lectures and for online and hybrid courses; test-item files; PowerPoint lecture slides; images for course Web pages.
- StudySpace allows students to test their knowledge of the subject and informs them of what they need to emphasize; provides students with a study plan to become more proficient in the subject.
  - Video exercises that allow students to view videos and to discover how the presentations relate to key concepts being covered.
  - Quiz+ allows students to test their knowledge and refers to specific textbook pages where the information may be found.
  - Chapter outlines.
  - Flashcards.
  - Policy debate, including "you decide" exercises.
  - "Get involved" exercises.
  - Simulations of political situations.
  - American politics news RSS (Really Simple Syndication) feed offers blog entries, news headlines, and audio and video presentations.

Alternatives to Standard American Politics and Government Textbooks

AM GOV 2011

Author:	Losco Baker
Publisher:	McGraw-Hill, 2011
Major theme:	The paperback text focuses directly on youth political participation, including current articles about contemporary issues.

Key features

- "Global Perspectives" discusses political trends in other nations; for instance, "Political Advertising in Scandinavia," "Changing Patterns of Political Participation," and "Military Expenditures."

- "Portrait of an Activist" describes historical and contemporary political figures.
- "Obama at Midterm": Brief treatments of topics related to President Barack Obama's first two years in office (for instance, "Federalism Under Obama," "Civil Liberties Issues," and "Obama and the Media").
- "Current Controversy": Specific topics that have generated disagreement on such issues as civil liberties and civil rights, equal state representation in the U.S. Senate, and interest group lobbying reform.
- "Citizenship Quiz": Several brief quizzes drawn from the U.S. Citizenship and Immigration Services test for citizenship.
- *National Journal* articles that supplement textbook topics.

Additional materials

- GradGuru Web site allows students to help each other in the course by sharing notes and information.

Democracy For the Few, ninth edition

Author:	Michael Parenti
Publisher:	Wadsworth, 2010
Major theme:	Although the authors of most American politics and government textbooks claim to present a neutral view of the topics covered, Parenti asserts that they "are merely conventional," and hence are "apologists for the existing social order," simply describing the status quo and thus tacitly accepting the present governing system and disseminating an essentially orthodox interpretation of U.S. politics. Parenti claims that many of these authors present such status quo views as the following:

- The large number of nonvoters are essentially satisfied with the existing social conditions.

- The system of lobbying is conducive to democracy because it contributes to representative government by providing vital information to office holders.
- A powerful executive is an advantage in a democracy because the president responds to the general national interest.
- The exclusion of third parties from the electoral process helps to maintain a stable political system.

Key features

Topics that provide a critical perspective on U.S. politics and government:

- "A Constitution for the Few" (Chapter 4)
  - Class Power in Early America
  - Containing the Spread of Democracy
  - Fragmenting Majority Power
- "Rise of the Corporate State" (Chapter 5)
  - War against Labor, Favors for Business
  - Pliable Progressives and Red Scares
- "Politics: Who Gets What?" (Chapter 6)
  - Welfare for the Rich
  - Taxes: Helping the Rich in Their Time of Greed
  - Unkind Cuts, Unfair Rates
- "Health and Human Services: Sacrificial Lambs" (Chapter 7)
  - The Poor Get Less (and Less)
  - Social Security: Privatizing Everything
  - Creating Crises: Schools and Housing
  - "Mess Transit"
- "Military Empire and Global Domination" (Chapter 11)
  - A Global Kill Capacity
  - Pentagon Profits, Waste and Theft
  - Economic Imperialism
  - Global Bloodletting

From Parenti's point of view, the U.S. political system has fallen seriously short of what should be expected of a democracy. However, in order to fulfill a key purpose of an American government textbook, which is to encourage political engagement among students instead of increased cynicism and withdrawal, the author recognizes that he must offer some avenue for effective political participation. Therefore, Parenti claims that the textbook "tries to strike a balance"; "it tries to explain how democracy is incongruous with modern-day capitalism and is consistently violated by a capitalist social order, and yet how democracy refuses to die and continues to fight back and even make gains despite the great odds against popular forces."

The Irony of Democracy: An Uncommon Introduction to American Politics, ninth edition

Authors:	Thomas R. Dye, Harmon Zeigler, and Louis Schubert
Publisher:	Cengage Learning, 2011
Major theme:	The text approaches U.S. government and politics from an elitist perspective, focusing on the role that elites have played in maintaining democratic politics by taking key roles in political decision making historically and in contemporary U.S. politics. The chapters follow this theme; for instance, "The Founding Fathers: The Nation's First Elite" (chapter 2); "Elite-Mass Communication" (chapter 5); "Congress: The Legislative Elite"(chapter 8); and "The United States as Global Elite" (chapter 14). However, in order to abide by the key purpose of such courses to encourage political engagement, the authors include an epilogue titled "What Can Students Do?"

Key features

- ABC News DVDs include video clips and President Barack Obama speeches.
- "Joinin": Software that allows the instructor to poll students with "clicker" hardware.
- "Political Theater 2.0": A three-DVD series containing video clips from the public sector, including political advertisements, speeches, and interviews.
- "Focus boxes treat text subjects in greater detail.
- "In Brief" boxes summarize a subject that is treated in the text.

7

Directory of Organizations

The organizations listed here include noted historical groups in which young people played key roles, as well as current groups that have memberships composed primarily of youth or that have as their major objective encouraging youth political engagement. Some organizations have a substantive objective such as supporting a political party, attaining a policy outcome, or furthering an ideological position. Others have the more procedural mission of increasing young people's participation in politics and civic affairs as a crucial element in maintaining a democratic political system that accurately reflects the informed views of the general population. Groups also differ in that some are focused on engaging young people in politics who previously have been nonparticipants, while others provide training and guidance for more effective participation among those already interested and engaged in the political realm.

Advocates for Youth (AY)
http://www.advocatesforyouth.org

Advocates for Youth (AY) was established in 1980 as the Center for Population Options, which indicates the organization's primary focus: advocating a more progressive view of the sexual behavior and health of youth. The organization has opposed federal funding for "abstinence-only-until-marriage" sex education programs, supporting instead more comprehensive sex education programs for youth. Although primarily an advocacy organization that represents a particular issue regarding young people, AY publicizes three core values: rights, respect, and responsibility that require active youth involvement. These values are operationalized by the group's mission of "involving [youth] in the design, implementation and evaluation of programs and policies that affect their health and well-being." AY states that it has for more than 25 years represented the views of young people regarding reproductive and health issues, including assisting college students to support more foreign aid for family planning and HIV/AIDS prevention. The organization founded Amplify, an Internet-based organizing and communication network, to assist youth activists in the United States and worldwide to build a grassroots movement.

American Youth Congress (AYC)

Established in 1935, the American Youth Congress (AYC) served as a coalition of youth organizations during the Great Depression. The AYC represents the most significant example of youth activism before the 1960s. Notably, the AYC gained the support of Eleanor Roosevelt, wife of President Franklin Delano Roosevelt, which gave the organization significant political influence. Among its causes, the organization lobbied for social justice and called for greater federal funding of education and an end to the requirement that male college students participate in the Reserve Officer Training Corps (ROTC). In 1936, the AYC released a Declaration of the Rights of American Youth, proclaiming what the members considered the basic rights of young people. In 1939, the organization claimed a membership of more than 4.5 million with more than 500 affiliated organizations. As World War II approached, the AYC opposed conscription and supported U.S. neutrality in the war then raging in Europe. As membership grew, groups on the left of the political spectrum, including the Young Communist League, comprised an ever larger proportion of the membership, and the leadership became more extremist. Joseph Cadden and Joseph Lash, director and secretary respectively, were accused of being associated with communist organizations. The U.S. House of Representatives Un-American Activities Committee and its chair, Martin Dies, attacked the organization for what they claimed was communist infiltration of the group. The committee subpoenaed group leaders to testify before the committee. Eleanor Roosevelt ceased defending the organization when members became involved in anti-Roosevelt activities. Support for the AYC diminished, and by late 1941, the organization ceased operations. In 1940, *Time* magazine, reporting on the AYC's sixth annual convention, commented that the purpose of the organization was "to give Youth a chance to shoot its mouth off," a statement that perhaps represented the attitude of many at that time toward young people and their efforts to participate in politics.

Bus Project
http://busproject.org

Established in 2001 in Oregon, the Bus Project (or Federation) attempts to engage young people in electoral politics, political action, and civic participation. The project states that it mobilizes "thousands of volunteers for political action and civic engagement." The organization facilitates the activities of state groups that conduct programs, such as Bus Trips, Trick or Vote Halloween Canvassing (for which the organization received the 2009 Reed Award from *Politics* magazine as the best get-out-the-vote effort), and Alternative Candidate Debates, each of which is most conducive to local rather than national political circumstances. The project has substantive goals such as an improved educational system, an economy that provides jobs, access to affordable health care, and the assurance of a fair election system. The organization summarizes these objectives in the "Six E's": education, environment, economic strength, equal rights, election reform, and "'ealth care." The Bus Project attempts to connect people in urban, rural, and suburban areas in order to bring together those of differing backgrounds to work for a common objective. The organization also strives to activate young people, many of whom readily volunteer for civic activities but tend not to take part in election campaigns and issue advocacy.

Campus Compact
http://www.compact.org

In 1985, the presidents of Brown, Georgetown, and Stanford universities, along with the president of the Education Commission of the States, established Campus Compact as an organization committed to encouraging and facilitating campus-based civic engagement and to providing students with educational experiences that develop civic and social responsibility. Now a coalition of more than 1,100 college and university presidents representing approximately 6 million students, Campus Compact encourages the development of public and community service programs intended to develop the citizenship skills of students. Campus Compact offers resources and training to faculty who are interested in adding civic and community-based learning to the curriculum, and helps them to combine community activities with their teaching and research. The organization also assists colleges and universities in developing campus-community alliances to establish programs in such areas as public education, health care, the environment, homelessness, literacy, and assistance to the elderly. Campus Compact provides various kinds of support to individual schools, including scholarships as incentives to students to become more involved in civic engagement. Campus Compact reports that more than 98 percent of member institutions have initiated at least one community partnership.

Center for Information and Research on Civic Learning and Engagement (CIRCLE)
http://www.civicyouth.org

The Center for Information and Research on Civic Learning and Engagement (CIRCLE), established in 2001 with a grant from the Pew Charitable Trusts, conducts research and data analysis on civic education, investigates the effects of campaigning directed toward young people, and serves as a source of training and assistance for more than 300 organizations that offer assistance to youth. CIRCLE has concluded that both the Democratic and Republican parties can benefit from devoting greater resources to reaching out to youth. The organization has published research papers dealing with the engagement of young people. In 2003, CIRCLE, in cooperation with the Carnegie Corporation of New York, issued a report on civic education from kindergarten through 12th grade in which recommendations were made. Following release of the report, the two organizations helped to establish Campaign for the Civic Mission of Schools, in which more than 40 organizations have called for increased support for civic education from state and local governments. In 2006, CIRCLE issued the results of the National Civic and Political Health Survey, which examined the level and type of youth participation in politics and local communities and youth attitudes toward government and political issues. One 2007 paper, titled "Improving Textbooks as a Way to Foster Civic Understanding and Engagement," discussed a test of the effectiveness of three different explanations of direct and representative democracy in a group of 10th graders. Students were assigned a reading on one of the three explanations, and then all students were given the same assignment in order to measure their understanding of, and interest in, engaging in civic-related activities.

CIRCLE affirms the conclusion that the acquisition of knowledge about civics and government is important to youth political participation and that students also need to acquire skills and attitudes conducive to civic engagement. Other CIRCLE reports have found that the use of media in curricula tends to increase aspects of civic engagement and political knowledge, and that participation in some extracurricular activities is associated with higher rates of voting. A 2010 working paper reported the five-year evaluation of a study in which students were assigned to groups of 100–150 students that discussed government-related issues for one hour each week. The researchers discovered that community service participation rates increased 23 percent.

College Democrats of America (CDA)

College Democrats of America (CDA), established in 1932 to involve young people in Franklin Roosevelt's presidential election campaign, is the youth division of the Democratic National Committee. The organization has a national office in addition to local and state chapters. CDA holds a national convention each year, at which workshops are held on such topics as effective campaigning, and prominent Democratic politicians and officeholders present motivating speeches. Each year delegates to the national convention elect members of the executive board. A national council, composed of officers from each state, also provides direction for the organization. CDA distributes guides to students that offer practical advice about organizing a chapter. There are several caucuses within CDA for such groups as African Americans; Hispanics; military veterans; women; people of faith; those with disabilities; and lesbian, gay, bisexual, and transgender members. Although CDA is expected to follow the lead of the Democratic National Committee, in 1967 organization members decided to oppose President Lyndon Johnson's policy of military involvement in Vietnam, a stance that at the time resulted in the Democratic Party cutting the organization's funding. As with College Republicans, CDA campus chapters generally become more active during election campaigns, when members strive to engage students in campaigns at the local, state, and national levels to support the party's candidates and to get voters to the polls on election day. In addition to encouraging fellow students to register to vote, college chapters support passage of legislation that benefits students.

CDA encourages members to engage in grassroots politics by, for instance, offering guidelines for writing letters to the editor of campus as well as local and national newspapers and magazines. CDA's website contains advice about how to register to vote, including information about eligibility requirements and deadlines, and guidance for citizens residing outside the country ("Democrats Abroad") about casting an absentee ballot. The organization expresses pride in the level of voter turnout among young people in the 2008 presidential election, claiming that the youth vote was crucial to Democratic victories in several states. CDA has celebrated the accomplishments of the first two years of the Barack Obama administration and the Democratic-controlled 111th Congress, including passage of legislation instituting credit card reform, student loan reform, repeal of the "Don't ask, don't tell" policy regarding gays and lesbians in the military, health care reform, and Senate approval of the new START treaty with Russia limiting nuclear weapons.

College Republican National Committee (CRNC)

James Francis Burke established the College Republican National Committee (CRNC) in 1892. Presently the organization claims more than 200,000 members at approximately 1,500 colleges and universities. The CRNC maintains a national office in Washington, D.C., and has elected officers, including a national chairman and co-chairman, secretary, and treasurer, as well as a professional staff. Each state has its own organization, including a state chairman and executive committee. The CRNC, state federations, and campus organizations recruit members and engage them in political activities and the advocacy of conservative principles. The campus organizations become especially active during election campaigns, working to elect Republican candidates by distributing campaign literature, visiting neighborhoods, and phoning prospective voters. The organization provides students with training in electoral politics, thus providing them with an entrance into political activism after graduation. In the 2010 election campaign, CRNC field representatives, in a program called Operation Red November, mobilized nearly 15,000 volunteers to campaign for Republican candidates. The CRNC estimates that field representatives and volunteers directly contacted more than 2 million prospective voters.

Common Cause
http://www.commoncause.org

John Gardner founded Common Cause in 1970 to increase citizen influence on the political process and to hold elected officials accountable to the public for their actions. Common Cause has approximately 400,000 members and 36 state organizations. In 2000, the organization established a tax-exempt public education and research branch, the Common Cause Education Fund. The organization states that in striving for reform in the political process, it uses "grassroots organizing, coalition building, research, policy development, public education, lobbying, and litigation." Common Cause works to increase public participation and confidence in self-governing; to limit the influence of money in elections and government policy making; to assure fair, open, and honest elections; and to guarantee the civil liberties and civil rights of citizens. Members of the national governing board, who serve three-year terms, oversee the operation of the organization. Although not directly involved in youth political engagement, and young people as such do not play a distinct role in the organization, the efforts of Common Cause to bring about election reform speak to many youths' disengagement from the political process. The organization has called for improving voter registration policies by passing legislation at the federal and state levels to augment voting machine accuracy and security, instituting more stringent rules to hold election officials accountable to the public, and excluding partisan bias from election administration.

Common Cause has supported passage of legislation requiring that voting machines produce a paper record of votes and that random audits be conducted to check for machine malfunction or hacking. The organization also supports reform of the redistricting process in which legislative district lines are drawn. Common Cause holds that by removing the electoral process from partisan legislatures and establishing instead independent redistricting commissions, partisan gerrymandering can be minimized. Common Cause supports reform of the Electoral College in order to ensure that the popular vote winner is elected president. Asserting that there is no pervasive evidence of voter fraud, the organization opposes passage of restrictive voter identification laws that tend to discourage certain groups of citizens, such as minorities and low-income citizens, from voting.

Federalist Society for Law and Public Policy Studies
http://www.fed-soc.org

The Federalist Society was founded in 1982 to support conservatives and libertarians who wish to participate effectively in the public policy process. The society is composed of three divisions: the lawyers division, the faculty division, and the student division. The student division is composed of more than 10,000 law students at 196 American Bar Association–accredited law schools and additional chapters at international law schools, non-accredited law schools, branch campuses of accredited schools, and some undergraduate schools. Society members hold three basic principles: that the primary purpose of governing institutions is to maintain freedom, that a central ingredient of the U.S. Constitution is the separation of governing powers, and that the judiciary has the responsibility of determining specifically "what the law is, not what it should be." The student chapters host various events that emphasize these principles. The faculty division plays an important role by encouraging the development of traditional legal scholarship among faculty members and among students. The society assists members to become actively engaged at the community level and to take part in local, state, and national affairs.

Generational Alliance (GA)
http://www.generationalalliance.org

In 2005, three youth-oriented organizations, Young People For, the League of Young Voters Education Fund, and the Movement Strategy Center, joined forces to create Generational Alliance (GA) as an organization dedicated to facilitating coordination among youth organizations. The alliance has come to represent collaborative activities among 15 national organizations. Participating organizations include the United States Student Association Foundation; the Center for Progressive Leadership; the National Association for the Advancement of Colored People (NAACP), Youth and College Division; Democracia USA; and Campus Progress. The alliance brings together organizations with distinct emphases, including community-based youth organizing, campus organizing, general youth voter programs, and advocacy groups. Member groups have collaborated in several areas, including curriculum development, regional conferences, membership training, leadership development, issue advocacy, and fund-raising. A common youth agenda includes such issue concerns as comprehensive health care, affordable high-quality education, voting rights and election reform, clean energy, creating a safer world, and affordable housing.

The alliance has backed several national legislative initiatives, including the DREAM (Development, Relief, and Education for

Alien Minors) Act, which would allow undocumented students who have graduated from high school to attend college and to move toward citizenship; the Responsible Education about Life Act, which would support comprehensive sex education rather than abstinence-only programs; and the Youth Promise (Prison Reduction through Opportunities, Mentoring, Intervention, Support, and Education) Act that is intended to deal with the basic causes of youth crime. The alliance promotes the activities of member organizations, such as the Center for Progressive Leadership's New Leaders Fellowship Program, which finds paid internships and entry-level positions for minority and female students and leaders.

Head Count
http://www.headcount.org

Musician Andy Bernstein established Head Count in 2004 as an organization committed to encouraging democratic participation by registering voters at music concerts and introducing civic participation at these concerts. The organization is composed of a few full-time workers; more than 75 volunteers, including community organizers and graphic designers, who provide leadership; and a 20-member board of directors, including Andy Bernstein, Peter Bahouth of U.S. Climate Action Network, Mark Brownstein of the Disco Biscuits, Dave Marguiles of High Sierra Music Festival, and Jonathan Schwartz of Sirius XM. Several rock musicians allow representatives of Head Count to set up a voter registration table at concerts and invite the audience to become registered voters. The organization has 4,000 volunteers who take part in the registration effort and 80 musicians who have agreed to allow audience members at their concerts to register to vote, to write a letter to Congress, or to join e-mail lists on particular issues. Among the issues the organization emphasizes are food and farm policy, health care, personal liberty, human rights, environmental sustainability and conservation, and climate change. Head Count believes that this tactic will result in musicians and their fans becoming a politically influential group that will "turn every election into a pop-culture event."

Institute for Humane Studies (IHS)
http://www.theihs.org

F. A. "Baldy" Harper, a former economics professor at Cornell University, established the Institute for Humane Studies (IHS) in

1961 as an organization dedicated to promoting "peace, prosperity, and social harmony" through research and education activities that focus on the concept of freedom. The IHS states that it contributes to the intellectual development of students and scholars who appreciate the value of freedom and its practical contribution to modern society and hence who are likely to engage in political activity to advance the classical liberal position. The institute awards Humane Studies fellowships to qualified undergraduate and graduate students principally in the fields of economics, philosophy, law, business, political science, history, and sociology who are engaged in "liberty-enhancing" research. In 2010, the institute awarded fellowships ranging from $2,000 to $15,000 each to 180 students.

The institute invites fellowship winners to present their research at an annual research colloquium or to attend a discussion colloquium, cosponsored by Liberty Fund and devoted to the works of Friedrich Hayek. The organization also invites undergraduate and graduate students to IHS summer seminars at which participants learn about classical liberal principles. The topics of the 12-week-long seminars vary according to the career paths and academic fields of the participants. In 2011, the IHS scheduled 12 seminars on such topics as liberty and society; the tradition of liberty; and career-oriented seminars in journalism, public policy, and academics. The institute asks college faculty to encourage students to apply for the seminar program, and grants full scholarships for lodging, meals, and course materials. The IHS also offers weekend seminars that deal with the historical, economic, and philosophical grounds of liberty and the concept's relationship to contemporary political issues. The seminars include lectures and discussion, along with social events in the evening.

Intercollegiate Studies Institute (ISI)
http://www.isi.org

Frank Chodorov established the Intercollegiate Studies Institute (ISI) in 1953 to facilitate the dissemination of conservative economic, political, and moral ideals on college campuses. William F. Buckley Jr., a noted conservative commentator, became the institute's first president. The institute works to develop in young people an appreciation for the principles of limited government, individual liberty, the rule of law, a free market economy, personal responsibility, and fundamental moral standards. Volunteer representatives of the institute are active on more than 900 campuses and the organization claims more than 65,000 student and faculty adherents across the nation. Each year ISI conducts more than 300 programs, including lectures, debates, conferences, and summer schools. ISI notes that President Ronald Reagan selected former institute members to take leadership positions in his administration. The institute distributes its major publication, *The Intercollegiate Review*, to 50,000 students and faculty. The journal, which is published twice each year, contains essays and commentary dealing with politics, economics, culture, and history.

Leadership Institute (LI)
http://www.leadershipinstitute.org

Morton C. Blackwell founded the Leadership Institute (LI) in 1979 to train young conservatives in methods of influencing public policy through active participation. The LI serves as a means of generating future conservative public policy leaders who support free enterprise, traditional values, limited government, and a strong national defense. The institute recruits young conservatives to the organization's 41 educational programs, which offer training in such areas as campaign leadership; broadcast journalism; grassroots activism, campaigning, fundraising, and get-out-the-vote efforts; Internet activism; public relations; public speaking; and youth leadership. The institute has placed graduates of its training programs in various areas of public policy making and in the news media. The organization reports that at least 555 LI graduates are presently serving in state legislatures and that at least 90 of the Broadcast Journalism School graduates are employed in television news. The organization has provided small grants as start-up funding for more than 1,000 conservative campus clubs. The institute also provides funding to students to begin a campus publication as a conservative voice on campus and offers advice to students about receiving university funding for their publication projects.

League of Young Voters (LYV)
http://theleague.com

Founded in 2003, the League of Young Voters (LYV) encourages young people to engage in democratic politics in order to initiate desired change at the local, state, and national levels. Noting that one-third of young people from 18 to 24 years old are not in college, the LYV focuses mainly on non-college youth, especially those living in low-income communities and those who are minority group members. The organization attempts to engage youth in politics by focusing on issues most likely to affect the lives of young people and by providing training in the skills necessary for effective political participation and political organization. During election campaigns, the league organizes efforts at the local level to encourage youth to vote. Following elections, the LYV maintains a focus on engaging youth and emphasizes local issues that are especially important to young people, such as job creation, the prevention of violence, the cost of higher education, and juvenile justice. The league attempts to build relationships among youth from different racial, class, and cultural backgrounds. The league has developed leadership training programs, including the five-day Tunnel Builder Institute electoral "bootcamp," a 10-week practical training program to develop leaders, and online programs to prepare young people for voter turnout efforts. In addition to nonpartisan educational programs and youth engagement efforts, the organization maintains a political action committee that supports candidates in order to influence the outcome of elections. In cooperation with local groups, the league has developed an online voter guide site, TheBallot.org, which has communicated more than 270 voter guides in 33 states.

Mobilize.org
http://mobilize.org

David B. Smith and fellow students established Mobilize.org in 2002 on the campus of the University of California at Berkeley. Smith, a senior at the university, became politically active after receiving notification that college tuition would increase. In March 2002, Smith and several students from the Berkeley student government gathered at the state capitol in Sacramento to meet with elected officials. After more than 100 meetings of students with legislators, student tuition increases were suspended and the legislature passed a student housing bond that allowed the construction of additional student lodging. The meetings with the university administration and student government convinced Smith of the importance of political engagement. In 2005, Mobilizer.org staff members and interns developed the "Mobilizer's Guidebook," a resource that offers to young people practical instruction about the skills and techniques required to improve their communities and campuses. Among the steps to political activism, the guide discusses the topics of defining the mission to be accomplished, starting or joining a group, establishing goals, building a team, planning an event, engaging in advocacy, and raising funds.

The organization declares that its mission is "to improve the way democracy works by investing in Millennial-driven solutions" (millennials are defined as young people born from 1976 to 1996, which in 2011 were those between the ages of 15 and 35). The organization calls on young people to collaborate to pinpoint problems, offer solutions, and cooperate to establish the proposals on the college campus and in the community.

In 2010, Generation Engage (GenGage) merged with Mobilize.org. GenGage, founded in 2005, had worked to establish nonpartisan programs on election, civic, and educational issues in order to advance engagement opportunities for young people. The John S. and James L. Knight Foundation, which had funded GenGage, continued to support Mobilize.org. Mobilize.org began Democracy 2.0, a project to highlight the ways in which the democratic process and U.S. political institutions benefit, or fail to benefit, the goals and interests of young people. The organization developed the Democracy 2.0 Declaration, which details the impediments to youth engagement in the political process. The organization holds Democracy 2.0 Summits at which young people make presentations and the organization announces the funding of projects dealing with such topics as the financial health of the nation, the problems facing young veterans, and the influence of money on politics.

National Youth Rights Association (NYRA)
http://www.youthrights.org

The National Youth Rights Association (NYRA), established in 1998, works for the recognition of civil rights and civil liberties for young people, especially those less than 18 years old; challenges what it considers age discrimination against young people; and assists youth in defending their legal rights. The association claims to have 10,000 members in organization chapters throughout the nation. NYRA's organizational structure includes a board of directors, a board of advisors, and a staff including a president, vice president, secretary, and executive director. The members of the board of directors range in age from 14 to more than 30. Organization members elect the officers at each annual meeting. Claiming that only young people can adequately represent their own interests, the organization supports lowering the voting age below 18. The NYRA also supports lowering the minimum age for drinking alcoholic beverages, defends student rights, and advocates the right of young people to run for elective office. The NYRA opposes juvenile curfew laws that the organization believes unfairly limit young people's freedom of movement, and has challenged such laws in the courts. The association has challenged the right of states to limit the sale of video games based on age. In November 2010, the association held a rally at the U.S. Supreme Court building to support free speech, oppose video game censorship, and call for lowering the voting age. The association's basic position on the place of youth in contemporary society definitely has supporters, and various organizations have lowered the age at which persons may participate as full members. However, others who are skeptical of the group's aims argue that questions need to be confronted regarding just how low the minimum age for voting and other activities usually associated with adults should be set, and what constitutes being sufficiently responsible to engage fully in such activities.

New Leaders Council (NLC)
http://www.newleaderscouncil.org

Established in 2005, the New Leaders Council (NLC) offers training opportunities for young people to become political leaders and entrepreneurs in industry and in the civic and political realms. To accomplish this goal, the council has created the NLC Institute, which conducts a political entrepreneurship training program. Each year every regional institute trains approximately 20 promising young professional leaders, aged 22 to 35. This age range is higher than that targeted by other organizations because the council focuses on people who already have completed their undergraduate and graduate education (although the NLC does not require a college degree) and are already engaged in a profession, such as finance, law, journalism, medicine, the mass media, nonprofit management, and small business.

Unlike many other youth-oriented organizations, the council focuses on those young people who already show promise of high levels of civic engagement. The organization chooses a diverse group of fellows with regard to race, gender, and sexual orientation. Those chosen as fellows spend one weekend per month for five months in training programs that involve personal leadership development, entrepreneurship, marketing, fund-raising, advances in communications, and political management. Each fellow has the opportunity to meet with local and national officials and is assigned a mentor. Those who have completed the program maintain their contacts with the NLC, contributing resources, time, and expertise to the training of new fellows. The organization has a national board of directors, and each NLC chapter has an advisory board that includes established leaders and elected officials who assist in fund-raising. In August of each year, the organization holds a leadership retreat to plan for the coming year's institutes and to encourage discussion among the chapter leaders.

Rock the Vote
http://www.rockthevote.com

Established in 1990, Rock the Vote works to increase the political influence of young citizens by conducting registration campaigns and get-out-the-vote efforts, by pressuring political candidates to focus attention on gaining the votes of young people, and by persuading public officials to address those issues of special importance to youth. In cooperation with various companies and media celebrities, Rock the Vote has created public service announcements for such television networks as MTV, BET, and Fox. The organization provides information about mobilizing young voters through such techniques as phone calling and canvassing and such newly developed techniques as social network development, online advertising, e-mail communication, and mobile phoning. In 2008, Rock the Vote published the guide *Winning Young Voters Handbook*, which provides practical information for election campaigns, organizations, and political parties about registering 18 to 29 year olds and getting them to vote. Because young people tend to move frequently, Rock the Vote has focused on re-registering those who have changed their residence in order to increase voter participation in this age group.

In 2007, Rock the Vote distributed *Young Voter Mobilization Tactics II*, which reported that more campaigns had experienced greater success in mobilizing the youth vote by using such techniques as person-to-person contact as well as online social networking. In 2008, the organization experimented with the influence of text messaging on voter turnout and discovered that sending messages had a positive influence on registration and that messaging the day before the election resulted in higher turnout rates. Rock the Vote notes that increasing the political engagement of young people in current elections will increase the probability of participation in future elections: voting and other forms of political participation tend to become habitual activities. Rock the Vote regularly conducts polls among those aged 18 to 29 to determine which issues young people consider important, and the opinions they have on these issues; their vote intentions in pre-election surveys; and the attitudes of various minority groups.

Skyline Public Works (SPW)
http://www.skylinepublicworks.com

Deborah Rappaport, along with her husband Andy, established Skyline Public Works (SPW) in 2003 as an organization that supports expanded civic participation, especially within the progressive movement. SPW has provided financial support for political entrepreneurs who are committed to the progressive movement. Skyline has offered administrative and grant making support to the Rappaport Family Foundation, an organization that provides grants to nonprofit organizations involved in promoting civic engagement. In accord with its advocacy of progressive causes, SPW has commissioned studies dealing with how the Democratic Party can achieve electoral victories by appealing to young people for support, and it commissioned a voter mobilization study in 2004 investigating attempts to reach out to young people from 18 to 29 years old to persuade them to vote.

The organization's study of Democrats and electoral victory notes that young people should not be regarded as identical in interests and concerns. Rather, those aged 18 to 29 can vary according to the stage in life they find themselves and what life-changing events they may be experiencing, such as marriage, divorce, entering or leaving school, changing employment, and relocation. The report concludes that in order for Democrats to appeal to and mobilize young people, they must understand the issues, such as the minimum wage, unemployment, and military service, that concern particular segments of this age group. In addition, the report emphasizes that new modes of communication, including the Internet, text messaging, blogs, and podcasts, should be used to reach young people. The report emphasizes the value of peer-to-peer contact to provide information about the political candidates and the issues of greatest concern particularly to young people. The organization's website contains an application form for those wishing to receive funding.

Student Environmental Action Coalition (SEAC)
http://www.seac.org

The Student Environmental Action Coalition (SEAC) describes itself as a student-run network of progressive organizations and individuals who work to end environmental injustice. The coalition began in 1988 when students at the University of North Carolina at Chapel Hill suggested in a notice placed in *Greenpeace Magazine* that students interested in environmental concerns could form a network for sharing information. SEAC ultimately grew into a coalition of several hundred groups in junior high schools, high schools, colleges, and local communities. At the national level, a national council coordinates the coalition's activities. The previous year's board members select the current membership. Each member of the national council becomes involved in one of four working groups: finance, communications, materials, and "collective liberation."

SEAC has publicized 14 organizational principles, including first and primarily fighting environmental degradation, but also supporting human and animal rights, fighting racism and sexism, demanding corporate responsibility, and maintaining a diverse membership. In the organization's first years, groups established recycling programs in high schools and colleges. Coalition members have used direct action tactics to achieve the organization's goals. For instance, in 1992, the New York branch of the coalition, which included 120 schools, worked to stop the construction of a dam in Canada that would flood the Cree Nation land. Groups have instituted recycling programs at high schools and colleges. One of the organization's current campaigns is to oppose mountaintop removal as a method of coal mining because of its harmful environmental consequences.

Student Nonviolent Coordinating Committee (SNCC)

In 1960, students who had participated in sit-ins at segregated lunch counters in Greensboro, North Carolina, and Nashville, Tennessee, met with Ella Baker, executive secretary of the Southern Christian Leadership Conference (SCLC), on the campus of Shaw University in Raleigh, North Carolina, where they established the

Student Nonviolent Coordinating Committee (SNCC). Organization members participated in various political activities, including voter registration, rallies, and demonstrations to bring segregation to an end. The organization attracted many young blacks to the organization and its activities, including several sit-ins at department stores in Atlanta, Georgia, and mass demonstrations.

With the selection of Stokely Carmichael (aged 25) in 1966, and then H. Rap Brown (aged 24) in 1967, as the organization's chair, SNCC became more radicalized. Carmichael advocated racial separatism rather than integration and supported black power, including the use of violence for legitimate self-defense. During Brown's tenure as chair, the organization cooperated more closely with the Black Panther Party, the members of which rejected the nonviolent strategy that was included in the organization's 1960 statement of purpose. In 1968, Brown changed "Nonviolent" to "National" in the organization's name. Both Carmichael and Brown became involved in the Black Panther organization. Soon after Brown left SNCC, the organization dissolved.

Student PIRGs
http://www.studentpirgs.org

Student PIRGs (Public Interest Research Groups), begun in the early 1980s, are primarily groups organized at the state level that mobilize young students to examine and propose solutions to such issues as rising education costs, environmental protection and global warming, consumer protection, and homelessness. However, the organizations do not take an official position on any legislation and do not endorse any candidates. Recognizing that those aged 18 to 29 have demonstrated a low voter turnout rate relative to other age groups, that citizen participation contributes to a healthy democracy, and that political leaders pay greater attention to groups with higher voter turnout, Student PIRGs have worked to increase participation among youth. In 1983, the PIRGs conducted the National Student Campaign for Voter Registration, which the organization credits with registering approximately one million young people to vote. In 2003, Student PIRGs began the New Voters Project, an initiative to register young people and encourage them to vote on election day.

The organization reports that the voter turnout rate among those 18 to 25 years old increased in the 2004 and 2008 presidential elections and also in the 2006 midterm election. During the 2008 presidential primary campaign, Student PIRGs organized 500 student volunteers in 28 states to attend various campaign events and asked candidates their stands on issues of concern to youth. Student PIRGs contacted local voter registrars to assure that young voters would not experience voter registration problems at the polls, and monitored polling places to determine if young voters were experiencing any difficulties in casting their ballot. Although turnout declined in 2010 compared to the previous off-year congressional election in 2006, the organization notes that the youth vote increased in those precincts where students engaged in New Voters Project registration efforts and get-out-the-vote drives. New Voters Project campaigns were conducted in at least 19 states.

Students for a Democratic Society (SDS)

Students for a Democratic Society (SDS), established in the early 1960s, represented the core of the so-called New Left. The organization began as the Student League for Industrial Democracy, an offshoot of the League for Industrial Democracy. At its first convention in 1962, SDS adopted the Port Huron Statement, a political manifesto initially written by Tom Hayden, who was 23 years old at the time. Among its pronouncements, the statement critically examined U.S. foreign policy, the nuclear arms race, racial discrimination, and economic inequality. Events, particularly the civil rights movement and U.S. military involvement in Vietnam, significantly influenced the path the organization followed and divided the membership according to which issues were considered primary and what strategies (including violence) were considered appropriate.

More than 200 delegates representing at least 32 colleges and universities attended the organization's second convention in summer 1963. Delegates decided to elect national officers each year, a policy that certainly was considered more democratic, but which undoubtedly contributed to a lack of consistent leadership at the national level and disagreement over the direction the organization should pursue. By 1966, SDS focused a great deal of attention on such college campus issues as military recruitment and school administrations that cooperated with the Selective Service System by providing academic rankings of students subject to the draft. In 1967, spurred on by a desire to make the organizational structure more democratic, the convention eliminated the offices of president and vice president. SDS organizations on various college campuses spearheaded protests against the draft and the war, and the organization participated in the October 21, 1967, March on the Pentagon, which attracted approximately 100,000 participants. At the organization's ninth national convention in summer 1969, the presence of various factions within SDS resulted in a chaotic situation that led to the formation of two separate SDS organizations. One of the factions, the Worker-Student Alliance (SDS-WSA), remained active until 1974, when the national organization decided to disband, with local groups establishing themselves as branches of the International Committee Against Racism (InCAR). More militant groups, such as the Weathermen, embraced more extreme tactics, including bombing campaigns. Some of the earlier members of SDS, such as Tom Hayden, subsequently entered mainstream politics, running for public office. The youthfulness and political inexperience of members, along with commitments to particular ideological causes, contributed to the disorganization within SDS. And perhaps disillusionment with more moderate strategies led either to radicalization or withdrawal from active involvement.

Students for Liberty (SFL)
http://studentsforliberty.org

Students for Liberty (SFL) originated in the 2007 Institute for Humane Studies Koch Summer Fellowship. In July several students participated in a discussion of procedures that student organizations can use to advance the idea of liberty most effectively. Four students, Alexander McCobin, Sloane Frost, Pin-Quan Ng, and Sam Eckman, who were joined by Richard Tracy, formed an executive board to schedule a Students for Liberty Conference. The conference was held at Columbia University in February 2008, with 100 students from 42 schools attending. On the last day of the conference, the executive board announced that the Liberty Conference would be expanded to become SFL, an organization to provide support for students interested in the ideal of liberty.

The executive board established the Campus Coordinator Program, an initiative that trains young people to become campus coordinators who assist student groups in their designated region, help to form new student groups, and facilitate the planning of SFL regional conferences. The ultimate objective of campus coordinators is to stimulate interest in individual liberty and economic freedom on college campuses. Following preparatory training in the spring of each year, participants attend a retreat during the summer. Among the desired qualifications, program members are expected to have at least one year of experience leading a pro-liberty student group, possess the ability to manage several projects simultaneously, and have the motivation to complete projects with minimal supervision.

SFL has begun to distribute an annual publication, *Journal of Liberty and Society*, which contains academic articles written by students. A faculty committee composed of scholars with expertise on the topic of liberty reviews submitted papers. SFL also offers the opportunity for students to submit brief pieces (750 words or less) to the organization's Liberty Forum Online. The organization encourages contributors to explore new ideas, engage in debates, and comment on others' submissions. A panel of SFL executive board members reviews pieces before being posted.

21st Century Democrats
http://www.21stcenturydems.org

The mission statement of 21st Century Democrats states that the purpose of the organization is to build "a 'farm team' of progressive populists who will be the future leaders of the Democratic Party." The organization concentrates on training field organizers and leaders who can attain higher offices at all levels of government, following in the footsteps of such progressive Democrats as Senator Barbara Boxer (D-CA), Senator Tom Harkin (D-IA), and former Texas agriculture commissioner Jim Hightower.

21st Century Democrats also takes part in training campaign staff that assist in electing progressive candidates. The organization wishes to nurture candidates who believe that government plays an important role in the nation, and who will support public policies that contribute to the values of "equality, opportunity, compassion, justice, and fairness." The organization states that it has trained thousands of high school and college students as well as party activists and has found political jobs with progressive leaders for hundreds of these individuals. Candidates in primaries as well as general elections receive support, and major efforts are expended in contributing to the campaigns of candidates challenging incumbents and protecting Democratic incumbents who face serious election challenges. Those who complete the organization's training program are considered part of the alumni network and receive continuing assistance in gaining employment in politics.

United States Student Association (USSA)
http://www.usstudents.org

According to the United States Student Association's (USSA) statement of belief, the organization is committed to training and organizing student leaders to participate in extending access to higher education opportunities to disadvantaged groups and, more generally, to work for social justice. The organization was initiated in 1946 as a result of a conference held in Prague, Czechoslovakia, at which students from more than 35 countries met to establish the International Union of Students. Later that year, several hundred students met in Chicago to begin the process of establishing a U.S. organization, and the following summer a constitutional convention was held to establish the National Student Association (NSA), the forerunner of the USSA. Although many early members argued that the new association should remain nonpolitical, the NSA took a public stand against segregation in educational institutions. In 1951, the organization condemned the anti-communist activities of Senator Joseph McCarthy, and in 1953 the group denounced apartheid in South African universities. However, the organizational leadership maintained moderate political stances, and in fact during the 1950s a small group of officers collaborated with the Central Intelligence Agency.

In the 1960s, the NSA became more politically active in a liberal direction. In 1967, the organization approved a resolution supporting the Black Power movement, and in 1968, opposing U.S. involvement in Vietnam, the association began an effort to prevent President Lyndon Johnson from being re-nominated for the presidency. In 1978, the NSA met with a group that had left the organization in 1971 and reunited to form the USSA. The association continued its political activism, especially regarding efforts to encourage diversity on college campuses. In 1989, the USSA congress required that "people of color" hold half the positions on the board of directors. Subsequently, the organization mandated that board representation be guaranteed to women, lesbians, gays, and bisexuals. Today, the USSA prides itself on being the nation's "oldest, largest, and most inclusive national student-led organization."

Voto Latino (VL)
http://www.votolatino.org

Rosario Dawson and Maria Teresa Kumar established Voto Latino in 2004 as an organization dedicated to engaging young Latinos in the political process. During the 2010 election campaign, Voto Latino conducted an online voter registration effort. The organization encouraged adherents to make sure that they had registered to vote, and then prompted them to send messages to others, encouraging them to register. Voto Latino offered prizes to those who succeeded in persuading at least 10 others to register to vote. Voto Latino also participated in the design of a voter guide that discussed what to expect on the November ballot and explained to young people the importance of the elected positions. The organization claims that the Latino vote determined the outcome of several elections in 2010. For instance, Jerry Brown, who was elected governor of California, received 86 percent of the Latino vote and Latinos composed 18 percent of the electorate. Also in California, Barbara Boxer gained re-election to the U.S. Senate and received 86 percent of the Latino vote. In Nevada, Voto Latino notes, Senate majority leader Harry Reid scored a narrow victory in his reelection campaign for the Senate, receiving 90 percent of the Latino vote. Voto Latino notes additional Democrats and Republicans whose electoral victories were assured by Latino support. Voto Latino's fundamental message to public officials is that they should acknowledge the interests of Latinos, and the organization's message to Latinos is that their vote can be a crucial factor in the outcome of elections.

Voto Latino takes positions on public policy issues. It supported passage of the DREAM (Development, Relief and Education for Alien Minors) Act, organizing phone banks and letter writing campaigns. When the U.S. Senate defeated the measure, executive director Maria Teresa Kumar announced that the Latino community "will not forget those political leaders who today chose to obstruct progress for personal gain," thus indicating that Voto Latino will continue its efforts to register young voters who would cast ballots in the interest of the Latino community. Voto Latino also has opposed passage in various states of legislation similar to Arizona's controversial law that, until a court injunction prevented its enforcement, granted to police officers the authority to arrest suspected illegal aliens.

Young Americans for Freedom (YAF)
http://www.yaf.com

Young Americans for Freedom (YAF) began in 1960 when a group of 90 conservative young people met at William F. Buckley's home in Sharon, Connecticut. The group developed a list of principles, called the Sharon Statement, which proclaims that American youth have the responsibility to profess certain fundamental values, including the right to freedom from the limitations of unaccountable power. The statement also contained the assertion that political and economic freedom are closely related, that the U.S. Constitution is the best governing instrument ever devised, and that Communism is "the greatest single threat" to liberty. The organization held its first national convention in 1962. YAF began publication of *New Guard* magazine to express the group's position on various political issues. Throughout its history, YAF has attempted to offer young people with conservative views an alternative to the more liberal youth organizations, particularly on college campuses.

During the tumultuous years of U.S. involvement in Vietnam, YAF members, unlike such organizations as Students for a Democratic Society (SDS), supported the objective of victory over communism in Southeast Asia. The group also worked for a constitutional amendment to allow voluntary prayer in the public schools and for gun rights. YAF became a voice of opposition to the activities of the National Student Association on college campuses. During President Jimmy Carter's administration, YAF opposed transferring control of the Panama Canal to Panama and the Strategic Arms Limitation Talks treaties. The group strongly supported Ronald Reagan for the presidency, and several group members received appointments in the Reagan administration. During the 1990s, YAF engaged in recruitment campaigns on more than 75 college campuses and conducted campaigns against various liberal causes. In 2009, the organization co-sponsored a New York rally to oppose the Barack Obama administration's intention of trying terrorists in the domestic court system; in 2010, the organization supported the Tea Party movement, and YAF executive director Jordan Marks spoke at the Tea Party convention; and YAF opposed Obama's nomination of Elena Kagan to the U.S. Supreme Court, claiming that she adhered to a socialist ideology.

Young Americans for Liberty (YAL)
http://www.YALiberty.org

Following U.S. Representative Ron Paul's (R-TX) failed campaign for the Republican presidential nomination in 2008, young people who worked in the youth section of Paul's campaign (estimated at 26,000 students) formed the nucleus of Young Americans for Liberty (YAL). Jeff Frazee, a Texas native and graduate of Texas A&M University who worked as national youth coordinator in the Paul presidential campaign, spearheaded the formation of YAL. In December 2008, Paul sent an e-mil message to supporters announcing the official establishment of the organization. Frazee, YAL's executive director, sees the mission of the new organization to be similar to that of the Leadership Institute (LI), where he previously served as deputy campus services coordinator. YAL's objective is to "identify, train, and place conservatives in media, public policy, and government." The training involves instruction in libertarian philosophy as well as techniques for winning elections. Unlike the LI, YAL assumes the role of supporting and opposing candidates for public office. YAL's print publication, *Young American Revolutionary*, contains articles by and about young as well as veteran libertarians and encourages student involvement in the organization's activities. Daniel McCarthy, the former Internet communication coordinator for Paul's presidential campaign, edits the publication. YAL maintains a close relationship with the Paul organization, which contributed $25,000 to help the group begin operations and also granted YAL access to Paul's donor list to help the group solicit funds.

According to YAL's statement of principles, the organization adheres to the natural rights of life, liberty, and property. However, with these freedoms comes responsibility to maintain "high moral character and conduct." Young people who support limited government and classical liberalism are encouraged to become members. The organization's principles include the beliefs that "government is the negation of liberty"; "voluntary action is the only ethical behavior"; "respect for the individual's property is fundamental to a peaceful society"; "violent action is only warranted in defense of one's property"; and "the individual owns his/her body and is therefore responsible for his/her actions."

A national committee and an executive committee govern the organization. The national committee is composed of 21 individuals who approve the annual budget and program of activities, including the national convention. Committee members include the national chair, seven regional directors, seven at-large members, and six appointed members. The executive committee, led by the executive director, administers the organization's daily operations and provides support for YAL chapters. The national field director supervises the creation of new chapters and maintains communication with regional groups. YAL's libertarian principles may place the organization in opposition to other conservative groups on such social issues as gay rights and the advisability of existing drug laws. The organization maintains an application form on its website and encourages interested persons to establish new college chapters.

Young America's Foundation (YAF)
http://www.yaf.org

M. Stanton Evans, a conservative journalist, established Young America's Foundation (YAF) in 1977. For more than 30 years, Ron Robinson has served as the foundation's president. The organization endeavors to foster in young people an appreciation for the principles of individual freedom, free enterprise, traditional values, and a strong national defense. YAF organizes conferences and seminars, produces educational materials, and offers internships to students. In 1998, the foundation acquired President Ronald Reagan's ranch, *Rancho del Cielo*, in California, as the organization's headquarters. YAF pursues President Reagan's objective of conveying conservative ideals to young people and offers support to campus conservative organizations. Two of the organization's publications, *Conservative Guide to Campus Activism* and *Campus Conservative Battle Plan*, offer to students information about creating a campus conservative club, promoting a campus event, gaining media attention, and avoiding some of the common mistakes that campus activists often make. YAF recommends to students a strategy of aggressive activism, which involves pursuing a proactive strategy of attacking opponents and provoking controversy to gain publicity.

YAF's National Journalism Center conducts a 12-week program in which interns hear talks from leading journalists and public policy analysts and engage in current events and policy discussions. Interns spend most of the time during the program gaining practical experience with a mass media firm. The organization has established the National Conservative Student Conference and the National High School Conference, each of which meets annually in Washington, D.C. The YAF expects that the experience will give graduates of the program an advantage in gaining employment in the mass media.

Young Communist League USA (YCL)
http://www.yclusa.org

The Young Communist League (YCL) describes itself as a multiracial organization of the working class, including in its membership employed and unemployed workers and high school and college students. The YCL states that its objective is to further the interests of young people, to advance the cause of the working class, and to transform the United States through democratic means into a socialist society. The league can trace its roots back to the early 20th century and the establishment of the first Communist Party organizations in the United States. As with the Communist organizations, given official government sanctions, youth branches found it difficult to organize and retain members. A convention of 14 delegates was held in 1922 to establish the YCL. However, the organization maintained a highly secret status, which made it difficult to attract new members. The organization was disbanded in 1923, when the Young Workers League of America (YWL), which was established in 1922, continued as the main Communist youth organization. YWL membership included those between 14 and 30 years of age. In 1929, the youth organization reclaimed the title Young Communist League, and with the Great Depression, the organization experienced membership growth. However, in 1943, the YCL, along with the Communist Party (CPUSA), was dissolved. In 1949, subsequent to the reestablishment of the CPUSA, the Labor Youth League was established, an organization that also ended in dissolution following the Hungarian revolution against Soviet dominance and the publication of revelations about political repression in the Soviet Union under Joseph Stalin. A new organization formed in the 1960s, and in 1985, the youth organization became the Young Communist League once again.

Today the league invites youth to become members by paying dues of $24 per year. Membership includes a subscription to the organization's magazine, *Dynamic*. Members are invited to charter a local YCL club. The YCL reports the organization's position on various issues in the United States and worldwide, taking positions not unlike those of more mainstream organizations. For instance, in 2010, the league supported congressional passage of the DREAM Act, which would provide a path to citizenship among young illegal aliens who serve in the military or are college students. Although they did not take part in organizing the event, YCL members attended the 2010 One Nation Rally in Washington, D.C. As do more mainstream youth organizations, the YCL calls on young people to vote and engage in campaigning.

Young Democrats of America (YDA)

Founded in 1932, Young Democrats of America (YDA) works to activate younger voters and to support policies favorable to young people. The organization welcomes as members those identifying with the Democratic Party who are less than 36 years old. At a national convention every two years, YDA elects national officers—including a president and executive vice president—in addition to two representatives to the Democratic National Committee (DNC). The national board is composed of these officers plus six representatives from associated organizations. The organization has an appointed executive director and a full-time staff of approximately 9 and more than 100 part-time organizers.

YDA rather than College Democrats of America played the more significant role in mobilizing the youth vote during the 2000 election. However, the DNC, with which YDA was tied financially and strategically, tended not to emphasize efforts to mobilize young voters, due in part to limited financial resources as well as the assessment that a large proportion of young people did not vote. Concerned about minimal financial support from the DNC, and the expectation that the Bipartisan Campaign Reform Act of 2002 would limit even further the financial health of the organization, YDA leadership decided to sever the organization's formal ties with the DNC. YDA reformed as a nonfederal political action committee under the federal tax code, section 527, which allowed the organization to raise unlimited funds from donors rather than depending on the DNC. YDA would no longer be permitted to endorse individual candidates but rather would provide more general support for the Democratic agenda and develop its own strategies for engaging youth in politics. YDA has an annual budget of more than $1 million and a membership of more than 150,000 in approximately 1,200 chapters, and attempts to organize in areas where the Democratic Party previously has had weak support.

Young Elected Officials (YEO) Network
http://www.yeonetwork.org

In 2006, the People for the American Way Foundation, a liberal political group, established Young Elected Officials (YEO) Network to support progressive elected officials no more than 35 years old, a group that, according to the organization, composes nearly 5 percent of all elected officials at the local, state, and national levels. The network notes that more than 50 percent of presidents, members of Congress, and governors were between the ages of 18 and 35 when they first were elected to public office. The organization strives to help in preparing young office holders for long-term leadership roles. The network provides the opportunity to public officials to communicate with one another, to develop leadership skills, and to interact with public policy organizations. The organization also offers networking opportunities through conferences and communication channels offered by websites, newsletters, and online forums. The network prepares training materials that are presented at conferences and teleconferences that assist officials to develop skills in such areas as communication technology, the use of the mass media, coalition building, and debate. The organization is creating a page on their website, titled "YEO Interactive" (http://www.yeonetwork.org/content/yeo-interactive), at which public officials may share policy recommendations, take part in discussions, share resources, and see the YEO Network's events calendar.

Young People For (YP4)
http://www.youngpeoplefor.org

The liberal group People for the American Way Foundation established Young People For (YP4) in 2004 in order to "invest in the next generation of leaders and build a long-term national network for young progressives." YP4 offers opportunities for young political activists to communicate with other young people and organizations; plan projects; and acquire leadership, communication, organizing, and advocacy abilities. The organization works to develop young leaders who can create positive social changes in their local communities and in the nation as a whole. Each year, YP4, in cooperation with Young Elected Officials (YEO) Network, conducts the Front Line Leaders Academy, in which 20 young people receive training from successful political campaign professionals to become political candidates and campaign leaders. YP4 senior fellows design "Little Black Books," which are guides for campus organizers and student leaders. The books present information about organizing skills and contain case studies offered by campus activists. The topics covered in such books include advocacy and lobbying, event planning, media and messaging, coalition building, and professional writing. "YP4 Toolkits" focus on political issues, using case studies. Information about tactics, conferences, potential allies, and scholarships is also included. The organization holds a national summit each year, in which fellows who have been active during the first four months of their fellowship share strategies to bring about change in their communities.

Young Politicians of America (YPA)
http://www.ypa.org

Young Politicians of America (YPA) began in 1998 with a group of high school students meeting to discuss ways of addressing the lower level of political awareness and participation among young people compared to fairly high levels of voluntary community service in this same age group. The organization believes that without the appropriate political background, volunteer activities fail to serve a greater social and political purpose. The organization seeks to widen young people's understanding of democracy and to make them aware of government's role in dealing with social problems. YPA includes civic clubs in high schools and colleges, each of which is composed of young people aged 14 to 22. The organization works to make young people aware of their political responsibilities and to reestablish respect for the vocation of politics. Members are encouraged to regard themselves as public servants in their local communities.

YPA service chapters have been established in high schools and colleges around the nation, with from 15 to 50 students in each chapter (or club). Chapter members initiate community service projects while at the same time engaging in political discussions about the role of government in the particular service area. Each service chapter is required to meet weekly to discuss current political issues; to complete each month at least one community service-learning activity; and report to the national YPA organization each month about the meetings and service activities. Each member is required to complete a monthly assignment and link the experience to the relevant level of government, whether local, state, or national, thus linking community service to political discussion. For instance, YPA suggests that volunteer work at a local senior center could lead to a discussion of Medicare.

Young Voter PAC
http://www.youngvoterpac.org

Young Voter PAC is a political action committee that works to engage young people in politics in order to help Democratic candidates win elections. The organization represents a relatively new focus for the Democratic Party, which in the past was faulted for neglecting young people both as a source of votes and as a constituency with issue concerns. Given the low voter turnout among young people relative to older citizens, neither major political party has experienced great success in mobilizing this age group. However, the organization observes that voter turnout among young people increased significantly in recent elections, noting that in 2008, 85 percent of young adults had registered to vote, which represents a 5 percent increase in two years. Therefore, young people have become a crucial source of electoral support.

Young Voter PAC conducts investigations of the values and concerns of young people and provides the information to progressive candidates to assist them in winning support from young voters. The organization also has explored different media techniques for reaching young people. Young Voter PAC encourages candidates to develop a campaign strategy that includes appeals to young people between 18 and 30 years of age and offers financial assistance and consulting services to help candidates communicate with and develop support among young voters. The organization encourages voter registration drives and helps to publicize, especially through the Internet, candidate positions on issues considered of special importance to youth. Young Voter PAC notes that young people generally take more liberal stances on issues than do older age cohorts and therefore increasing the number of young voters is likely to benefit the Democratic Party and develop a coalition of voters in the future who are inclined to vote for Democratic candidates.

Youth for Western Civilization (YWC)
http://www.westernyouth.org

Kevin DeAnna, a graduate student at American University, established Youth for Western Civilization (YWC) in 2006 as a nonprofit education foundation. YWC states that its mission is "to organize, educate and train activists dedicated to the revival of Western Civilization." The organization began holding events on university campuses in 2008, hosting speakers such as conservative congressmen Tom Tancredo (R-CO) and Virgil Goode (R-VA), and Bay Buchanan, U.S. treasurer during the Ronald Reagan administration, conservative activist, media commentator, and sister of social conservative Patrick Buchanan. Organization members have initiated debates on such issues as illegal immigration, multiculturalism, and the value of classical education. Although organization members support limited government and fiscal conservatism, their major focus is social conservative causes. YWC opposes "radical multiculturalism, political correctness, racial preferences, mass immigration, and socialism" and also opposes what it considers "the insane and extreme anti-Western bigotry on college campuses." YWC considers Western civilization to be composed of the Greco-Roman, Christian, and folk traditions and the resulting social norms and practices that developed in Europe and those areas of the world settled by Europeans.

Youth Franchise Coalition (YFC)

In 1969, 23 organizations, including influential civil rights and educational groups, came together to form the Youth Franchise Coalition (YFC) as the major national organization advocating the lowering of the minimum voting age to 18. The coalition included such organizations as the Committee for Community Affairs, Democratic Party Citizens Division, National Association for the Advancement of Colored People (NAACP), National Education Association (NEA) and its Project 18, United States Youth Council, and Let Us Vote (LUV). Several other groups became affiliated with YFC in the pursuit of the 18-year-old vote. Youth members of the coalition diverged from those engaged in protests against the Vietnam War in both strategy and objective. They engaged in traditional lobbying activities to achieve the right of youth to engage in traditional electoral politics. YFC's major purpose was to maintain communication among the various associated organizations and to provide advice and materials to local groups. Ian R. MacGowan, who was 29 years old in 1969, served as the executive director of the Washington, D.C., office. The coalition followed two strategies to achieve its goal: (1) to lobby state legislatures to lower the minimum voting age, and (2) to lobby Congress to propose a constitutional amendment that would establish a national minimum voting age. The strategies were interconnected, in that coalition members believed that if states approved lower minimum ages, Congress would be more likely to propose an amendment. The YFC collected data about each U.S. senator's and representative's views regarding voting age and transferred the information to state and local members of participating organizations. During 1970 and 1971, the coalition followed a complex strategy of supporting state efforts to lower the minimum voting age, advocating the inclusion of a minimum voting age in legislation renewing the Voting Rights Act, and encouraging Congress to propose a constitutional amendment. The YFC ultimately achieved its objective in June 1971 when the Ohio legislature became the 38th state to ratify the proposed amendment, thus adding the Twenty-Sixth Amendment to the Constitution.

Youth Service America (YSA)
http://www.ysa.org

Youth Service America, established in 1986, works in the United States and other countries to assist organizations that are concerned with developing the ability of young people to engage in community service. YSA has the goal of making service learning widely accessible to young people. YSA has established several initiatives to promote youth civic engagement. The organization conducts public mobilization campaigns to encourage youth commitment to community engagement and to publicize the contributions that young people have made. Each April, YSA sponsors Global Youth Service Day, during which young people participate in service projects aimed at improving their communities. In the Semester of Service program, which begins in January and ends in April of each year, the organization encourages students aged 5 to 25 to participate in a service-learning project. The organization's Civic Engagement Initiative fosters further youth involvement in areas of concern by volunteering in election campaigns and voting. Each year, YSA offers several grant programs, giving to young people resources to identify community needs, offer new solutions, and involve other youth in the projects. The organization distributes *National Service Briefing*, a weekly online newsletter that provides information about future programs, relates youth service experiences, and announces future events relevant to youth service programs. YSA offers an online project planning instrument that assists young people in developing a service project (http://www.servenet.org/planit).

8

Resources

The resources listed in this chapter include a wide variety of topics that are related to youth and political participation. Some citation subjects, although not dealing directly with youth political engagement (such as general studies of voting behavior, the effects of newly introduced electronic communication tools on political participation, electoral rules, and campaign strategies) have considerable relevance for youth as well as the general population regarding the perception of the importance of one's vote and hence the likelihood of political engagement and casting a ballot.

Print Resources

Books

Alvarez, R. Michael, and Thad E. Hall. *Electronic Elections: The Perils and Promises of Digital Democracy.* Princeton, NJ: Princeton University Press, 2010.

The shift in recent years toward the use of electronic voting machines has raised concerns that such systems could experience breakdowns in which votes are destroyed, or the systems could be intentionally compromised, or "hacked." On the basis of their analysis of electronic voting, Alvarez and Hall conclude that the advantages of the new systems outweigh the claimed drawbacks. They also suggest ways in which voting technology might be improved and recommend strategies for evaluating the new voting systems. Although other analysts conclude that attacks on electronic voting systems are a real possibility, there appears to be agreement that confident participation in democratic politics depends on the maintenance of voting systems that accurately and honestly report voters' choices.

Amato, Theresa. *Grand Illusion: The Myth of Voter Choice in a Two-Party Tyranny.* **New York: New Press, 2009.**

Theresa Amato, Ralph Nader's former campaign manager when Nader ran for the presidency in 2000 and 2004, details the extreme difficulties, both administrative and legal, a third-party candidate experiences getting on the ballot in all states. The author argues that voters should be given a greater number of candidate choices in elections and recommends reforms to achieve that objective. She advocates a plan to institute federal administration and financing of elections.

American Democracy Project. *Electoral Voices: Engaging College Students in Elections.* **New York: American Association of State Colleges and Universities, 2006.**

This "best practices guide" presents accounts of various youth-mobilization efforts initiated at colleges and universities. Individual articles deal with such topics as voter registration, voter education, and the assessment of electoral engagement efforts. An appendix contains numerous case studies of political engagement projects on university campuses.

Azocar, Patricio Aylwin. *Youth Voter Participation: Involving Today's Young in Tomorrow's Democracy.* **Stockholm, Sweden: International IDEA, 1999.**

Azocar employs a comparative analysis of parliamentary elections in 15 European democracies to emphasize the importance of electoral politics and the potential consequences of failing to participate. The author discusses programs that countries such as Chile, South Africa, and the United States have established to expand voter participation among young citizens, and offers various proposals to increase youth involvement in electoral politics.

Baildon, Mark, and James S. Damico. *Social Studies as New Literacies in a Global Society: Relational Cosmopolitanism in the Classroom.* **New York: Routledge, 2011.**

Baildon and Damico develop a new approach to understanding social studies teaching and learning that they believe will endow students with the ability to flourish in a changing world. Students must be prepared to deal with new Web-based technologies and to manage new media. The authors present examples of teachers and students striving to deal with the challenges they face in a cosmopolitan environment.

Barany, Zoltan, and Robert G. Moser, eds. *Is Democracy Exportable?* **New York: Cambridge University Press, 2009.**

The essays in this volume explore the possibilities of promoting democratic principles in developing countries. The authors investigate the often cited structural preconditions to democracy, including an appropriate political culture and civil society as well as the presence of institutions and political processes crucial to democratic development, such as a constitution, electoral rules, and a stable economic system. These treatments also contribute to a better understanding of political participation in countries already considered democracies.

Baringhorst, Sigrid, Veronika Kneip, and Johanna Niesyto, eds. *Political Campaigning on the Web.* **New Brunswick, NJ: Transaction Publishers, 2009.**

The contributors to this volume offer perspectives on political campaigning via the Internet, presenting a comparative examination of Internet use by various political actors. The essays discuss the effect of Web campaigning on democracy and thus provide insights into the potential influence of this medium on citizens' level of political engagement.

Bartels, Larry M. *Unequal Democracy: The Political Economy of the New Gilded Age.* **Princeton, NJ: Princeton University Press, 2010.**

Focusing on the interaction of politics with economics, Bartels discusses the role that economic interests and concerns have played in U.S. politics. Bartels primarily emphasizes the apparent gap between citizens' commitment to egalitarian values and a seemingly inconsistent acquiescence with expanding economic inequality, and speculates about which political party is more likely to bring about economic well-being. However, the discussion is relevant to the role that citizens generally can play in the political process where significant economic inequalities exist.

Bauerlein, Mark. *The Dumbest Generation: How the Digital Age Stupefies Young Americans and Jeopardizes Our Future.* New York: Tarcher, 2009.

Bauerlein offers a more pessimistic view of the influence of such communication technologies as instant messaging, e-mail, chat rooms, and blogs on the level of political engagement of young people. The availability of these various means of electronic communication and access to knowledge notwithstanding, the author argues that the members of the present younger generation are less informed about politics, less literate, and more focused on themselves. With the use of social networking sites, young people concentrate not on broadening exposure to the larger world but on themselves and their limited group of friends.

Baumgartner, Jody C., and Peter L. Francia. *Conventional Wisdom and American Elections: Exploding Myths, Exploring Misconceptions.* Second edition. Lanham, MD: Rowman and Littlefield, 2010.

Baumgartner and Francia investigate several topics that, they claim, have been subject to misunderstandings, such as campaign finance reform, strategies for choosing a vice presidential candidate, media bias, negative campaigning, independent voters, and polling. The book is intended to help students to think more clearly about elections as well as the discipline of political science.

Baym, Geoffrey. *From Cronkite to Colbert: The Evolution of Broadcast News.* Boulder, CO: Paradigm Publishers, 2010.

Baym views the history of news broadcasting as a series of "paradigm shifts" that have altered the ability of citizens to acquire knowledge about the political process. The broadcast media have evolved from an era of a few networks to the "multichannel era" and ultimately to the "truly post-network age," characterized by rapidly changing communication practices. Jon Stewart's *The Daily Show* and Stephen Colbert's *The Colbert Report* represent a blending of news reporting and entertainment that Baym acknowledges may amount to a genuine form of political journalism, especially for younger citizens.

Berelson, Bernard R., Paul F. Lazarsfeld, and William N. McPhee. *Voting: A Study of Opinion Formation in a Presidential Campaign.* Chicago: University of Chicago Press, 1954.

This volume is a relatively early examination of voting behavior based on a 1948 empirical study conducted in Elmira, New York, during the presidential campaign. The authors investigate the influences on voting choice, including social class, religious affiliation, employment status, and the mass media. The authors also identify age as a variable that influences vote choice as well as the decision whether to vote.

Bhavnani, Kum-Kum. *Talking Politics: A Psychological Framing of Views from Youth in Britain.* **New York: Cambridge University Press, 2010.**

Bhavnani's book, originally published in 1991, examines the views that young people in Great Britain have about politics. In order to avoid the limitations of fixed-response survey methods, the author uses open-response interviews to investigate youth attitudes on such topics as unemployment, voting, racism, and democracy.

Birch, Sarah. *Full Participation: A Comparative Study of Compulsory Voting.* **New York: United Nations Publications, 2009.**

Noting that approximately one-quarter of all democracies have instituted some form of compulsory voting, Birch investigates the consequences of this interesting method of increasing voter turnout. The author presents the historical background to compulsory voting, the arguments for and against its use, and its influence on such political factors as election campaigns, political attitudes, electoral legitimacy, and policy outcomes. Other researchers have recommended the enactment of compulsory voting, but in the case of the United States, constitutional and practical issues would appear to militate against its adoption.

Brunell, Thomas. *Redistricting and Representation: Why Competitive Elections Are Bad for America.* **New York: Routledge, 2008.**

Contrary to the objective of making legislative districts as competitive as possible, which, some argue, increases the probability of higher rates of voter turnout, Brunell contends that a better strategy is to include in each district as many voters of the same party as possible. The author discusses theories of democracy and representation, principles of redistricting, and the claimed benefits and disadvantages of drawing gerrymandered legislative district boundaries.

Bugh, Gary, ed. *Electoral College Reform (Election Laws, Politics, and Theory).* **Farnham, UK: Ashgate, 2010.**

The contributors to this volume examine the origins and operation of the electoral college and possible changes in the method of electing the president. The essays highlight the reasons that many call for reform, the influence of the electoral college on campaigns and policy making, the prospect of a constitutional amendment to alter the system, and possible ways of altering the electoral system without a constitutional amendment. The key question for those supporting greater democratization is: would changing the electoral college result in greater voter participation?

Bullock, Charles S., III. *Redistricting: The Most Political Activity in America.* **Lanham, MD: Rowman and Littlefield, 2010.**

Politically motivated redistricting plans are often mentioned as a reason for political cynicism and low voter participation. Bullock investigates the processes for redrawing congressional, state legislative, and local legislative district lines and discusses the major court cases that have established guidelines for redistricting. Bullock also notes the consequences of previous redistricting efforts.

Campbell, Tracy. *Deliver the Vote: A History of Election Fraud and American Political Tradition—1742–2004.* **New York: Basic Books, 2006.**

Given the hypothesis that perceptions of the integrity of the political process generally and the electoral system in particular can influence the willingness of citizens to engage in politics, Campbell's treatment of election fraud is highly relevant to the topic of political participation. Campbell discusses such undemocratic activities as vote buying, stuffing ballot boxes, and disfranchising and intimidating voters, which the author claims have been used extensively in elections and persist to the present day.

Caplan, Bryan. *The Myth of the Rational Voter: Why Democracies Choose Bad Policies.* **Princeton, NJ: Princeton University Press, 2008.**

Caplan concludes from his research that voters, viewed as rational and self-interested persons, have little motivation to become informed about political issues because they realize that their individual vote is highly unlikely to determine the outcome of an election, which leads to a condition of "rational ignorance."

Therefore, voters are inclined to act irrationally because their vote decisions tend to be based on biased and uninformed understandings, and these biases allow voters to support policies that do not serve their interests. It would appear that the rational ignorance phenomenon would also lead many who lack basic knowledge of politics and political issues not to participate at all.

Cassino, Dan, and Yasemin Besen-Cassino. *Consuming Politics: Jon Stewart, Branding, and the Youth Vote in America.* Madison, NJ: Fairleigh Dickinson University Press, 2009.

Employing interviews with young people, the authors explore the reasons why many youth fail to engage in the political realm. They conclude that for young people, politics is less an end in itself than an object of consumption, and that sources such as Jon Stewart's *The Daily Show* may be an effective way for them to acquire knowledge about politics.

Charlton, John. *Don't You Hear the H-Bomb's Thunder? Youth and Politics on Tyneside in the Late Fifties and Early Sixties.* London: Merlin Press, 2010.

Relying on interviews with those who participated in the youth movement, Charlton examines the stormy politics of the 1950s and 1960s in northeast England and the rise of New Left politics among British youth who were aroused by the perceived threat of nuclear warfare. The author includes accounts of "Ban the Bomb" demonstrations and the disruptions caused by youth in the Labor Party.

Chesney, James D., and Otto Feinstein. *A Guide to Civic Literacy.* Englewood Cliffs, NJ: Prentice Hall, 1995.

This booklet is an earlier practical guide to political engagement intended as a supplement to an American government and politics textbook. Chesney and Feinstein define civic literacy as the skills a citizen should develop in order to function effectively in a democracy. Among the skills the authors discuss are familiarity with the various stages of building a political agenda, acquiring partners and developing a coalition, conducting voter registration drives, and mobilizing voters.

Cohen, Cathy J. *Democracy Remixed: Black Youth and the Future of American Politics.* New York: Oxford University Press, 2010.

Barack Obama's successful run for the presidency notwithstanding, Cohen argues that racial divisions have not been eliminated. Black youth continue to experience high rates of unemployment and imprisonment and low levels of political trust in government and politics generally.

Cohen, Robert. *Freedom's Orator: Mario Savio and the Radical Legacy of the 1960s.* **New York: Oxford University Press, 2009.**

Cohen's biography describes the transformation of Mario Savio from the son of a working-class family in Queens, New York, to leader of the 1960s Free Speech Movement at Berkeley University. The book contains a selection of Savio's speeches given during the student protests against the university's policy of limiting political expression on campus.

Colby, Anne, Elizabeth Beaumont, Thomas Ehrlich, and Josh Corngold. *Educating for Democracy: Preparing Undergraduates for Responsible Political Engagement.* **San Francisco, CA: Jossey-Bass, 2007.**

Colby et al. report on the results of the Political Engagement Project, which investigated college-level education techniques to provide students with knowledge and skills for democratic participation. The authors conclude from programs at various colleges and universities that education for political engagement has positive effects on students' political understanding, skills, and motivation to become involved in the public sphere.

Colby, Anne, Thomas Ehrlich, Elizabeth Beaumont, Jason Stephens, and Lee S. Shulman. *Educating Citizens: Preparing America's Undergraduates for Lives of Moral and Civic Responsibility.* **San Francisco, CA: Jossey-Bass, 2010.**

Colby et al. discuss the importance of civic learning and present educational strategies instituted at various universities and colleges to increase community engagement. The authors present an explanation for why they think civic engagement and ethical discernment declined on college campuses and recommend a strategy for increasing the participation of institutions of higher learning in public affairs.

Coleman, Stephen, and Jay G. Blumler. *The Internet and Democratic Citizenship: Theory, Practice and Policy.* **New York: Cambridge University Press, 2009.**

Coleman and Blumler explore the potential of the Internet for making significant contributions to public communications and hence to enhancing democracy. Recognizing that the operation of democracy in contemporary society faces severe limitations, the authors propose the development of an online civic commons that citizens can access to offer responses to government decisions.

Coles, Robert. *The Political Life of Children.* **Boston: Atlantic Monthly Press, 2000. First published in 1985.**

Coles conducted focused interviews with children in various countries, including Nicaragua and the United States, to gain an understanding of children's views on political subjects. The author concludes that children often acquire a surprising level of political awareness, even as early as the age of five. Although children often develop attitudes different from their parents, Coles notes that unfortunately they often take on the biased perspectives of adults on such issues as race.

Connery, Michael. *Youth to Power: How Today's Young Voters Are Building Tomorrow's Progressive Majority.* **Brooklyn, NY: Ig Publishing, 2008.**

Connery, co-founder of Music for America, an organization that has worked to increase youth voter turnout, argues that grassroots organizers are using the Internet to engage young people in civic activity, a trend he believes will reverse the reported withdrawal of youth from politics in recent decades. The author presents interviews conducted with those active in the youth movement.

Cultice, Wendell W. *Youth's Battle for the Ballot: A History of Voting Age in America.* **Westport, CT: Greenwood Press, 1992.**

Cultice presents a thorough historical treatment of the question of the minimum voting age and the push for the 18-year-old vote. The author notes that the argument for voting age was often associated with the minimum age for military service. Youth activism and protests against U.S. involvement in Vietnam in the 1960s spurred the movement toward reducing the minimum voting age. Cultice examines youth voting behavior from ratification of the Twenty-Sixth Amendment establishing the 18-year-old vote to the early 1990s.

Currinder, Marian. *Money in the House: Campaign Funds and Congressional Party Politics.* **Boulder, CO: Westview, 2008.**

Currinder's empirical research has led her to conclude that the significance to political candidates of raising campaign funds and the increasing importance of internal campaign fund raising has altered the political structure of the U.S. House of Representatives and now dominates congressional party politics.

Dahlgren, Peter. *Media and Political Engagement: Citizens, Communication, and Democracy.* **New York: Cambridge University Press, 2009.**

Dahlgren confronts the phenomenon of decreased social and political involvement in Western democracies, focusing on the mass media's role in influencing civic engagement. The author investigates the cultural foundations of political participation and explores the promise of interactive media in both heightening traditional political engagement and providing new ways in which citizens may become involved in politics.

Daling, Tjabel. *Costa Rica: A Guide to the People, Politics and Culture.* **New York: Interlink Books, 2002.**

Daling presents an overview of Costa Rica, a country that has experienced a stable democracy for more than 50 years. The author discusses the country's history, political development, culture, and major aspects of the economy, including coffee growing and exports, eco-tourism, and the government's role in economic affairs.

Dalton, Russell J. *The Good Citizen: How a Younger Generation Is Reshaping American Politics.* **Revised edition. Washington, DC: CQ Press, 2008.**

Contrary to the conclusion that young people are uninformed about public affairs and uninterested in political participation, Dalton argues that the present generation of young people is politically active in areas other than electoral politics. The author perceives a shift from a traditional "duty-based citizenship" to "engaged citizenship" that involves non-electoral activities such as protests and boycotts, a less deferential attitude toward political authority, a skeptical view of government officials, and identification with and concern for the well-being of other people.

Delgado, Melvin, and Lee Staples. *Youth-Led Community Organizing: Theory and Action*. New York: Oxford University Press, 2007.

Delgado and Staples, prominent in the field of community organization, discuss youth-led organizing that increases youths' community influence and also facilitates contributions young people can make to their communities. The authors provide descriptions of group activities and offer insights into establishing effective youth organizations.

Delli Carpini, Michael X., and Scott Keeter. *What Americans Know about Politics and Why It Matters*. New Haven, CT: Yale University Press, 1997.

The authors explore the level of citizens' political knowledge, using survey data gathered over five decades. They discover that although U.S. citizens tend to have relatively low levels of political knowledge, they do possess a certain level of political awareness, which varies according to demographic characteristics. For instance, younger people, along with African Americans and the poor, possess lower levels of knowledge than other groups.

Doppelt, Jack C., and Ellen Shearer. *Nonvoters: America's No-Shows*. Thousand Oaks, CA: Sage Publications, 1999.

Starting with the very low voter turnout rate in the United States, Doppelt and Shearer provide a discussion of the characteristics of nonvoters and possible explanations for their nonparticipation. The authors categorize nonvoters into five groups: "doers," "unplugged," "irritable," "don't knows," and "alienated." Various explanations for nonvoting include unrealistically high expectations for political action that lead to withdrawal, and very low levels of political knowledge that limit the ability of a person to follow an election campaign.

Eisner, Jane. *Taking Back the Vote: Getting American Youth Involved in Our Democracy*. Boston, MA: Beacon Press, 2004.

Eisner, recognizing that youth often do not participate in politics, claims that older citizens who are engaged in politics prefer the low participation rates among young people. The author points to such factors as the mass media and negative campaigning to explain low rates of youth participation and suggests such reforms as instituting same-day registration and increasing personal contact with the political realm.

Ellis, Andrew, Maria Gratschew, Jon H. Pammett, and Erin Theisen. *Engaging the Electorate: Initiatives to Promote Voter Turnout from Around the World, Including Voter Turnout Data from National Elections Worldwide 1945–2006.* Stockholm, Sweden: International IDEA, 2007.

The authors employ several case studies of electoral politics to investigate strategies that election officials and public interest groups use to halt the decline in voter participation experienced in many countries. Among the steps taken are information and advertising campaigns, grassroots organizing, the introduction of mock elections in schools, programs to offer inducements to citizens to participate, and entertainment events to attract young people.

Fahmy, Eldin. *Young Citizens: Young People's Involvement in Politics and Decision Making.* Farnham, UK: Ashgate Publishing, 2006.

Fahmy, noting that many young people in Great Britain, as in other countries, appear to have disengaged from political participation, investigates the attitudes that youth have toward politics and the British government. The author evaluates the likelihood that more young people can become politically active.

Farah, George. *No Debate: How the Republican and Democratic Parties Secretly Control the Presidential Debates.* New York: Seven Stories Press, 2004.

Since the 1960 election, debates have become expected events in the presidential campaign. However, Farah argues that the Democratic and Republican parties have, with few exceptions, successfully excluded from the debates candidates of other political parties, thus transforming the debates into "manufactured bipartisan press conferences" and limiting the issues that are subject to public discussion. The debates tend not to spark high interest in the electorate or encourage high levels of voter participation.

Franklin, Mark N., ed. *Voter Turnout and the Dynamics of Electoral Competition in Established Democracies Since 1945.* New York: Cambridge University Press, 2004.

The contributors to this volume investigate the relationship between voter turnout and the general health of a democracy. Individual essays examine the causes of low voter turnout and suggest methods of mitigating these factors. The editor concludes that declining turnout can be attributed to institutional factors, particularly a lack of electoral competition that discourages many potential voters from participating.

Frederick, Brian. *Congressional Representation and Constituents: The Case for Increasing the U.S. House of Representatives.* **New York: Routledge, 2009.**

Frederick investigates the relationship between constituency size and several variables related to representation, including the estimated effects of electoral competition, responsiveness of policy choices to constituencies, constituent contact with representatives, and citizen approval of representatives. Frederick concludes that the size of the U.S. House of Representatives should be increased so that the legislative body may represent more effectively the U.S. population.

Gastil, John, E. Pierre Deess, Philip J. Weiser, and Cindy Simmons. *The Jury and Democracy: How Jury Deliberation Promotes Civic Engagement and Political Participation.* **New York: Oxford University Press, 2010.**

Gastil et al. defend the traditional belief that jury service increases knowledge of public affairs and encourages civic and political engagement. The authors support their position with in-depth interviews, juror surveys, and voting records indicating that serving on a jury can result in significantly increased turnout, greater political activity, and heightened community involvement.

Gelman, Andrew. *Red State, Blue State, Rich State, Poor State: Why Americans Vote the Way They Do.* **Princeton, NJ: Princeton University Press, 2009.**

Gelman focuses his investigation of survey and election data on the relationship among class, culture, and voting behavior. He transcends the red state–blue state (Republican state–Democratic state) model to determine how individual voters behave and compares his findings with such countries as Mexico and Canada. Although more wealthy citizens tend to vote Republican, a wealthy state does not necessarily back the Republican Party, as the case of Connecticut illustrates. A key factor appears to be not only which political party the wealthy and less affluent support, but who is more likely to participate in electoral politics.

Gerken, Heather K. *The Democracy Index: Why Our Election System Is Failing and How to Fix It.* Princeton, NJ: Princeton University Press, 2009.

Gerken argues that the creation of a democracy index that ranks state and local governments according to their level of democracy can result in a rivalry among governing units to introduce democratic reforms, including an improved electoral system.

Giroux, Henry A., and Susan Searls Giroux. *Take Back Higher Education: Race, Youth, and the Crisis of Democracy in the Post-Civil Rights Era.* New York: Palgrave Macmillan, 2006.

Giroux and Giroux argue that corporations are attempting to mold higher education according to a business model and that cultural conservatives are undermining academic freedom by attacking higher education institutions as anti-American supporters of multiculturalism. The authors urge educators to resist such attacks and to support an educational model that prepares students for informed public engagement and political involvement based on a commitment to democratic principles.

Green, Donald P., and Alan S. Gerber. *Get Out the Vote: How to Increase Voter Turnout.* Second edition. Washington, DC: Brookings Institution, 2008.

The authors' findings are based on analysis of the results of techniques used in several election campaigns to increase voter turnout. Green and Gerber evaluate the cost-effectiveness of such voter mobilization strategies as door-to-door canvassing, sending e-mail messages, and making telephone calls. Additional tactics analyzed include use of the mass media, organizing events such as candidate forums, and holding election day festivals.

Gutman, Amy. *Democratic Education.* Princeton, NJ: Princeton University Press, 1999. First published in 1987.

In an attempt to develop a democratic theory of education, Gutman discusses a number of issues, including a democratic argument against book banning, the place of teachers' unions in education, public financing of private schools, and the policy of affirmative action in university admissions. Gutman identifies as purposes of higher education the instruction of officeholders and the encouragement of freedom of association.

Hanmer, Michael J. *Discount Voting: Voter Registration Reforms and Their Effects.* **New York: Cambridge University Press, 2009.**

Hanmer investigates the effects that registration laws have on the makeup of the electorate, voter turnout, and the strategies that political parties choose to pursue. The author concludes that the effects of registration laws are not as significant as previous studies suggest, and recommends a shift away from voter registration reform to other approaches for increasing voter turnout.

Henderson, Lesley, Craig Murray, Julian Petley, and Mike Wayne. *Television News, Young People and Politics: Generation Disconnected.* **New York: Palgrave Macmillan, 2010.**

Henderson et al. investigate the level of disaffection that young people in the United Kingdom feel toward the traditional political process. The authors focus attention on the way in which television broadcasts portray the political process and young people themselves, and on how young citizens use the mass media to become informed about politics.

Hess, Diana E. *Controversy in the Classroom: The Democratic Power of Discussion.* **New York: Routledge, 2009.**

On the basis of empirical research conducted in schools around the nation, Hess argues for introducing the treatment of controversial issues in curricula as a key ingredient in democratic education. The author maintains that the skilled inclusion of controversial issues can provide training in the democratic process and can assist in developing in young people the ability to engage in and improve their communities.

Hess, Robert, and Judith Torney. *The Development of Political Attitudes in Children.* **Piscataway, NJ: Aldine Transaction, 2005.**

Hess and Torney present the results of an extensive study of 12,000 elementary school students in eight U.S. cities. Building on Fred Greenstein's earlier more limited investigation, *Children and Politics*, which focused on one city, the authors examine the influence of several variables, including social class, intelligence, and religious affiliation, on the development of political attitudes.

Hill, David. *American Voter Turnout: An Institutional Perspective.* **Boulder, CO: Westview, 2006.**

Hill examines the low voter turnout rate in the United States compared to other industrialized nations, focusing primarily on the institutional arrangements that result in a situation that discourages many from participating in electoral politics. The author analyzes the effects of such aspects of the U.S. political process as registration requirements; the single-member district system of electing representatives, including the electoral college; and separation of powers. Recognizing that more effective means of increasing voter participation, such as abolishing the Electoral College, are highly unlikely to be adopted, Hill recommends more modest reforms, such as allowing election day registration and introducing Internet voting.

Hindman, Matthew. *The Myth of Digital Democracy.* **Princeton, NJ: Princeton University Press, 2008.**

Hindman criticizes the often-made claim that the Internet is leading to more democratic modes of political interaction among citizens. According to the author, corporate-controlled media have not experienced a decrease in their share of the audience, nor have ordinary citizens increased their political voice. Hindman's argument is especially relevant to younger citizens, who are more likely than older age cohorts to rely on new technology for communication.

Howard, Philip N. *The Digital Origins of Dictatorship and Democracy: Information Technology and Political Islam.* **New York: Oxford University Press, 2010.**

Howard examines the use of innovative communication technologies in the development of democratic processes in Muslim countries. The author concludes from his study of 74 countries with large Muslim populations that online forums have encouraged the organization of activist movements supporting democratic development. Howard's discussion potentially has wider application to the contribution that technology may make to democratic processes in political systems generally.

Howe, Brendan, Vesselin Popovski, and Mark Notaras, eds. *Democracy in the South: Participation, the State, and the People.* **New York: United Nations University Book, 2010.**

The contributors to this volume examine the difficulties of democratic development in non-Western parts of the world. The essays focus on nine case studies from African, Latin American, and Asian nations. The authors elucidate the practice of democracy outside the standard Western understanding. The essays can contribute to a comparative understanding of political participation.

Invernizzi, Antonella, and Jane Williams, eds. *Children and Citizenship.* **Thousand Oaks, CA: SAGE Publications, 2008.**

These essays offer a comparative treatment of the place children take in society, their rights, and their status as citizens. Individual essays deal with educating children for citizenship and developing political literacy, the dilemmas involved in children's participation, and the language of children's rights. In dealing with the citizenship of children, this volume provides a link between childhood and adult political engagement.

Jamieson, Kathleen Hall, ed. *Electing the President 2008: The Insiders' View.* **Philadelphia: University of Pennsylvania Press, 2009.**

Following the November 2008 election, Jamieson and Brooks Jackson of FactCheck.org organized a conference composed of the major election strategists and consultants of both major political parties to analyze the campaign and election results. Participants discussed such topics as the major decisions made during the campaign, campaign spending, press coverage, and the influence of the Internet on the election. The book includes a DVD that contains selected portions of the event.

Kasniunas, Nina, and Daniel M. Shea. *Campaign Rules: A 50-State Guide to Campaigns and Elections in America.* **Lanham, MD: Rowman and Littlefield, 2009.**

Kasniunas and Shea provide detailed information about campaigns and elections for each state, including electoral turnout data; election outcomes; voting regulations; rules for becoming a candidate; rules regulating campaign finance; information about judicial elections; rules governing party primaries; and ballot initiative data. Such information is of special value to younger voters, who likely are less familiar with the details of the electoral process.

Kenski, Kate, Bruce W. Hardy, and Kathleen Hall Jamieson. *The Obama Victory: How Media, Money, and Message Shaped the 2008 Election.* **New York: Oxford University Press, 2010.**

Kenski, Hardy, and Jamieson employ results of the National Annenberg Election Survey and interviews with campaign advisers in their investigation of the role the mass media, money, and campaign communication played in the outcome of the 2008 election. The authors focus on such topics as the Barack Obama campaign's strategy for communicating the candidate's message, the vice presidential nominees, and the issue of race. Mobilization of groups, including younger citizens, played a key role in the election outcome.

Kirshner, Benjamin, Jennifer L. O'Donoghue, and Milbrey W. McLaughlin, eds. *Youth Participation: Improving Institutions and Communities, New Directions for Youth Development.* **New York: Jossey-Bass, 2003.**

This volume of essays is based on the proposition that the civic development of youth crucially depends on their participation in community affairs. The contributors discuss a variety of activities that can qualify as participation. They note that youth participation has faced several barriers, including cultural beliefs about the abilities of adolescents. In order to overcome such barriers, youth organizations, community development groups, schools, and governing agencies have worked to include young people in leadership and decision making roles.

Koon, Tracy H. *Believe, Obey, Fight: Political Socialization of Youth in Fascist Italy, 1922–1943.* **Chapel Hill, NC: University of North Carolina Press, 1985.**

This historical description of fascist Italy provides an account of how an authoritarian regime attempted to socialize its young people. Koon discusses the role of the fascist party, the educational system, youth groups, and the mass media in socializing young people. In youth organizations, young people received physical, military, and political training. Koon notes that although Benito Mussolini's regime experienced some success in instilling conformity among youth, the failures of the regime led to disillusionment.

Kornbluh, Mark L. *Why America Stopped Voting: The Decline of Participatory Democracy and the Emergence of Modern American Politics.* **New York: New York University Press, 2000.**

Writing prior to the modest increase in voter turnout in more recent elections, Kornbluh notes the pervasiveness of nonvoting in contrast to the much higher rates of voting in the 19th century. The author observes that the decline in voter turnout was gradual and no specific political cause can be determined. Kornbluh attributes the decline in mass participation to general social transformations that occurred in the late 19th and early 20th centuries.

Kropf, Martha E., and David C. Kimball. *Helping America Vote: The Limits of Election Reform.* **New York: Routledge, 2010.**

Kropf and Kimball examine the Help America Vote Act (HAVA) of 2002, its purposes, and consequences. The authors note that given the difficulties experienced with voting equipment, especially in the 2000 elections, the legislation focused mainly on technological improvement. Various electoral problems, such as ballot design and the partisanship of election administrators, still remain, as well as the political conflict between those arguing for greater ballot access and those concerned with voter fraud.

Leighley, Jan E., ed. *The Oxford Handbook of American Elections and Political Behavior.* **New York: Oxford University Press, 2010.**

This edited work covers the various approaches to studying political behavior and U.S. elections. Individual articles treat such subjects as low voter turnout, voter registration, voting technology, campaign influences on vote choice, local elections and judicial contests, primary elections, voter mobilization, redistricting, the role of money in elections, and the U.S. electoral system compared to other nations.

Levi, Margaret, James Johnson, Jack Knight, and Susan Stokes, eds. *Designing Democratic Government: Making Institutions Work.* **New York: Russell Sage Foundation, 2008.**

The essays in this volume focus on how formal and informal institutional organization influences the character of democratic government. The authors attempt to determine the way in which established procedures either encourage or hamper electoral participation and other forms of political activity in order to identify possible political reforms to enhance democracy.

Levine, Peter. *The Future of Democracy: Developing the Next Generation of American Citizens.* **Boston, MA: Tufts University Press, 2007.**

Levine discusses ways of involving students more deeply in politics and civic affairs through the use of such activities as field trips, mock elections, and service projects. Not only schools but also families, churches, communities, and political and governing institutions are urged to become involved in developing a sense of civic responsibility in young people, a task that the author considers crucial to maintaining a democratic system.

Levinson, Sanford. *Our Undemocratic Constitution: Where the Constitution Goes Wrong (And How We the People Can Correct It).* **New York: Oxford University Press, 2006.**

Levinson presents several criticisms of the U.S. Constitution that lead him to the conclusion that citizens should work toward fundamental changes in the document. Such provisions as mandating for each state equal representation in the Senate and electing the president through the complex electoral college are aspects of the Constitution that critics often cite as undemocratic restrictions on the electoral system that reduce the value of electoral participation and arguably reduce voter turnout.

Lewis-Beck, Michael S., William G. Jacoby, Helmut Norpoth, and Herbert F. Weisberg. *The American Voter Revisited.* **Ann Arbor: University of Michigan Press, 2008.**

The authors return to Angus Campbell, Philip Converse, Warren Miller, and Donald Stokes's noted election study, *The American Voter*, using current election and survey data to characterize the contemporary U.S. voter. The authors conclude that the characteristics and behavior of contemporary voters closely resemble that of voters in the 1950s.

Loader, Brian D., ed. *Young Citizens in the Digital Age: Political Engagement, Young People and the New Media.* **New York: Routledge, 2007.**

Although the voter turnout rate among those 18 to 25 years old consistently falls below that of older age groups, Loader argues that youth, who are experiencing political socialization through newly developed media, can become more politically active. New media technologies may be used to engage young people more extensively in democratic politics.

Loeb, Paul Rogat. *Soul of a Citizen: Living with Conviction in Challenging Times.* **Second edition. New York: St. Martin's Press, 2010.**

Concerned about social isolation and the increasing income gap between rich and poor, Loeb presents an alternative vision of political activism that emphasizes community involvement. The author recounts cases of successful activism and encourages students to resist possible disappointment and disillusionment and to continue taking action in difficult situations.

Macedo, Stephen, ed. *Democracy at Risk: How Political Choices Undermine Citizen Participation and What We Can Do About It.* Washington, DC: Brookings Institution Press, 2005.

Contributors to this volume focus on the ill effects of low citizen participation in politics and community affairs, and what strategies may be implemented to increase civic engagement. Their major focus is on reforming political institutions and policies that discourage civic involvement, that enhance political inequality, and that dampen interest in election campaigns and substantive policy discussion.

Maisel, L. Sandy. *American Political Parties and Elections: A Very Short Introduction.* New York: Oxford University Press, 2007.

Noting the low voter participation in U.S. elections, Maisel suggests that the lack of competition is a key reason. Low competition could be due to a condition in which a large proportion of citizens identify with neither of the two major political parties, but those two parties win the vast majority of elections. Maisel also notes that incumbents tend to receive the lion's share of campaign contributions, and independent groups often have more influence on electoral outcomes than political parties or candidates' own organizations. This discussion offers some plausible reasons why young people tend not to participate in politics.

Margolis, Michael, and Gerson Moreno-Riaño. *The Prospect of Internet Democracy.* Surrey, UK: Ashgate, 2009.

Margolis and Moreno-Riaño examine the prospect that the Internet will enhance democracy in the United States. Although the Internet offers greater opportunities to citizens, political parties, and interest groups, the authors question whether developments in information and communication technologies will result in fundamental changes in democratic politics.

Mark, David. *Going Dirty: The Art of Negative Campaigning.* **Updated edition. Lanham, MD: Rowman and Littlefield, 2009.**

Mark examines the history of negative campaigning and details some better-known case studies. The author concludes that attacks can be effective if well-timed but that ill-conceived attacks can lead to voter backlash against the negative tactics. A key question is whether such negative campaigning has a dampening effect on voter turnout, especially among younger citizens.

Marsh, David, Therese O'Toole, and Su Jones. *Young People in the UK: Apathy or Alienation?* **New York: Palgrave Macmillan, 2007.**

Rather than focusing on engagement with the traditional political realm, the authors focus on the way in which young people approach politics. Using as variables class, gender, ethnicity, and age, the authors conclude that rather than being apathetic, many young people are alienated from the mainstream political process, which they consider unresponsive to their concerns.

McClafferty, Brett. *The Age of Politics.* **Bloomington, IN: Author House, 2008.**

McClafferty relates his political activities in electoral politics as a student at Cleveland State University in 2007. Becoming involved in local politics in the city of Streetsboro, he concluded that none of the mayoral candidates was sufficiently qualified. McClafferty decided that he, at the age of 18, would become a mayoral candidate in the primary election. In a field of eight candidates, he lost the election by just one vote. That summer McClafferty established Young Citizens for a Better Streetsboro, a political action committee of 32 members, to defend the rights of young people.

McDonnell, Lorraine M., P. Michael Timpane, and Roger Benjamin, eds. *Rediscovering the Democratic Purposes of Education.* **Lawrence: University Press of Kansas, 2000.**

Concerned that those engaged in public education have neglected the goal of imparting civic values, instead focusing narrowly on preparing students for employment, the editors have gathered together nine essays that offer suggestions for reviving the democratic objectives of educational institutions. The contributors deal with such topics as vouchers, charter schools, national testing standards, and the place of deliberation in a democratic society.

McKay, George, ed. *DIY Culture: Party and Protest in Nineties Britain*. New York: Verso, 1998.

Contributors to this volume, who are political activists, evaluate the political involvement of British youth in the 1990s and the DIY (Do-It-Yourself) counterculture movement. The authors present from a variety of political perspectives their perception of alternatives to the mainstream political process.

Milbrath, Lester W., and M. L. Goel. *Political Participation: How and Why Do People Get Involved in Politics?* Second edition. Chicago: Rand McNally, 1977.

Milbrath and Goel discuss the fundamental factors associated with political participation, including personal factors such as basic beliefs and attitudes, external stimuli such as contact by political party representatives who encourage voting, and environmental factors such as the rules that either promote or discourage political engagement. The authors help to place the subject of youth political participation in the context of civic engagement.

Nie, Norman H., Jane Junn, and Kenneth Stehlik-Barry. *Education and Democratic Citizenship in America*. Chicago: University of Chicago Press, 1996.

Observing that formal education plays a crucial role in developing active citizens and that those with a higher level of education tend to be more engaged in civic affairs and are more knowledgeable, the authors investigate the causal links between education and democratic citizenship, which includes both political participation to achieve individual objectives as well as commitment to democratic values. Those with higher levels of education have a greater probability of achieving more prestigious social and economic status and the social connections that facilitate civic engagement.

Nie, Norman H., Sidney Verba, and John R. Petrocik. *The Changing American Voter*. Enlarged edition. Cambridge, MA: Harvard University Press, 1979.

The authors provide a comprehensive interpretation of national election data. They discuss possible changes in the electorate from the 1950s to the 1970s, including the decline of political party identification among voters and the rise of issue voting. The authors note the consistent finding that younger people are less likely to vote than older age cohorts. Nie, Verba, and Petrocik continue the tradition of major election analyses that reached a high level of sophistication with Angus Campbell, Philip E. Converse, Warren E. Miller, and Donald E. Stokes's *The American Voter* (1960).

Niemi, Richard G., and Jane Junn. *Civic Education: What Makes a Student Learn?* **New Haven, CT: Yale University Press, 2005.**

Niemi and Junn analyze data resulting from tests measuring the level of knowledge about civics among high school seniors and relate these scores to level of interest in politics, the organization of civics courses, and student–teachers ratios. The authors conclude that civic education does contribute to political knowledge, and present suggestions to improve civic learning in the public schools.

Nimmo, Dan. *The Techniques of Modern Election Campaigns.* **New Brunswick, NJ: Transaction Publishers, 2001.**

Nimmo presents an analysis of political management and consulting, a profession that has expanded substantially in recent years. The author notes the effects of professional consulting on the operation of campaigns and communication. A significant question regarding citizen participation that arises from Nimmo's critique is whether the increasing professionalization of electoral politics spurs more widespread political involvement or discourages citizen engagement in politics.

Nordlinger, Gary, and Dennis W. Johnson. *Campaigning in the Twenty-First Century: A Whole New Ballgame.* **New York: Routledge, 2010.**

Candidates for political office traditionally have used campaigning to mobilize citizens to cast a vote. Nordlinger and Johnson explain the way in which sophisticated techniques such as online fund-raising and Internet communication along with the introduction of technological tools by political parties and interest groups have altered the political campaign. Various political actors use such techniques to identify and communicate with voters, discover their preferences, and motivate them to go to the polls. The question remains whether the use of new technologies will increase overall voter turnout.

Norrander, Barbara. *The Imperfect Primary: Oddities, Biases, and Strengths of U.S. Presidential Nomination Politics.* New York: Routledge, 2010.

In her examination of the presidential primary system, Norrander observes that the reforms of the 1970s produced several unintended consequences that led to calls for further reforms. Therefore, the author recommends careful consideration of additional reform proposals to improve a system that resulted from inadequate planning and consideration of possible unforeseen consequences. She investigates more pragmatic and incremental changes, given that wholesale changes are unlikely to be adopted. Norrander's treatment of electoral reform is relevant to the question of increasing voter participation, particular among the younger population.

Overton, Spencer. *Stealing Democracy: The New Politics of Voter Suppression.* New York: Norton, 2008.

Overton conducts a critical examination of elections in the United States, noting that there are 4,600 different state and local election systems, with a wide variety of voting machines, ballot design, and recount procedures. However, most U.S. election systems have in common the single-member district plurality method of electing representatives, an arrangement that allows for the drawing of noncompetitive representative districts that tend to dampen voter turnout. The author notes that given the traditional support for states' rights, nationwide electoral reform to achieve fair voting procedures is likely not to occur. Therefore, Overton focuses on a defense of existing policies, such as the 1965 Voting Rights Act, that are intended to protect the right to vote.

Perry, James L., and Steven Jones, eds. *Quick Hits for Educating Citizens: Successful Strategies by Award-Winning Teachers.* Bloomington: Indiana University Press, 2006.

Based on the conviction that community engagement is necessary to sustain democratic values and that civic engagement is a crucial aspect of educating people to citizenship, the 58 essays in this edited volume provide faculty and administrators in higher education with ideas for including civic education in the curriculum. The essays offer strategies for engaging students in community activities beyond formal classes.

Poundstone, William. *Gaming the Vote: Why Elections Aren't Fair (And What We Can Do About It)*. **New York: Hill and Wang, 2008.**

Focusing his attention on the problem of assuring that elections reflect the will of voters, Poundstone examines the effects of plurality elections in which the candidate with the most votes wins. The author analyzes the advantages and potential disadvantages of instant runoff voting and, due to flaws in the system, tends to support range voting, which involves rating candidates on a scale. With regard to young people, Poundstone recommends incremental improvements in the electoral system, realizing that voting involves more than a rational individual casting a ballot; it involves joining in a collective activity to which individuals make a commitment.

Powell, G. Bingham. *Elections as Instruments of Democracy: Majoritarian and Proportional Visions*. **New Haven, CT: Yale University Press, 2000.**

Noted political scientist G. Bingham Powell presents a comparative analysis of elections as crucial mechanisms of democratic governance in 20 democracies. The author contrasts majoritarian systems with proportional representation ones. Many political scientists claim that the United States would be better served with a proportional system, which would grant to minor political parties a greater opportunity to elect representatives, and hence would provide greater incentive to citizens to participate in electoral politics.

Powell, William. *The Anarchist Cookbook*. **Springdale, AR: Ozark Press, 2002. First published in 1970.**

Powell wrote this brief 160-page book in the late 1960s when he was a teenager disaffected by U.S. military involvement in the Vietnam War. The book provides information gleaned from library sources, including decommissioned government manuals, about conducting terrorist operations. Topics include bomb making, setting booby traps, and preparing ricin as a biological warfare agent. Some have claimed that the volume inspired several terrorist bombings in the United States and around the world. Although Powell subsequently disavowed the book and requested that the publisher discontinue sales, it still remains in print.

Print, Murray, and Henry Milner, eds. *Civic Education and Youth Political Participation*. Rotterdam, the Netherlands: Sense Publishers, 2009.

The essays in this edited volume investigate young people's disengagement from democratic politics and presents the results of civic education research on programs intended to culminate in increasing political participation among youth.

Putnam, Robert D. *Bowling Alone: The Collapse and Revival of American Community*. New York: Simon and Schuster, 2001.

Putnam presents detailed evidence that organized community life in the United States has declined since the end of World War II. The author attributes this troubling change to various factors, including the rise of television as a primary entertainment medium, the two-career family, expansion of the suburbs and frequent mobility, and differing values held by the younger generation. Altered voting patterns can in part be attributed to the decline in community. Putnam recommends remedies, including educational programs that emphasize engagement and subsidized community service projects.

Ravitch, Diane, and Joseph P. Viteritti, eds. *Making Good Citizens: Education and Civil Society*. New Haven, CT: Yale University Press, 2003.

Contributors to this volume investigate various aspects of the relationship between education and citizen engagement. Among the topics discussed is the problem of encouraging honesty and other values of civic engagement when students observe corrupt practices in the political arena. Individual essays deal with such topics as religion and civic engagement and placing civic education within an international context.

Richie, Robert, and Steven Hill, eds. *Reflecting All of Us: The Case For Proportional Representation*. Boston: Beacon Press, 1999.

The essays in this volume investigate the potential consequences of shifting from a single-member district system of electing representatives to a form of proportional representation. Supporters of proportional representation argue that the current system results in voter apathy and many voices being ignored, and that a proportional system would lead to higher voter turnout because election outcomes would more accurately reflect voter preferences.

Rigby, Ben. *Mobilizing Generation 2.0: A Practical Guide to Using Web2.0 Technologies to Recruit, Organize and Engage Youth.* **Hoboken, NJ: Jossey-Bass, 2008.**

Rigby discusses the various opportunities that recently developed media technology offers for recruiting, organizing, and mobilizing young political participants. The author provides descriptions of, and advice about using, such techniques as blogging, social networking, and sharing videos and photographs to attract young supporters.

Rimmerman, Craig A. *The New Citizenship: Unconventional Politics, Activism, and Service.* **Fourth edition. Boulder, CO: Westview Press, 2010.**

In this supplementary textbook, Rimmerman investigates the various ways in which citizens engage in the discourse and action of politics and community affairs. The author relates the effect that political events have on college students, highlights groups in which college students participate, and suggests ways of overcoming apathy toward politics.

Saha, Lawrence J., Murray Print, and Kathy Edwards, eds. *Youth and Political Participation.* **Rotterdam, the Netherlands: Sense Publishers, 2008.**

Focusing primarily on Australia, the editors have collected a group of essays that explore the ways in which young people participate in politics, and investigate the reasons why many youth fail to become engaged politically. The essays examine such topics as the process by which young people become legally eligible to vote and the ways in which social institutions contribute to political learning.

Shapiro, H. Svi, ed. *Education and Hope in Troubled Times: Visions of Change for Our Children's World.* **New York: Routledge, 2009.**

Contributors to this edited volume contemplate the prospects and objectives of public education and investigate the basic meaning of education in the context of challenging circumstances students will find themselves. The changes in education policy the volume explores can be considered an important element in civic engagement in a rapidly evolving world.

Shenkman, Rick. *Just How Stupid Are We? Facing the Truth About the American Voter*. New York: Basic Books, 2009.

Shenkman argues that as the electoral process has gained in significance in recent decades, voters have become less knowledgeable about politics and hence more open to manipulation. The author notes that most citizens lack such basic information as who their congressional representative is and hence lack the ability to vote in either their own or the nation's best interest. Shenkman describes the ways in which politicians have deluded the public through professional marketing campaigns and the distribution of misinformation, and suggests a path that voters can take to gain the knowledge necessary to become informed and effective participants in the political process.

Sherrod, Lonnie R., Judith Torney-Purta, and Constance A. Flanagan, eds. *Handbook of Research on Civic Engagement in Youth*. San Francisco, CA: Wiley, 2010.

The editors and contributors to this large volume are guided by the maxim that a fundamental requirement of a democratic system is citizens who are engaged in the political process. The essays deal with various aspects of the subject of civic engagement, including theoretical, empirical, and normative questions. One essay discusses civic engagement in Mexico, and another examines the civic activities of immigrant youth in the United States.

Smith, Graham. *Democratic Innovations: Designing Institutions for Citizen Participation*. New York: Cambridge University Press, 2009.

Graham examines several innovations that various countries have introduced to involve greater numbers of citizens in the making of political decisions. The author's examples include participatory budgeting in Brazil; citizens' assemblies on electoral reform in Canada; the use of the initiative in California and Switzerland that allows citizens to take part directly in passing legislation; and prospects for the use of the Internet to expand political participation.

Spannring, Reingard. *Youth Participation: Social Capital and Political Engagement of Young People in Western Europe*.

Saarbrücken, Germany: Suedwestdeutscher Verlag fuer Hochschulschriften, 2009.

Spannring examines factors related to age and political participation in Western Europe, including young people's views of politics and actual political engagement, and differences in participation levels based on age categories. The author notes that although European youth tend to view politics skeptically, he finds no overall trend toward disinterest in politics.

Spannring, Reingard, Günther Ogris, and Wolfgang Gaiser, eds. *Youth and Political Participation in Europe: Results of the Comparative Study EUYOUPART.* Leverkusen Opladen, Germany: Barbara Budrich Publishers, 2008.

This volume presents the results of the European Union project Political Participation of Young People in Europe, which involved intensive interviews, focus group discussions, and surveys of those 15 to 25 years old. The countries involved in the investigation were Austria, Estonia, Finland, France, Germany, Great Britain, Italy, and Slovakia. The essays examine such topics as socialization and the transmission of values to the younger generation by parents, peer groups, the educational system, and voluntary groups.

Smith, Raymond A. *The American Anomaly: U.S. Politics and Government in Comparative Perspective.* Second edition. New York: Routledge, 2010.

This supplementary text for college courses analyzes the U.S. political system in comparison with other countries. Smith focuses on constitutional structures, governmental institutions, and political participation in the United States compared and contrasted with countries in Western and Eastern Europe, the Middle East, Africa, Asia, Latin America, and North America. The author provides insights into many unique aspects of the U.S. political system, including possible explanations for the lower level of political participation.

Streb, Matthew J. *Rethinking American Electoral Democracy.* New York: Routledge, 2008.

In a volume intended for college courses, Streb investigates various aspects of the U.S. electoral system, such as the costs of voting, influences on voter turnout, voting technology, redistricting, presidential primaries, the electoral college, and campaign finance. Focusing on possible reforms to the electoral system, Streb broaches the question of the ultimate value of further democratizing the electoral system.

Sunstein, Cass R. *Republic 2.0*. Princeton, NJ: Princeton University Press, 2009.

In this treatment of the potentially negative effects technology can have on public discourse, Sunstein refers to the huge choices individuals have available to acquire news and information. However, they also have the ability to filter out alternative viewpoints and simply to reinforce existing ideological positions. In order to sustain democratic discourse, Sunstein argues that different groups must expose themselves to diverse views.

Thomasson, Jacques, ed. *The European Voter*. New York: Oxford University Press, 2006.

Contributors to this volume provide a comparative analysis of voting behavior in European countries, testing the hypothesis that social changes have led to modified voting behavior, including lower turnout rates. The authors conclude that another explanation—that changes in voting behavior have resulted from the changed offerings of political parties—better explains the altered patterns of voting behavior.

Wattenberg, Martin P. *Is Voting for Young People? With a Postscript on Citizen Engagement*. New York: Pearson Longman, 2008.

In his search for the causes and consequences of low voter participation, Wattenberg focuses on a generally limited level of political knowledge among young people that can be attributed to a shift in the prevalent medium for receiving news. The author considers various ways of increasing voter turnout, including compulsory voting. Wattenberg recognizes that, despite troubling rates of voter participation, young people demonstrate increased participation in non-electoral forms of political engagement.

Wayne, Stephen J. *Is This Any Way to Run a Democratic Election?* Fourth edition. Washington, DC: CQ Press, 2010.

In this supplementary textbook, Wayne examines the various aspects of campaigns, elections, and government policy making, and focuses on the divergence between the perfect model of a political process and its actual operation. Wayne discusses the role of the media in the 2008 election campaigns, the campaign financing system, and how the conduct of the 2008 presidential primaries may influence future nomination contests. The willingness of young people and citizens generally to take part in campaigns and elections may depend in part on the extent to which the electoral process coincides with reasonable expectations for the way in which elections should be conducted.

Whitney, Susan. *Mobilizing Youth: Communists and Catholics in Interwar France.* **Durham, NC: Duke University Press, 2009.**

Whitney presents an account of the role that adults played in influencing youth activism in France in the 1920s and 1930s. Communists and Catholics competed to recruit young people to their respective organizations, the Young Communists and the Young Christian Workers. The author places these mobilization efforts in the context of the time period, which included the devastating effects of the Great Depression.

Winburn, Jonathan. *The Realities of Redistricting: Following the Rules and Limiting Gerrymandering in State Legislative Redistricting.* **Lanham, MD: Lexington Books, 2009.**

Winburn examines the redistricting process in 2000, using as case studies the states of Georgia, Idaho, Indiana, Kentucky, Michigan, Ohio, Texas, and Washington. The author focuses on the legal and political contexts of the redistricting process and analyzes the ability of nonpartisan principles to limit partisan gerrymandering.

Winograd, Morley, and Michael D. Hais. *Millennial Makeover: MySpace, YouTube, and the Future of American Politics.* **New Brunswick, NJ: Rutgers University Press, 2008.**

Morley and Hais speculate about the influence that new communication technologies will have on the generation that is coming of age after the turn of the century. In contrast to the baby boomer generation and similar to the generation of the 1930s, the authors predict that the new millennial generation will emphasize social unity and the resolution of fundamental economic and political issues.

Wood, B. Dan. *The Myth of Presidential Representation.* **New York: Cambridge University Press, 2009.**

In his investigation of presidential responsiveness to public opinion in policy making, Wood discovers little evidence that presidents follow citizen preferences. The author's research raises questions about the belief that presidents are representatives of the whole community. Instead of following a centrist strategy of compromise, there appears to be evidence that presidents instead tend to adhere to partisan positions. Wood's investigation may be relevant to questions about the withdrawal of many young people from political participation.

Yates, Miranda, and James Youniss, eds. *Roots of Civic Identity: International Perspectives on Community Service and Activism in Youth.* **New York: Cambridge University Press, 2006.**

This collection of essays describes the extent of youth participation in community affairs in various countries around the world. The authors emphasize the important role that actual participation in community affairs plays in the socialization process. Individual essays deal with such questions as defeating political corruption, surmounting disillusionment, and overcoming barriers to effective youth participation.

Youniss, James, Peter Levine, and Lee Hamilton, eds. *Engaging Young People in Civic Life.* **Nashville, TN: Vanderbilt University Press, 2009.**

The contributors to this volume direct their attention to the perception that young people, especially those with less education, frequently are uninformed about politics and are not engaged in civic affairs. One subject of the essays is the establishment of programs in poorer school districts that likely neglect civic education. Other essays deal with programs to engage youth in municipal boards and agencies, and civic education in Canada and Western Europe.

Zukin, Cliff, Scott Keeter, Molly Andolina, Krista Jenkins, and Michael X. Delli Carpini. *A New Engagement? Political Participation, Civic Life, and the Changing American Citizen.* **New York: Oxford University Press, 2006.**

The authors examine changes in citizen participation in the United States. They attribute those changes to generational diversity, including differing perceptions of government and varying social and cultural experiences. Zukin et al. conclude that generational diversity is significant to political engagement and therefore greater attention should be paid to the decreasing political engagement of young adults. However, the authors emphasize the distinction between political and civic engagement; although young people participate less politically, they do volunteer for various community activities.

Nonprint Resources

DVDs and Videotapes

"Campaign Ads/The New Gilded Age" (Bill Moyers *Journal*)

Date: 2008
Source: Films for the Humanities and Sciences
Website: http://ffh.films.com/

In the first portion of this video, Bill Moyers discusses with Kathleen Hall Jamieson, a media and politics researcher, the content of political ads that the Barack Obama, Hillary Clinton, and John McCain organizations used in the 2008 primary campaigns.

"Campaign Finance Reform and the Court" (Bill Moyers *Journal*)

Date: 2009
Source: Films for the Humanities and Sciences
Website: http://ffh.films.com/

Trevor Potter, president and general counsel of the Campaign Legal Center, and Floyd Abrams, partner and member of the executive committee at the law firm of Cahill, Gordon, and Reindel, present arguments for and against campaign finance reform and specifically about whether there should be a legal distinction between corporation and union expenditures, and individual spending with regard to campaign finance limitations. The U.S. Supreme Court, in *Citizens United v. Federal Election Commission* (2010) subsequently ruled that corporate funding of political broadcasts independent of candidates is protected under the First Amendment.

Citizenship and Civic Responsibilities

Date: 2010
Source: Films for the Humanities and Sciences
Website: http://ffh.films.com/

This program, also available via Films on Demand streaming video, explores the various meanings of citizenship and how those meanings have been shaped throughout U.S. history. The video asks what constitutes a "good citizen," focusing on personal rights and freedoms as well as duties the individual might be said to owe to society.

Iron Jawed Angels

> *Date*:   2004
>
> *Source*:   Home Box Office Films
>
> *Website*: ttp://store.hbo.com/detail.
>   php?p=100395&v=hbo_dvds

This portrayal of the fight for woman suffrage in the early 20th century features Hillary Swank as Alice Paul and Frances O'Connor as Lucy Burns, two activists who played key roles in the final push for adoption of the Nineteenth Amendment in 1920. This inspiring film demonstrates the high value many women at the time placed on acquiring the right to participate in electoral politics.

"John Nichols and Robert McChesney on the Media and Democracy" (*NOW* with Bill Moyers)

> *Date*:   2003
>
> *Source*:   Films for the Humanities and Sciences
>
> *Website*: http://ffh.films.com/

Nichols, McChesney, and Moyers discuss the potentially harmful effect that corporate interests can have on freedom of the press. Nichols and McChesney consider corporate control of the mass media to be a serious impediment to maintaining a democratic system.

"Jon Stewart on Humor and an Informed Public" (Bill Moyers *Journal*)

> *Date*:   2007
>
> *Source*:   Films for the Humanities and Sciences
>
> *Website*: http://ffh.films.com/

Bill Moyers interviews Jon Stewart, anchor for the entertainment-based news program *The Daily Show with John Stewart*. Moyers and Stewart discuss the possible reasons for the popularity of the show as a source of news. Many have noted the attraction the program has for younger citizens.

"Kathleen Hall Jamieson on Political Advertising" (*NOW* with Bill Moyers)

> *Date*:   2003
>
> *Source*:   Films for the Humanities and Sciences
>
> *Website*:   http://ffh.films.com/

Bill Moyers and media analyst Kathleen Hall Jamieson discuss the messages that sophisticated political advertisements are attempting to convey to the voter. Jamieson analyzes approximately 12 television commercials that politicians and interest groups have produced and discusses the importance of such ads for U.S. elections and politics.

Not for Ourselves Alone: The Story of Elizabeth Cady Stanton and Susan B. Anthony

> *Date*:   1999
>
> *Source*:   PBS Video
>
> *Website*:   www.shopPBS.com/teachers

This video follows the two giants of the struggle for woman suffrage, neither of which lived long enough to see the adoption of the Nineteenth Amendment granting women the right to vote. Such treatments can provide inspiration for students to value voting rights and other forms of political participation.

One Woman, One Vote

> *Date*:   1995
>
> *Source*:   PBS Video
>
> *Website*:   www.shopPBS.com/teachers

This video traces the 70-year effort in which women engaged to attain the right to vote. The story begins with the Seneca Falls Convention in 1848 and ends with the final battle in 1920 against both men and women who were opposed to woman suffrage that resulted in passage of the Nineteenth Amendment.

Please Vote for Me

> *Date*:   2007
>
> *Source*:   Amazon.com
>
> *Website*:   www.amazon.com/Please-Vote-Sub-Luo-Lei/dp/
>   B0019Z3P5W

Documentary filmmaker Weijun Chen chronicles an elementary school election in a third grade class in Wuhan, China. This highly praised film portrays a limited example of democracy in an otherwise authoritarian regime. One female and two male candidates compete for the votes of their classmates to be elected class monitor. The video depicts the campaign tactics used by the candidates (including lobbying fellow students and heckling opponents' speeches) and the involvement of teachers and parents in the election campaign.

"Politics, Reforming Washington, and Voting" (Bill Moyers *Journal*)

Date: 2008
Source: Films for the Humanities and Sciences
Website: http://ffh.films.com/

In this segment that was filmed prior to the 2008 election, Moyers first discusses the implications of electing either the first black president or the first female vice president. Moyers then discusses with public interest group activists Bob Edgar (Common Cause) and Joan Claybrook (Public Citizen) the possibility that campaign spending by influential groups may block genuine political reform in the nation's capital.

"The Press and the Campaign/Rage on the Radio" (Bill Moyers *Journal*)

Date: 2008
Source: Films for the Humanities and Sciences
Website: http://ffh.films.com/

As the fall 2008 presidential campaign continues, Bill Moyers discusses Barack Obama's and John McCain's campaign strategies with National Public Radio reporter Brooke Gladstone and journalist Les Payne. They note the difficulty of providing accurate reporting in the context of the candidates' competing campaign messages.

Recall Florida

Date: 2008
Source: Jezebel Productions
Website: www.jezebel.org

This video, directed by Greta Schiller, documents former Attorney General Janet Reno's 2002 grassroots campaign to win the Democratic Party nomination for governor of Florida. The film claims to reveal flaws in the use of new voting technology, highlights the question of soft (unregulated) money in campaigns, and discusses the problem of low voter turnout.

The Right to Count

> *Date*:   2005
> *Source*:   Roaming Video
> *Website*:   roamingvideo.com

In reaction to the push for improved voting machines that has resulted in the introduction of computer systems and sophisticated software, many have questioned whether election results can be manipulated. Several computer scientists present evidence that electronic voting machines and software are unreliable. The video also contains testimony from representatives of voting machine manufacturers and election officials who defend electronic voting systems. Questions raised in this video about assuring the integrity of the electoral system are relevant to efforts to engage youth in politics.

The Social Network

> *Date*:   2010
> *Source*:   Sony Pictures
> *Website*:   www.sonypictures.com

This film presents the fictionalized story of Mark Zuckerberg's role in creating Facebook while a student at Harvard University. The film depicts the incredibly fast expansion of Facebook from a campus networking website to an international phenomenon worth billions of dollars.

Voting: A Right and a Responsibility

> *Date*:   1996
> *Source*:   Films for the Humanities and Sciences
> *Website*:   http://ffh.films.com/

The program explains why young people should vote. Beginning with a history of voting in the United States, the video provides examples of close elections and asks students to consider how history might have been altered had election results been different. Also presented is information about how to register and vote and how to use a voting machine. Students also are provided with information about critically evaluating candidates based on issue positions and experience.

Wild in the Streets

Date: 1968
Source: MGM Video and DVD
Website: www.moviesunlimited.com

This film presents a simplistic scenario of youth ("everyone under 30") taking over the U.S. government. Rock star Max Frost organizes young people to demand that the voting age be lowered to 15 and ultimately that the Constitution be amended to reset the age qualification for national office at 14. The mandatory retirement age is lowered to 30 and those over 35 are placed in re-education camps where they receive doses of the psychedelic drug LSD.

Glossary

alienation   The sense of estrangement from the political process that individuals experience when they perceive that voting and other forms of political participation do not influence the governing process. Distrust of public figures, cynicism, and withdrawal from the political realm accompany alienation.

apportionment   The process of allocating representation geographically for Congress, state legislatures, and other representative bodies by establishing districts or precincts containing roughly equal populations.

civic duty   The obligation of citizens to engage in such public activities as voting. A major objective of the education system is to instill in young people the sense that they have a responsibility to be knowledgeable about public affairs and to become involved in politics.

civic virtue   Encompasses various characteristics of the individual that are considered crucial to being a good citizen, such as knowledge of politics, willingness to participate in community affairs, and self-restraint. Educational institutions and various voluntary organizations often regard the cultivation of such virtues as vital to the maintenance of democracy.

compulsory voting   An electoral system in which citizens are legally obligated to vote. Several countries, such as Australia, Belgium, and Greece, require electoral participation. However, the penalties for failing to vote usually are minimal or nonexistent. Some have argued that introducing a mandatory voting law in the United States would result in increased voter turnout, especially among young people.

contested election   An election in which more than one candidate claims to have won, a circumstance that leads to a recount or a court's determination of the winner. Because of the doubts that may be raised about the honesty and accuracy of the vote counting procedure, such an election may result in voter disaffection and withdrawal from the electoral process.

counterculture A term that refers to the attitudes and actions of many young people in the 1960s who expressed, in words and deeds, a rejection of mainstream social and political beliefs. The political relevance of the counterculture gained expression in illegal drug use; freewheeling sexual mores; protests against the Vietnam War and censorship in literature, music, and the mass media; and rejection of mainstream political engagement.

dealignment The increasing tendency of voters not to identify with a particular political party and thus to use party identification less as a cue for vote choice. Some election researchers identify this phenomenon as one explanation for lower voter turnout, especially among young people, who are less inclined to have strong party ties.

deliberative democracy A governing system combining elements of participatory democracy with representative democracy that provides individuals with the opportunity to engage in reasoned discussion about issues facing the community. Supporters argue that this form of democracy offers the average citizen more meaningful opportunities for political participation and thus encourages political engagement, and ultimately increases the legitimacy of resulting legislation and public policy.

disfranchisement The loss of voting rights. Convicted felons and those who lose citizenship may legally be denied voting rights. Many are disfranchised simply by their failure to become a registered voter. A key activity of many groups concerned with youth political participation is to register young people in order to assure that they are not disfranchised.

Duverger's law A social science generalization, drawn from the writings of Maurice Duverger, a French sociologist, asserting that single-member district plurality electoral systems result in two-party systems. When this system is used, additional (or third) political parties have great difficulty in getting members elected to legislative seats. Opponents of the system contend that those who do not support the two major parties tend to withdraw from electoral politics because no alternative parties have a chance of electoral victory. However, in some countries that use the single-member district system, such as England, third parties have experienced modest electoral success.

elite theory The view that a relatively small group of people in government, the economy, and the professions (including the military and the mass media) collaborate to make the most important decisions for a society. Whether true or false, such a view may contribute to cynicism and hence discourage political engagement among the general population.

gerrymandering Drawing electoral district boundaries in a way that increases the chances a political party, group, or candidate has of winning elections.

GOTV   The acronym for get-out-the-vote campaigns that political parties and other organizations conduct during the week or so before election day to encourage people to go to the polls. GOTV campaigns involve contacting people by various methods, including personal communication with friends and acquaintances, volunteer phone calls, mailings, door hangers, e-mail messages, and rallies. Such campaigns also include providing transportation to the polls on election day. Infrequent voters may be targeted to offer them information about their voting rights and the voting process. Some youth organizations emphasize GOTV campaigns over electronic media advertising as the most important means of encouraging young people to vote.

Help America Vote Act   Federal legislation approved in 2002 that attempted to remedy the inefficiencies in the electoral system that could lead to inaccurate counting of ballots and that may discourage citizens from participating in elections. Funds were provided to assist state and local governments in purchasing electronic or optical scan devices to replace punch card and other voting systems, and in establishing standards for election administration and voter registration.

incumbency effect   The advantage that current public officials (incumbents) have in running for reelection. Special interests tend to support incumbents, and incumbents generally are better known to voters than are any challengers. This advantage may deter those wishing to run against the sitting public official from entering the race, and also discourage voters from casting a ballot because the incumbent has a prohibitive advantage.

information overload   The condition in which individuals find themselves when they encounter many more sources of information than they can assimilate. Although new communication technologies have been touted as important contributions to political engagement, some argue that the sheer abundance of information sources may result in confusion and hence less political involvement, especially among young people who tend to be adept at using new technologies.

Mixed electoral systems   Electoral arrangements that combine some variation of proportional representation and district representation to determine the allocation of seats in the legislature. In an election, each voter casts two ballots: one for a candidate to serve as a district representative and the other for a political party list of candidates. The system attempts to combine the perceived advantages of each method; proportional representation grants legislative seats to a party in proportion to its support in the electorate, and district representation makes a representative more accountable to a specific constituency. To assure greater proportionality in representation, the total number of seats a party receives may be reduced by the number of district seats the party won. A less proportional outcome occurs if a party's district seats are simply added to the number of seats determined by proportional representation.

National Voter Registration Act (NVRA)   Legislation passed in 1993 that is meant to encourage voter registration by mandating that states permit registration by mail or in person at various government offices, such as driver's license bureaus (hence the legislation often is referred to as the Motor-Voter Act).

negative advertising   Campaign advertisements that present a derogatory view of the opponent rather than a positive perception of the candidate running the ad. Some researchers have claimed that such ads, by increasing cynicism, contribute to lower voter turnout.

participatory democracy   A version of direct democracy advocated by youth activists in the 1960s and 1970s that involves the establishment of institutions and procedures that provide the opportunity for individuals and groups to take part directly in political decision making rather than depending solely on representatives to reflect their views.

plurality system   An electoral system in which the candidate who receives the largest number of votes, whether or not it is a majority, wins the election. As the number of candidates vying for an elected office increases, there is a smaller chance that any one of them will receive a majority of the votes.

political apathy   The situation in which an otherwise eligible citizen fails to vote due to lack of interest in the election. Political apathy may result from overall satisfaction with the status quo or from disillusionment with the political process. Get-out-the-vote campaigns are intended to overcome citizen apathy, as are various proposals to reform the electoral system.

political efficacy   A measure of the degree to which individuals believe they can influence such political activities as nominating and electing candidates and affecting government policy making. The lower individuals' level of political efficacy, the less likely they are to engage in politics.

political socialization   The process, from childhood through adulthood, by which individuals gain all sorts of knowledge and attitudes about politics. Various individuals, groups, and institutions serve as agents of socialization, conveying, whether intentionally or not, the knowledge and attitudes about politics. Commonly recognized agents are family, public schools, peer groups, colleges and universities, and the mass media. The propensity to engage in politics results in part from the nature of an individual's political socialization experiences.

Port Huron Statement   The declaration of principles that Tom Hayden and other members of Students for a Democratic Society (SDS) developed at a meeting held in Port Huron, Michigan, in June 1962. The statement affirmed the principles of freedom, equality, and democratic government, and claimed that the current U.S. social, economic, and political system fell far short of meeting these requirements of a good society. In the search for democratic alternatives, the members of SDS asserted the importance of universities and alliances between students and faculty that would explore avenues for realizing human potential. Fundamental to achieving that potential is the establishment of participatory democracy, which involves all individuals having the opportunity to participate in communal policy making. The statement provided inspiration for much of the New Left actions during the 1960s, including the civil rights movement, protests against the Vietnam War, and campaigns to democratize university administrations.

proportional representation   A system of representation in which legislative seats are allocated to political parties or groups based on the percentage of votes each party wins in the election. A variety of such systems have been developed that more or less accurately translate the proportion of the popular vote into a proportion of the representation in the legislature. Third parties have a greater opportunity of gaining legislative seats with this system than with the single-member district plurality system. This characteristic of proportional representation leads some political analysts to argue that its use in the United States would lead to increased participation among young people who do not have a strong commitment to either of the two major parties.

responsible party government   A political principle that emphasizes uniform party support in the legislature for a public policy agenda. Guided by this principle, political parties would provide voters with clear policy options and therefore distinct voting options at election time. Reformers argue that the implementation of this principle would encourage greater citizen participation.

Sharon Statement   The declaration of conservative principles that the organizers of Young Americans for Freedom developed during an initial meeting held at William F. Buckley's home in Sharon, Connecticut, in September 1960. The statement affirms that political freedom and economic freedom are inseparable; that the purpose of government is to protect freedom, to maintain internal order and national defense, and to administer justice; that the U.S. Constitution is the best instrument ever conceived for establishing government authority; and that the market economy is the best system for maintaining personal freedom, perpetuating constitutional government, and meeting human needs. Ever since its adoption, the statement has provided inspiration for conservative youth groups and young people.

Twenty-sixth Amendment   Ratified in 1971, this amendment to the U.S. Constitution granted the right to vote to citizens between the ages of 18 and 20. Prior to ratification of this amendment, the predominant minimum voting age in the United States was 21.

voter identification laws   State laws that require prospective voters to supply some form of identification to confirm that they are legally registered to vote. Opponents of such laws argue that voter fraud does not represent a serious problem and that such laws discourage voter participation. Given low voter turnout rates, they argue that a far more important objective is to implement programs to encourage citizen participation. The U.S. Supreme Court, in *Crawford v. Marion County Election Board* (2008), upheld an Indiana law requiring voters to present photo identification before being allowed to cast a ballot.

voter registration   The requirement that individuals take the initiative in having their name placed on a list of eligible voters before they are allowed to cast a ballot. In the United States, this process is the responsibility of each individual, while in many other countries, the government assumes this responsibility. Voter registration requirements have been considered a reason for low voter turnout. Since the 1960s, states have liberalized registration requirements by introducing automatic re-registration, allowing registration by mail and at remote sites, and reducing the time period between the registration deadline and the election. The liberalization steps notwithstanding, proponents of greater voter turnout argue that voter registration requirements still dampen voter turnout, noting that in other Western democracies, the government assumes the responsibility of establishing and maintaining a voter registration list. At least nine states have instituted election day registration, and North Dakota has no voter registration requirement.

Yippies   In December 1967, Abbie Hoffman and Jerry Rubin along with three others established the Youth Independent Party, or "Yippies," a counterculture group that advocated the establishment of alternative institutions to those currently existing. Members ignored traditional politics, instead conducting their campaigns as theater. In 1968, they nominated a pig for president to demonstrate their dissatisfaction with the existing electoral system and participated in the antiwar demonstrations in Chicago during the Democratic National Convention. Although segments of the party continued, its appeal subsided quickly at the end of the 1960s.

Index

About the Author

Glenn H. Utter, professor of political science at Lamar University, was educated at Binghamton University, the University of Buffalo, and the University of London. Utter specializes in modern political theory and American political thought. He wrote *Mainline Christians and U.S. Public Policy* (2007); edited *Culture Wars in America* (2010); cowrote *Encyclopedia of Gun Control and Gun Rights* (2000, 2011), *Campaign and Election Reform* (1997, 2008), *The Religious Right* (1995, 2001, 2007), *Conservative Christians and Political Participation* (2004), and *Religion and Politics* (2002); and coedited *American Political Scientists: A Dictionary* (1993, 2002). He has written several articles for political science journals and other scholarly publications.